GUIDED FLIGHT DISCOVERY

INSTRUMENT COMMERCIAL SYLLABUS

Jeppesen is a registered trademark of Jeppesen Sanderson, Inc. All other trademarks, registered trademarks, product names, and company names or logos mentioned herein are the property of their respective owners.

All rights reserved. No part of this publication may be reproduced, stored in a retrieval system, or transmitted in any form or by any means, electronic, mechanical, photocopying, recording, or otherwise, without the prior permission of the publisher.

The charts, tables, and graphs used in this publication are for illustration purposes only and cannot be used for navigation or to determine actual aircraft performance.

Cover Photo
Piper Mirage in flight courtesy of Piper Aircraft, Inc.

978-0-88487-228-3

Jeppesen
55 Inverness Drive East
Englewood, CO 80112-5498
Web site: www.jeppesen.com
Email: Captain@jeppesen.com
Copyright © Jeppesen
All Rights Reserved.
Published 1998, 1999, 2000, 2001, 2002, 2003, 2004, 2006, 2012, 2015, 2016
Printed in the United States of America

10001785-004

Preface

The *Instrument/Commercial Syllabus* has been specifically developed to meet the requirements of Title 14 CFR, Part 141, Appendices C, D, and I, which apply to Instrument Rating, Commercial Pilot Certification, and Aircraft Class Rating Courses, respectively. The syllabus refers to specific 14 CFR parts and regulations as Federal Aviation Regulations (FARs). It is important that instructors refer to the pertinent sections of the regulations during the conduct of the course. This will ensure that all aeronautical knowledge areas, flight proficiency, and experience requirements have been included during training and are documented in appropriate records. The terminology for maneuvers and procedures listed in the syllabus is aligned with the "tasks" which are published in applicable FAA Airman Certification Standards.

The syllabus is arranged with separate ground and flight training segments which are taught concurrently. The Ground Training Syllabus is divided into five stages. Stages I, II, and III are for the instrument rating (airplane), and Stages IV and V are for commercial pilot (airplane single-engine). Stage VI of the Ground Training Syllabus is for the multi-engine rating. The Flight Training Syllabus includes Stages I, II, and III for the instrument rating and Stages IV, V, and VI for commercial pilot (airplane single-engine). Stage VII of the Flight Training Syllabus is for the multi-engine rating.

Computer-assisted training is incorporated into this syllabus to introduce concepts and enhance skills. The use of an aviation training device (ATD) is recommended for specified ground lessons and for use during flight lessons in the Instrument Course. This syllabus also contains provisions for use of a flight simulator or flight training device for instrument flight training. In the Commercial Course, provisions for a multi-engine rating are also included. Operators who wish to utilize these options should check the appropriate box(es) when they apply for Training Course Outline (TCO) approval. The student copy of the syllabus also should be marked accordingly.

- ☐ **This syllabus utilizes an ATD in the ground and flight training segments of the Instrument Rating Course.**
- ☐ **This syllabus utilizes a flight simulator or a flight training device for the flight training segments of the Instrument Rating Course.**

Instrument/Commercial Syllabus

Students possessing a private pilot certificate who want to obtain a commercial pilot certificate may enroll in the Instrument/Commercial Courses concurrently. Private pilots wanting to pursue only the instrument rating (airplane) may do so by completing Stages I, II, and III of the syllabus. In addition, students who possess a private pilot certificate with an instrument rating may pursue a commercial pilot certificate by completing Flight Stages IV, V, and VI of the syllabus for the **single-engine rating** and then continuing on through the multi-engine training in Stage VII to obtain a multi-engine rating. Students may begin the appropriate courses provided the school determines they meet the prerequisite knowledge, experience, and proficiency requirements for that rating or certificate. The stages a student must complete for the various courses are indicated below.

_____ is enrolled in the:
(Name)

❏ INSTRUMENT RATING COURSE
The student must hold a private pilot certificate and complete all of the instrument ground and flight training lessons in Stages I, II, and III of the *Instrument/Commercial Syllabus*.

❏ INSTRUMENT/COMMERCIAL COURSE
The combined Instrument/Commercial Course requires the student to hold a private pilot certificate and be concurrently enrolled in the Instrument Rating Course and the Commercial Pilot Certification Course. The student must complete all of the ground training lessons in Stages I through V and all of the flight training lessons in Stages I through VI in the *Instrument/Commercial Syllabus*.

MULTI-ENGINE RATING
To add a multi-engine rating to the commercial pilot certificate, the student must complete all of the ground training lessons in Stage VI and all of the flight training lessons in Stage VII of the *Instrument/Commercial Syllabus*.

❏ COMMERCIAL PILOT CERTIFICATION COURSE
The student must hold a private pilot certificate with an instrument rating and complete all of the ground training lessons in Stages IV, and V and all of the flight training lessons in Stages IV, V, and VI of the *Instrument/Commercial Syllabus*.

MULTI-ENGINE RATING
To add a multi-engine rating to the commercial pilot certificate, the student must complete all of the ground training lessons in Stage VI and all of the flight training lessons in Stage VII of the *Instrument/Commercial Syllabus*.

Instrument/Commercial Syllabus

Table of Contents

Introduction vi

Course Elements
Ground Training vi
Flight Training ix

Implementing the Courses
Credit for Previous Training... xii
Instrument/Commercial Course... xii
Instrument Rating Course.. xiii
Commercial Pilot Certification Course xiii
Part 61 Training xiv

Courses Overview
Instrument Rating Course.. xvi
Commercial Pilot Certification Course xix
Allocation Tables... xxii

Instrument Rating Course
Ground Training Syllabus 1
    Stage I 1
    Stage II 12
    Stage III... 23
Flight Training Syllabus 31
    Stage I 31
    Stage II 46
    Stage III... 56

Commercial Pilot Certification Course
Ground Training Syllabus 66
    Stage IV... 66
    Stage V.. 73
Flight Training Syllabus 88
    Stage IV... 88
    Stage V.. 105
    Stage VI.. 124

Multi-Engine Rating Course
Ground Training Syllabus (Stage VI)...................................... 141
Flight Training Syllabus (Stage VII).. 152

Appendix — Pilot Briefing Questions
Instrument Rating Course Briefings....................................... 171
Commercial Pilot Course Briefings... 176
Multi-Engine Rating Course Briefings.................................... 184

Introduction

The *Instrument/Commercial Syllabus* contains coordinated ground and flight training lessons. The lessons follow a careful, step-by-step progression of subject introduction and practice, incorporating academic assignments, the training airplane, and flight simulation devices where appropriate. The structure of the syllabus is not overly complex, but it does require a thorough understanding on the part of the instructor to achieve maximum benefit. When the principles and general order of the syllabus are followed, they make the difference between an effective program or a succession of lessons that lack order and direction. However, even though the ground and flight lessons are coordinated and arranged in a logical sequence, the syllabus should not be considered a rigid document. Any syllabus should be considered as an abstract or digest of the course of training. As such, it is important that flexibility be provided to adapt to individual student needs and/or the local training environment.

Course Elements

The *Instrument/Commercial Syllabus* utilizes separate ground and flight segments. It may be conducted as a combined ground and flight training program, or be divided into separate components. The course includes the latest FAA pilot certification requirements and a maximum of student-oriented instruction. The syllabus and support materials not only provide necessary information, but also guide the student through the course in a logical manner.

The basic syllabus is designed for the instrument rating (airplane) and the commercial certificate (airplane single-engine). However, additional ground training (Stage VI) and flight training (Stage VII) is included to add a multi-engine rating to your commercial certificate. Applicants may complete only the single-engine stages, or they may continue through the multi-engine training. In either case, at completion, the applicant will have complied with the training requirements of Part 141, Appendix C, Appendix D, and Appendix I.

GROUND TRAINING

In accordance with Part 141, ground school training is an integral part of pilot certification courses. The ground training syllabus has been designed to meet this requirement, and it may be coordinated with the flight training syllabus or used as a separate ground training course.

If the ground school is coordinated with the flight syllabus, each ground lesson is conducted at the point indicated in the Allocation Tables. This is the most effective method for course utilization, because the academic knowledge is obtained immediately prior to its application during flight training. However, to provide a degree of flexibility for adapting to individual student needs and the training environment, the syllabus lesson and stages may be altered with approval of the chief flight instructor. Any deviation should not disturb the course continuity or objective.

Instrument/Commercial Syllabus

When the course is presented as a formal classroom program, lessons should be followed as outlined. Each lesson may be presented in one classroom session, or it may be divided into two or more sessions, as necessary.

USING THE GROUND LESSONS

Ground lessons are based on Jeppesen Guided Flight Discovery (GFD) pilot courseware. Although each component of the GFD Instrument and Commercial courseware may be used separately, the effectiveness of the materials is maximized by using all of the individual elements together in an organized systems approach as described in this syllabus. The syllabus contains cross-references which direct the user to the appropriate GFD study materials for each lesson.

The student should complete the references in each ground lesson—the textbook and online learning center—prior to the classroom session or instructor briefing. The ground lessons include objectives, content, and completion standards. Instructors can use these components as a checklist to ensure that they cover the required material in each lesson. Instructors should introduce each lesson by outlining the subject material to be covered, the objectives, and the performance standards necessary for successful lesson completion. Each ground lesson also includes study assignments for the next lesson. The main components of the GFD Instrument and Commercial courseware are described below.

TEXTBOOKS

Prior to each ground lesson, the student should read and study the assigned textbook/eBook section or chapter, if appropriate. The *Instrument/Commercial* textbook/eBook is the main source of information for the first five stages of ground training. It is comprehensive and well-illustrated. The *Multi-Engine* textbook covers information necessary to complete the multi-engine stage of training. In addition, the FAR/AIM contains information essential for course completion.

THE JEPPESEN LEARNING CENTER ONLINE

Jeppesen's online instrument and commercial pilot ground schools provide academic and maneuvers training. They are powerful resources on their own or in combination with classroom training. The Jeppesen Learning Center complements the textbooks with lessons that explore the material with engaging multimedia presentations, practice opportunities, and exams.

QUESTIONS AND EXAMS

The final step is for the student to complete the appropriate textbook questions or online exams and discuss any incorrect responses with the instructor. This ensures student understanding prior to beginning the next ground lesson. When the lesson is complete, the instructor assigns the next textbook chapter and section(s) or online lesson(s) for out-of-class study. At the end of each stage, the student is required to successfully complete the stage exam outlined in the syllabus before the next ground training stage.

END-OF-COURSE EXAMS

When all the appropriate ground lesson assignments are complete, the student should take the end-of-course exam. The ground lesson assignments for the Instrument Rating End-of-Course Exam are completed in Stage III, and those for the Commercial Pilot (Airplane Single-Engine) End-of-Course Exam are completed in Stage V.

The ground training end-of-course exam for the combined Instrument/Commercial Course (Airplane Single-Engine) is administered following Stage V. The Commercial Pilot End-of-Course Exam serves as this final test. An additional end-of-course exam is also included for students completing the multi-engine rating. Following these tests, the instructor should assign each student appropriate subject areas for review.

PILOT BRIEFINGS

Pilot briefings are contained in the Appendix of this syllabus. Each briefing consists of a series of questions that provide comprehensive coverage of selected areas of instruction. The student should be provided with the appropriate briefing in advance. This allows the student to prepare properly by researching the answers and, therefore, gain optimum benefit from the briefing.

The briefings should be conducted as private tutoring sessions to test each student's comprehension. Every question should be discussed thoroughly to ensure the student understands the relevant information. The briefings are to be completed during the preflight orientation for the appropriate flight. Correct placement of the briefing sessions is indicated in the syllabus.

Altogether there are seven pilot briefings in the Instrument/Commercial Course (Airplane Single-Engine). The third one is the briefing for the FAA Instrument Rating Practical Test. It should be completed prior to the End-of-Course Flight Check in Stage III. The seventh briefing is for the FAA Commercial Pilot Practical Test (Airplane Single-Engine) and it should be completed before the single-engine End-of-Course Flight Check in Stage VI. Additional pilot briefings are included in the airplane multi-engine stage. During all of the pilot briefings, each subject area should be reviewed with the student to ensure complete understanding.

Instrument/Commercial Syllabus

FLIGHT TRAINING

The syllabus is divided into three stages for the instrument rating portion of the course and an additional three stages to complete the commercial portion. A seventh stage is provided for commercial students seeking a multi-engine airplane rating. Each stage builds on previous learning and, therefore, it is recommended they be completed in sequence.

Because the *Instrument/Commercial Syllabus* is to be used as a practical training guide, it is designed to allow a degree of flexibility in order to meet the needs of individual students. With the approval of the chief flight instructor, some lessons may be rearranged to suit training needs. However, it is the responsibility of the instructor to ensure the continuity of the learning blocks remains unaffected by the change. The following discussion presents a description of the primary areas of study in each stage.

STAGE I
Stage I of the syllabus is designed to provide the student with a strong foundation in attitude instrument flying and instrument navigation. At the completion of this stage, the student is thoroughly prepared for the introduction of holding patterns and instrument approach procedures.

STAGE II
During this stage, the student learns to perform holding patterns and instrument approaches. This training prepares the student for the introduction of IFR cross-country procedures in Stage III.

STAGE III
This stage of training teaches the student IFR cross-country procedures and provides a review of all previously learned maneuvers. Through the use of three instrument cross-country flights and review, the student is able to attain the proficiency level of an instrument-rated pilot.

The ground and flight training portions of the instrument course are completed in Stage III. The student should also successfully pass the FAA Instrument Rating Airman Knowledge Test and take the FAA Instrument Rating Practical Test at the completion of this stage.

STAGE IV
Stage IV builds upon previously learned ground and flight training. The student reviews and practices day and night VFR cross-country procedures to prepare for commercial pilot operations.

STAGE V
Stage V provides a thorough introduction and pilot-in-command checkout in the complex airplane. The remainder of the stage is devoted to the introduction and review of precision flight maneuvers.

Instrument/Commercial Syllabus

STAGE VI
Although no new maneuvers or procedures are introduced in Stage VI, practice of commercial maneuvers in the complex airplane is included. This is an important stage of training. It provides a review of the skills learned throughout the syllabus and prepares the student for the FAA practical test. If the student has not previously completed the FAA Instrument Rating Practical Test, both the Instrument and Commercial Practical Test Briefings that coincide with the End-of-Course Flight Check are to be utilized in this stage.

STAGE VII
Stage VII, which is for the multi-engine rating, provides a foundation for all relevant multi-engine maneuvers and procedures, including normal and engine-out operations. The final portion of Stage VII concentrates on multi-engine procedures in the IFR environment with both normal instrument approaches and engine-out instrument approach procedures.

PREFLIGHT DISCUSSION
Prior to each dual and solo flight, the instructor should provide the student with an overview of the subject matter to be covered during the lesson. The instructor should brief the student and explain the lesson objectives and completion standards. It is important that the instructor define unfamiliar terms and explain the maneuvers and procedures of each lesson. The Preflight Discussion should be tailored to the specific flight, the local environment, and the individual student.

AIRPLANE PRACTICE
The syllabus has been designed to enable practice of given procedures and maneuvers after the student has been introduced to the maneuver by the instructor. If a flight simulation device is used, the instructor is not relieved of teaching during flight lessons. However, the student is expected to grasp new techniques more easily having already been introduced to them in the simulation device. If simulation devices are not utilized, both introduction and practice are to be accomplished in the airplane.

USE OF A FLIGHT SIMULATOR, FTD, OR ATD
Some flight training time required for the Instrument Rating Course under Part 141, Appendix C may be conducted in an approved flight simulator, flight training device (FTD), and/or aviation training device (ATD).

A simulator is distinguished from an FTD by the simulator's motion cueing system. A flight simulator that meets the requirements of FAR 141.41(a) may be used for up to 50 percent of the required instrument flight training time.

An FTD is distinguished from most ATDs by the FTD's full-size replica of the instruments, equipment, panels, and controls of an aircraft, or set of aircraft, in an open flight deck area or in an enclosed cockpit. Advanced aviation training devices (AATDs) have similar capabilities as FTDs. An FTD that meets the requirements

Instrument/Commercial Syllabus

of FAR 141.41(a) or an AATD that meets the requirements of §141.41(b) may be used for up to 40 percent of the required instrument flight training time.

Basic ATDs (BATDs) can lack the physical controls contained in a simulator or FTD, or the device does not sufficiently replicate an aircraft cockpit to be an FTD. However, BATDs provide benefits such as versatility in lesson presentation, repositioning features, and freeze functions. A BATD that meets the requirements of §141.41(b), may be used for up to 25 percent of the required instrument flight training time. In addition, ATD training is included as part of selected ground lessons indicated in the Allocation Tables and in the individual ground lessons.

A combination of simulators, FTDs, and ATDs may be used for instrument flight training for the Instrument Rating Course; however, the total time in all of these devices may not exceed 50 percent of the required instrument flight training time and the total time in FTDs, AATDs, and BATDs may not exceed 40 percent of the required training time.

In addition, some flight training time required for the Commercial Pilot Certification Course under Part 141, Appendix D may be conducted in an approved flight simulator or flight training device (FTD). Up to 30 percent of the required flight training time may be met in the simulator and up to 20 percent of the required flight training time may be met in an FTD.

POSTFLIGHT DEBRIEFING

The Postflight Debriefing is as important as the Preflight Discussion. The student should perform a self-critique of maneuvers/procedures and single-pilot resource management (SRM) performance. This *learner-centered grading* is especially helpful in developing decision-making skills. If the student is having trouble mastering a certain skill, both the student and instructor should plan for improving the performance of that skill. An effective Postflight Debriefing increases retention and helps the student prepare for the next lesson.

STUDENT STAGE CHECKS

The stage checks in the *Instrument/Commercial Syllabus* are designed to identify deficiencies and to check the student's overall progress in accordance with Part 141. Each stage check is the responsibility of the chief flight instructor. However, the chief flight instructor may delegate the authority to conduct these tests to the assistant chief instructor or designated check instructor. This procedure provides close supervision of training and a second opinion on the student's progress. The stage check also gives the chief instructor an opportunity to check the effectiveness of the instructors and their teaching methods.

An examination of the building-block theory of learning will show that it is extremely important that the student's progress and proficiency are satisfactory before entering a new stage of training. Therefore, the next stage should not begin until the student successfully completes the stage check. Failure to follow this progression may defeat the purpose of the stage check and lead to overall course breakdown.

Instrument/Commercial Syllabus

Implementing the Courses

While the *Instrument/Commercial Syllabus* is intended to fulfill the requirements of a combined Instrument/Commercial Course, it may also be utilized for separate Instrument Rating or Commercial Pilot Certification Courses. This discussion explains the implementation of the combined Instrument/Commercial, as well as the separate Instrument Rating, and separate Commercial Pilot Certification Courses.

CREDIT FOR PREVIOUS TRAINING

According to FAR 141.77(c), when a student transfers from one FAA-approved school to another approved school, course credits obtained in the previous course of training may be credited for 50 percent of the curriculum requirements by the receiving school. However, the receiving school must determine the amount of credits to be allowed based upon a proficiency test, knowledge test, or both, conducted by the receiving school. A student who enrolls in a course of training may receive credit for 25 percent of the curriculum requirements for knowledge and experience gained in a Part 61 flight school, and the credit must be based upon a proficiency test, knowledge test, or both, conducted by the receiving school. The amount of credit for previous training allowed, whether received from an FAA-approved school or other source, is determined by the receiving school. In addition, the previous provider of the training must certify the kind and amount of training given, and the result of each stage check and end-of-course test, if applicable.

INSTRUMENT/COMMERCIAL COURSE

The Instrument/Commercial Course is designed for students who currently hold a private pilot certificate. The course includes a total of at least 65 hours of ground training and 155 hours of flight training. This total consists of 30 hours of ground training and 35 hours of flight training in Stages I, II, and III of the syllabus for the instrument rating segment. In addition, the commercial certification segment consists of 35 hours of ground training and 120 hours of flight training found in Stages IV, V, and VI.

Students adding a multi-engine rating to their commercial pilot certificate must complete Ground Stage VI, which includes 15 hours of ground training. They also must complete 15 hours of multi-engine flight training in Flight Stage VII.

The *Instrument/Commercial Syllabus* is presented in both an overview and a lesson-by-lesson format. The lesson sequence and content have been designed to provide the student with maximum academic and flight training prior to the introduction of new maneuvers or procedures. Therefore, the sequence of ground and fight training shown in the syllabus outline should not be altered significantly if the coordinated program is utilized.

Instrument/Commercial Syllabus

If absolutely necessary, the placement of ground lesson assignments may be changed to allow the student to progress more rapidly in the academic study than outlined in the course. If this method is used, the student should not be allowed to progress into the ground lesson assignments of the next stage until the flight lessons in the current stage of training are completed. This is important, because the student's recall of academic knowledge decreases with an increase in time between subject introduction during ground training and its application in flight training.

INSTRUMENT RATING COURSE

The Instrument Rating Course is presented first in the *Instrument/Commercial Syllabus*. It consists of a minimum of 30 hours of ground training and 35 hours of instrument flight training in Stages I, II, and III of the syllabus. During Stage III the student should pass the FAA Instrument Rating Airman Knowledge Test. At the completion of Stage III, the FAA Instrument Rating Practical Test should be taken.

The *Instrument Rating Syllabus* is presented in both an overview and a lesson-by-lesson format. The combined flight and ground training course includes the entire outline from Stage I through the completion of Stage III. The lesson sequence and content have been designed to provide the student with maximum academic and flight training prior to the introduction of new maneuvers and procedures. However, the sequence shown in the syllabus outline may be altered to meet special circumstances of the student or training environment.

NOTE: *Operators utilizing the ATD option in the Instrument/Commercial or Instrument Rating Course may credit ATD time for up to 10 percent of the required instrument flight training time and for up to 5 hours toward ground training requirements.*

COMMERCIAL PILOT CERTIFICATION COURSE

The Commercial Pilot Certification Course is presented in the next segment of the *Instrument/Commercial Syllabus*. It consists of a minimum of 35 hours of ground training and 120 hours of flight training in Stages IV, V, and VI. During Stage V, the student should pass the FAA Commercial Pilot Airman Knowledge Test. At the completion of Stage VI, the FAA Commercial Pilot Practical Test should be taken.

Students adding a multi-engine rating to their commercial pilot certificate must complete Ground Stage VI, which includes 15 hours of ground training. They also must complete 15 hours of multi-engine flight training in Flight Stage VII.

Instrument/Commercial Syllabus

The *Commercial Pilot Syllabus* is presented in both an overview and a lesson-by-lesson format. The lesson sequence and content have been designed to provide the student with maximum academic and flight training prior to the introduction of new maneuvers and procedures. While the syllabus provides a general training outline, the lesson sequence shown may be tailored to meet the individual needs of the student. Lessons 36, 37, 38, 39, 40 and 41 are designed to be solo cross-country flight lessons. However, these lessons may also be utilized for additional dual instruction to meet the proficiency requirements for the End-of-Course Flight Check and FAA practical test.

COMMERCIAL COURSE MULTI-ENGINE OPTIONS

The Allocation Tables for Flight Stages V, VI, and VII provide two options for completing a commercial certification course with a single-engine rating and a multi-engine rating. By shortening some of the single-engine flight lessons in Stage V and VI, the course is designed so that the student may earn the multi-engine rating without increasing the total flight time. The shortened times are listed in parenthesis in the Time Allocation tables. For Flight Stages V and VI, the student must select one of two flight times listed in many of the Allocation Table rows:

- To take the Commercial Pilot–Airplane Single-Engine Land Practical Test at the end of Stage VI, the student must complete the first flight time listed. After passing the practical test at the end of Stage VI, the student may continue training to add a multi-engine rating to the commercial certificate by completing Flight Stage VII. After completing the multi-engine rating course, the student takes the Commercial Pilot Airplane–Multi-Engine Land Practical Test.

- If the student chooses to complete the second flight time listed (shown in parentheses) for Flight Stages V and VI, the student must also complete the flight time in Stage VII to meet the total time required for commercial pilot certification. In this case, the student completes Stage VII before taking the Commercial Pilot–Airplane Single-Engine Land Practical Test and the Commercial Pilot Airplane–Multi-Engine Land Practical Test.

PART 61 TRAINING

The *Instrument/Commercial Syllabus* is designed to meet all of the requirements of Part 141, Appendices, C, D, and I. It may also be adapted to meet the requirements of Part 61. Part 61 incorporates greater aeronautical experience requirements than are found in Part 141. For example, as indicated in FAR 61.65 for an instrument rating, you must have at least 50 hours of cross-country time as pilot in command and 40 hours of actual or simulated instrument time in the areas of operation specified in the FARs. This includes at least 15 hours of instrument flight training from an authorized instructor in the aircraft category for which the instrument rating is sought. If your training is accomplished under Part 141, you must have 35 hours of instrument training from an authorized instructor in the areas specified in Part 141, Appendix C and need not comply with the 50-hour PIC cross-country requirement.

Instrument/Commercial Syllabus

Under Part 61, a commercial pilot applicant for an airplane category and single-engine class rating must log at least 250 hours of flight time as a pilot. This includes 100 hours in powered aircraft, of which 50 hours must be in airplanes. In addition, it must include 100 hours of pilot-in-command time, which includes at least 50 hours in cross-country flight of which at least 10 hours must be in airplanes. Further, 20 hours of flight training and 10 hours of solo flight also are required. Refer to FAR 61.125, 61.127, and 61.129.

Under Part 61, an applicant for a multi-engine class rating to be added to a pilot certificate must meet the requirements of FAR 61.63 (c). Essentially, there are no established minimum amounts of ground training or flight training time necessary in order to add an additional aircraft class rating to a pilot certificate. As a result, class ratings are often referred to as competency-based. Part 61 requires instruction be received appropriate to the desired rating, and that a flight instructor recommendation be obtained. Of course the appropriate practical test also must be successfully completed.

The ground training requirements under Part 61 specify that an applicant for a knowledge test is required to have a logbook endorsement from an authorized instructor who conducted the training or reviewed the person's home study course. The endorsement must indicate satisfactory completion of the ground instruction or home study course required for the certificate or rating sought. A home study course for the purposes of Part 61 is a course of study in those aeronautical knowledge areas specified in FAR 61.125, and organized by a pilot school, publisher, flight or ground instructor, or by the student. The Instrument/Commercial Course easily meets this requirement. As a practical consideration, students seeking pilot certification under Part 61 should receive some formal ground training, either in the classroom or from an authorized flight or ground instructor.

An applicant who applies for an additional class rating to be added on a pilot certificate need not take an additional knowledge test, provided the applicant holds an airplane, rotorcraft, powered-lift, or airship rating at that pilot certificate level.

Courses Overview

INTRODUCTION

The *Instrument/Commercial Syllabus* is designed to coordinate the academic study assignments and flight training required by pilots operating in an increasingly complex aviation environment. New subject matter is introduced during the ground lessons, which include the following:
1. In-depth textbook/eBook assignments
2. Ground lessons in the Jeppesen Learning Center online
3. Thorough instructor/student discussions
4. Textbook/eBook questions and online exams
5. Stage and end-of-course exams for evaluation and reinforcement

After completing the ground lesson, the student will apply these new principles in a simulation device or in the airplane during the flight lesson. The Allocation Tables indicate placement of the ground lessons when the coordinated sequence is used.

Optimum effectiveness is realized when ground lessons are completed just prior to the respective flight lessons, as outlined in the syllabus. However, it is also acceptable to present lessons in a formal ground school before the student is introduced to the airplane. If a considerable length of time has elapsed between the ground lesson and the associated flight, the instructor may wish to conduct a short review of essential material. Flight lessons should not be conducted until related ground lessons have been completed.

INSTRUMENT RATING COURSE

COURSE OBJECTIVE — The student will obtain the knowledge, skill, and aeronautical experience necessary to meet the requirements for an instrument rating (airplane).

COURSE COMPLETION STANDARD — The student must demonstrate through knowledge tests, flight tests, and appropriate records that he/she meets the knowledge, skill, and experience requirements necessary to obtain an instrument rating (airplane).

FLIGHT TRAINING COURSE OBJECTIVE — The student will obtain the aeronautical skill and experience necessary to meet the requirements for an instrument rating (airplane).

COMPLETION STANDARD — The student must demonstrate through flight tests and school records that the necessary aeronautical skill and experience requirements to obtain an instrument rating (airplane) have been met.

Instrument/Commercial Syllabus

GROUND TRAINING COURSE OBJECTIVE — The student will obtain the necessary aeronautical knowledge and meet the prerequisites specified in Part 141 for the FAA Instrument Rating Airman Knowledge Test.

COMPLETION STANDARD — The student must demonstrate through exams and school records that he/she meets the prerequisites specified in Part 141 and has the knowledge necessary to pass the FAA Instrument Rating Airman Knowledge Test.

STUDENT INFORMATION

COURSE ENROLLMENT
To enroll in the flight portion of the Instrument Rating Course, you must hold at least a private pilot certificate with an airplane category rating and a single-engine land class rating.

REQUIREMENTS FOR GRADUATION
To obtain an instrument rating, you must be able to read, speak, write, and understand the English language and hold a private pilot certificate with at least a third-class medical certificate. In addition, you must meet the aeronautical experience requirements specified in Part 141, Appendix C to be eligible for graduation.

LESSON DESCRIPTION AND STAGES OF TRAINING
This syllabus fully describes each lesson, including the objectives, references, topics, and completion standards. The stage objectives and standards are described at the beginning of each stage within the syllabus.

TESTS AND CHECKS
The syllabus incorporates stage and end-of-course flight checks in accordance with Part 141, Appendix C. These checks are given by the chief instructor, an assistant chief instructor, or check instructor designated by the chief instructor. The student will also complete the stage exams and pilot briefings that are described within the syllabus. In addition, the student must satisfactorily complete the end-of-course exam and end-of course flight check after completing all the stages.

Instrument/Commercial Syllabus

COURSES OVERVIEW

Curriculum Overview
Instrument Rating Course

Completion of this course is based solely upon compliance with the minimum requirements of FAR Part 141. The time tables are provided for guidance in achieving regulatory compliance.

GROUND TRAINING

	Ground Lessons	ATD	Briefings, Stage, and Final Exams	Ground Training Totals
STAGE I	8.0	(2.0)	1.0	9.0
STAGE II	10.0	(3.0)	1.5	11.5
STAGE III	6.0		3.5	9.5
TOTALS	24.0	(5.0)	6.0	30.0

FLIGHT TRAINING

	Instrument Training	Cross-Country Training	ATD	Flight Training Totals
STAGE I	13.0		As Required	13.0
STAGE II	11.0		As Required	11.0
STAGE III	11.0	(10.0)	As Required	11.0
TOTALS	35.0	(10.0)	As Required	35.0

NOTE: **Ground Training:**
1. Ground lessons may include class discussion or online lessons.
2. Operators using the ATD option may credit ATD time for up to 10 percent of the required instrument flight training time and for up to 5 hours toward ground training requirements. Suggested ATD hours for ground training are shown in parentheses.

NOTE: **Flight Training:**
1. Cross-country hours (shown in parentheses) are included in the instrument training time for Stage III and in the total flight training time.
2. All flight training in the Instrument Rating Course is dual.

Instrument/Commercial Syllabus

COMMERCIAL PILOT CERTIFICATION COURSE

COURSE OBJECTIVE — The student will obtain the knowledge, skill, and aeronautical experience necessary to meet the requirements for a commercial pilot certificate with an airplane category rating and a single-engine land class rating (and a multi-engine land class rating if completing the multi-engine training).

COURSE COMPLETION STANDARD — The student must demonstrate through knowledge tests, flight tests, and appropriate records that he/she meets the knowledge, skill, and experience requirements necessary to obtain a commercial pilot certificate with an airplane category rating and a single-engine land class rating (and a multi-engine land class rating if completing the multi-engine training).

FLIGHT TRAINING COURSE OBJECTIVE — The student will obtain the aeronautical skill and experience necessary to meet the requirements for a commercial pilot certificate with an airplane category rating and a single-engine land class rating (and a multi-engine land class rating if completing the multi-engine training).

COMPLETION STANDARD — The student must demonstrate through flight tests and school records that the necessary aeronautical skill and experience requirements to obtain a commercial pilot certificate with an airplane category rating and a single-engine land class rating (and a multi-engine land class rating if completing the multi-engine training) have been met.

GROUND TRAINING COURSE OBJECTIVE — The student will obtain the necessary aeronautical knowledge and meet the prerequisites specified in Part 141 for the FAA Commercial Pilot Airman Knowledge Test.

COMPLETION STANDARD — The student must demonstrate through knowledge tests and school records that he/she meets the prerequisites specified in Part 141 and has the knowledge necessary to pass the FAA Commercial Pilot Airman Knowledge Test.

STUDENT INFORMATION

COURSE ENROLLMENT
To enroll in the flight portion of the Commercial Pilot Certification Course, you must hold at least a private pilot certificate. In addition, you must hold an instrument rating or be concurrently enrolled in an instrument rating (airplane) course.

REQUIREMENTS FOR GRADUATION
To obtain a commercial pilot certificate, you must be at least 18 years of age and be able to read, speak, write, and understand the English language. In addition, you must have a valid FAA third-class medical certificate. However, to exercise

Instrument/Commercial Syllabus

the privileges of a commercial pilot you must possess a valid second-class medical certificate. In addition, you must meet the aeronautical experience requirements specified in Part 141, Appendix D, to be eligible for graduation.

LESSON DESCRIPTION AND STAGES OF TRAINING
This syllabus fully describes each lesson, including the objectives, references, topics, and completion standards. The stage objectives and standards are described at the beginning of each stage within the syllabus.

TESTS AND CHECKS
The syllabus incorporates stage and end-of-course flight checks in accordance with Part 141, Appendix D. These checks are given by the chief instructor, an assistant chief instructor, or check instructor designated by the chief instructor. The student will also complete the stage exams and pilot briefings that are described within the syllabus. In addition, the student must satisfactorily complete the end-of-course exam and end-of course flight check after completing all the stages.

Instrument/Commercial Syllabus

CURRICULUM OVERVIEW
Commercial Pilot Certification Course

Completion of this course is based solely upon compliance with the minimum requirements of FAR Part 141. The time tables are provided for guidance in achieving regulatory compliance.

GROUND TRAINING

		Ground Lessons	Stage and End-of-Course Exams	Briefings/ Debriefings	Ground Training Totals
	STAGE IV	9.0	1.0	As Required	10.0
	STAGE V	22.0	3.0	As Required	25.0
COMM'L SINGLE ENGINE →	TOTALS	31.0	4.0	As Required	35.0
MULTI-ENGINE →	STAGE VI	9.0	2.0	4.0	15.0

NOTE: Ground lessons may include class discussion or online lessons.

FLIGHT TRAINING

Dual | Solo

		Day Local	Day Cross X-C	Night	Complex	Multi-Engine	Instrument	Dual Stage Totals	Day Local	Day Cross X-C	Night	Solo Stage Totals	Dual/Solo Comb. Totals
	STAGE IV		8.0 (8.0)	5.0 (5.0)			As Required	13.0 (13.0)		34.0*	6.0	40.0	53.0 (53.0)
	STAGE V	20.0 (14.0)			10.0 (7.0)		As Required	20.0 (14.0)	9.0			9.0	29.0 (23.0)
	STAGE VI	20.0 (12.0)	2.0 (1.0)		5.0 (3.0)		As Required	22.0 (13.0)	16.0			16.0	38.0 (29.0)
SINGLE ENGINE →	TOTALS	40.0 (26.0)	10.0 (9.0)	5.0 (5.0)	15.0 (10.0)		As Required	55.0 (40.0)	25.0	34.0*	6.0	65.0	120.0 (105.0)
MULTI-ENGINE →	STAGE VII	(9.0)	(3.0)	(3.0)		(15.0)	As Required	(15.0)					(15.0)
COMBINED →	TOTALS	40.0 (35.0)	10.0 (12.0)	5.0 (8.0)	15.0 (10.0)	(15.0)	As Required	55.0 (55.0)	25.0	34.0*	6.0		120.0 (120.0)

NOTE:
1. * Indicates some solo cross-country hours may be used for additional dual instruction to meet the proficiency requirements for the End-of-Course Flight Check and FAA Commercial Pilot Practical Test.
2. In blocks where two times are shown, the first time is for students taking the Commercial Pilot–Airplane Single-Engine Land Practical Test at the end of Stage VI. If the student chooses to complete the second flight time listed (shown in parentheses) for Flight Stages V and VI, the student must also complete the multi-engine flight training time in Stage VII to meet the total time required for commercial pilot certification. For example, the dual time totals for Stages IV, V, and VI are 55.0 hours for students not completing the multi-engine training and 40 hours for those who will complete the remaining 15 hours in the multi-engine airplane during Flight Stage VII. In each case, the student will receive a minimum of 55.0 hours dual.
3. The 15 hours of flight time in Stage VII are all dual instruction in the multi-engine airplane.

xxi

Instrument/Commercial Syllabus

Allocation Tables

Lesson Time Allocation

Stage I

Ground Training					Lesson	Flight Training — Dual					Solo	
Ground Lessons	ATD	Pilot Briefings	Stage/Final Exams	Exam Debriefings		Day Local	Day Cross-Country	Night Local	Night Cross-Country	Instrument	Day Local	Day Cross-Country
1.0					GL 1 – Training/Opportunities/Human Factors							
1.0					GL 2 – Flight Instrument Systems							
1.0	As Req.				GL 3 – Attitude Instrument Flying							
					FL 1 – Preflight Procedures and Full Panel	1.0				1.0		
					FL 2 – Full Panel and IFR Systems	1.0				1.0		
1.0	As Req.				GL 4 – Instrument Navigation							
					FL 3 – Review Full Panel	1.0				1.0		
					FL 4 – Introduction to Partial Panel	1.0				1.0		
1.0					GL 5 – Instrument FARs							
1.0					GL 6 – Airports, Airspace, and Flight Information							
					FL 5 – Systems and Equipment Malfunctions	1.0				1.0		
					FL 6 – Full and Partial Panel	1.0				1.0		
1.0					GL 7 – ATC System							
					FL 7 – Review	1.0				1.0		
1.0					GL 8 – ATC Clearances							
					FL 8 – VOR Navigation	1.0				1.0		
		1.0	As Req.		GL 9 – Stage I Exam							
					FL 9 – NDB Navigation	1.0				1.0		
					FL 10 – GPS Navigation	1.0				1.0		
					FL 11 – Localizer Tracking	1.0				1.0		
					FL 12 – Partial-Panel Navigation	1.0				1.0		
					FL 13 – Stage I Check	1.0				1.0		
8.0	As Req.	1.0	As Req.		**Stage Totals**	13.0				13.0		

NOTE: 1. Ground lessons may include class discussion or online lessons.
2. The ATD may be used as required in the ground lessons indicated. Operators utilizing the ATD option in the Instrument/Commercial or Instrument Rating Course may credit up to 5 hours of ATD time toward ground training requirements.
3. The individual times shown on the Allocation Tables are for instructor/student guidance only; they are not mandatory for each ground lesson, flight lesson, or stage of training. At the completion of this course, the student must meet the minimum requirements of Part 141 for ground and flight training in order to graduate. Preflight and postflight briefings are as required.

COURSES OVERVIEW

Instrument/Commercial Syllabus

Lesson Time Allocation

Stage II

Ground Lessons	ATD	Pilot Briefings	Stage/Final Exams	Exam Debriefings	Lesson	Dual Day Local	Dual Day Cross-Country	Dual Night Local	Dual Night Cross-Country	Dual Instrument	Solo Day Local	Solo Day Cross-Country
1.0					GL 10 – Departure Charts and Procedures							
1.5					GL 11 – Enroute Charts and Procedures							
1.0	As Req.				GL 12 – Holding Procedures							
					FL 14 – VOR/NDB/GPS Holding	1.0				1.0		
					FL 15 – Localizer Holding	1.0				1.0		
					FL 16 – DME and Intersection Holding	1.5				1.5		
1.0					GL 13 – Arrival Charts and Procedures							
1.5					GL 14 – Approach Charts							
1.0					GL 15 – Approach Procedures							
1.0	As Req.				GL 16 – VOR and NDB Approaches							
				.5	Briefing – Instrument Approaches							
					FL 17 – VOR Approaches	1.0				1.0		
1.0	As Req.				GL 17 – ILS Approaches							
1.0					GL 18 – RNAV Approaches							
					FL 18 and 19 – RNAV (GPS) and/or NDB Approaches	2.0				2.0		
					FL 20 – ILS Approaches	1.0				1.0		
					FL 21 – Partial-Panel Approaches	1.0				1.0		
					FL 22 – Review Holding and Approaches	1.0				1.0		
		1.0	As Req.		GL 19 – Stage II Exam							
					FL 23 – Stage II Check	1.5				1.5		
10.0	As Req.	.5	1.0	As Req.	**Stage Totals**	11.0				11.0		

NOTE:
1. Ground lessons may include class discussion or online lessons.
2. The ATD may be used as required in the ground lessons indicated. Operators utilizing the ATD option in the Instrument/Commercial or Instrument Rating Course may credit up to 5 hours of ATD time toward ground training requirements.
3. The individual times shown on the Allocation Tables are for instructor/student guidance only; they are not mandatory for each ground lesson, flight lesson, or stage of training. At the completion of this course, the student must meet the minimum requirements of Part 141 for ground and flight training in order to graduate. Preflight and postflight briefings are as required.

COURSES OVERVIEW

xxiii

Instrument/Commercial Syllabus

COURSES OVERVIEW

Lesson Time Allocation

Ground Training						Flight Training — Dual				Flight Training — Solo	
Ground Lessons	ATD	Pilot Briefings	Stage/Final Exams	Exam Debriefings		Day Local	Day Cross-Country	Night Local	Night Cross-Country	Instrument	Day Local	Day Cross-Country

Stage III

Ground Lessons	ATD	Pilot Briefings	Stage/Final Exams	Exam Debriefings	Lesson	Day Local	Day Cross-Country	Night Local	Night Cross-Country	Instrument	Day Local	Day Cross-Country
1.0					GL 20 – Weather Factors and Hazards							
1.0					GL 21 – Printed Reports and Forecasts							
		.5			Briefing – IFR Cross-Country							
					FL 24 – IFR Cross-Country Procedures		1.0			1.0		
1.0					GL 22 – Graphic Weather Products							
					FL 25 – IFR Cross-Country		2.0			2.0		
1.0					GL 23 – Sources of Weather Information							
1.0					GL 24 – IFR Emergencies							
1.0					GL 25 – IFR SRM / IFR Flight Planning							
					FL 26 – Long IFR Cross-Country		3.0			3.0		
		1.0			Briefing – Instrument Rating Practical Test							
					FL 27 – IFR Cross-Country Review		2.0			2.0		
			1.0	As Req.	GL 26 – Stage III Exam							
					FL 28 – Stage III Check	1.5				1.5		
			1.0	As Req.	GL 27 – Instrument Rating End-of-Course Exam							
					FL 29 – End-of-Course Flight Check	1.5				1.5		
6.0		1.5	2.0	As Req.	**Stage Totals**	3.0	8.0			11.0		
24.0	(5.0)	2.0	4.0	As Req.	**Instrument Rating Course Totals**	27.0	8.0			35.0		

NOTE:
1. Ground lessons may include class discussion or online lessons.
2. The ATD may be used as required in the ground lessons indicated. Operators utilizing the ATD option in the Instrument/Commercial or Instrument Rating Course may credit up to 5 hours of ATD time toward ground training requirements.
3. The individual times shown on the Allocation Tables are for instructor/student guidance only; they are not mandatory for each ground lesson, flight lesson, or stage of training. At the completion of this course, the student must meet the minimum requirements of Part 141 for ground and flight training in order to graduate. Preflight and postflight briefings are as required.

Instrument/Commercial Syllabus

Lesson Time Allocation

Stage IV

Ground Training				Lesson	Flight Training — Dual					Flight Training — Solo		
Ground Lessons	Pilot Briefings	Stage/Final Exams	Exam Debriefings		Day Local	Day Cross-Country	Night	Complex	Instrument	Day Local	Day Cross-Country	Night
1.5				GL 28 – Airports/Airspace, Meteorology, VFR Charts								
1.5				GL 29 – Pilotage and Dead Reckoning								
	As Req.			Briefing – Cross-Country Procedures (VFR)								
				FL 30 – Day Cross-Country (VFR)		3.0			As Req.			
2.0				GL 30 – Aviation Physiology								
				FL 31 – Night Local			1.0					
2.0				GL 31 – Single-Pilot Resource Management								
				FL 32 – Night Cross-Country			4.0		As Req.			
2.0				GL 32 – Commercial FARs								
				FL 33 – Night Local Solo								1.5
				FL 34 – Night Local Solo								1.5
				FL 35 – Night Cross-Country Solo								3.0
		1.0	As Req.	GL 33 – Stage IV Exam								
				FL 36 – Cross-Country							5.0	
				FL 37 – Cross-Country							5.0	
				FL 38 – Cross-Country							5.0	
				FL 39 – Cross-Country							5.0	
				FL 40 – Cross-Country							5.0	
				FL 41 – Cross-Country							4.0	
				FL 42 – Cross-Country		3.0						
				FL 43 – Long Cross-Country							5.0	
				FL 44 – Stage IV Check		2.0						
9.0	As Req.	1.0	As Req.	**Stage Totals**		8.0	5.0				34.0	6.0

NOTE:
1. Ground lessons may include class discussion or online lessons.
2. The individual times shown on the Allocation Tables are for instructor/student guidance only; they are not mandatory for each ground lesson, flight lesson, or stage of training. At the completion of this course, the student must meet the minimum requirements of Part 141 for ground and flight training in order to graduate. Preflight and postflight briefings are as required.
3. Flight lessons 36 through 41 are designed for solo or dual flight as necessary to meet the proficiency requirements for the End-of-Course Flight Check and FAA Commercial Pilot Practical Test.

COURSES OVERVIEW

XXV

Instrument/Commercial Syllabus

COURSES OVERVIEW

Lesson Time Allocation

Ground Training					Flight Training						
					Dual					Solo	
Ground Lessons	Pilot Briefings	Stage/Final Exams	Exam Debriefings		Day Local	Day Cross-Country	Night	Complex	Instrument	Day Local	Day Cross-Country	Night

Stage V

Ground Lessons	Pilot Briefings	Stage/Final Exams	Exam Debriefings	Lesson	Day Local	Day XC	Night	Complex	Instrument	Solo Day Local	Solo Day XC	Solo Night
				FL 45 – Basic Flight Maneuvers					1.0			
2.0				GL 34 – High Performance Powerplants								
2.0				GL 35 – Environmental and Ice Control Systems								
2.0				GL 36 – Retractable Landing Gear								
			As Req.	Briefing – Complex Aircraft Transition								
				FL 46 – Complex	1.0 (1.0)			1.0 (1.0)				
				FL 47 – Complex	1.5 (1.0)			1.5 (1.0)	As Req.			
2.0				GL 37 – Advanced Aerodynamics and Accelerated Stalls								
				FL 48 – Complex	1.5 (1.0)			1.5 (1.0)	As Req.			
2.0				GL 38 – Predicting Performance								
2.0				GL 39 – Controlling Weight and Balance								
2.0				GL 40 – Maximum Performance Takeoffs and Landings								
				FL 49 – Complex	1.5 (1.0)			1.5 (1.0)				
				FL 50 – Complex	1.5 (1.0)			1.5 (1.0)				
				FL 51 – Stall/Spin Awareness	1.5 (1.0)							
			As Req.	Briefing – Commercial Flight Maneuvers								
2.0				GL 41 – Steep Turns and Chandelles								
				FL 52 – Steep Turns and Chandelles	1.5 (1.0)							
2.0				GL 42 – Lazy 8s, Pylon 8s, Steep Spirals, and Accuracy Landings								
				FL 53 – Lazy 8s, Pylon 8s, Steep Spirals, and Accuracy Landings	1.5 (1.0)							
				FL 54 – Review Commercial Maneuvers						1.0		
				FL 55 – Review Commercial Maneuvers						1.0		
				FL 56 – Review Commercial Maneuvers						1.0		
				FL 57 – Review Commercial Maneuvers	1.5 (1.0)				As Req.			
2.0				GL 43 – Emergency Procedures								
				FL 58 – Instrument/Commercial Review	1.5 (1.0)				As Req.			
2.0				GL 44 – Commercial Pilot SRM								
				FL 59 – Commercial Maneuvers						1.0		
				FL 60 – Commercial Maneuvers						1.0		
				FL 61 – Commercial Maneuvers						1.0		
				FL 62 – Commercial Maneuvers						1.0		
				FL 63 – Commercial Maneuvers						1.0		
				FL 64 – Commercial Maneuvers	1.5 (1.0)							
				FL 65 – Commercial Maneuvers	1.0 (1.0)							
				FL 66 – Complex	2.0 (1.0)			2.0 (1.0)	As Req.			
		1.0	As Req.	GL 45 – Stage V Exam								
		2.0	As Req.	GL 46 – Commercial Pilot End-of-Course Exam								
				FL 67 – Stage V Check (Complex)	1.0 (1.0)			1.0 (1.0)	As Req.			
22.0	As Req.	3.0	As Req.	Stage Totals	20.0 (14.0)			10.0 (7.0)	As Req.	9.0		

NOTE:
1. Ground lessons may include class discussion or online lessons.
2. The individual times shown on the Allocation Tables are for instructor/student guidance only; they are not mandatory for each ground lesson, flight lesson, or stage of training. At the completion of this course, the student must meet the minimum requirements of Part 141 for ground and flight training in order to graduate. Preflight and postflight briefings are as required.
3. In blocks where two times are shown, the first time is for students taking the Commercial Pilot–Airplane Single-Engine Land Practical Test at the end of Stage VI. If the student chooses to complete the second flight time listed (shown in parentheses) for Flight Stages V and VI, the student must also complete the multi-engine flight training time in Stage VII to meet the total time required for commercial pilot certification.

Instrument/Commercial Syllabus

Lesson Time Allocation

Ground Training					Flight Training							
					Dual				Solo		
Ground Lessons	Pilot Briefings	Stage/Final Exams	Exam Debriefings		Day Local	Day Cross-Country	Night	Complex	Instrument	Day Local	Day Cross-Country	Night

Flight Stage VI

				Lesson								
				FL 68 – Instrument/Commercial Review	2.0 (1.0)				As Req.			
				FL 69 – Instrument/Commercial Maneuvers/Procedures	2.0 (1.0)				As Req.			
				FL 70 – Commercial Maneuvers					2.0			
				FL 71 – Commercial Maneuvers					2.0			
				FL 72 – Commercial Maneuvers	2.0 (1.0)							
				FL 73 – Commercial Maneuvers					2.0			
				FL 74 – Commercial Maneuvers					2.0			
				FL 75 – Commercial Maneuvers					2.0			
				FL 76 – Commercial Maneuvers/Procedures	2.0 (1.0)				As Req.			
				FL 77 – Commercial Maneuvers/Procedures	2.0 (1.0)				As Req.			
				FL 78 – Complex Review	2.0 (1.0)			2.0 (1.0)				
				FL 79 – Solo Review						2.0		
				FL 80 – Solo Review						2.0		
				FL 81 – Solo Review						2.0		
				FL 82 – Complex Cross-Country		2.0 (1.0)		2.0 (1.0)	As Req.			
				FL 83 – Complex	1.0 (1.0)			1.0 (1.0)				
	As Req.			Briefing – Commercial Pilot Practical Test								
				FL 84 – Final Stage Review	2.0 (1.0)							
				FL 85 – Final Stage Review	2.0 (1.0)							
				FL 86 – Stage VI Check	1.5 (1.5)							
				FL 87 – End-of-Course Flight Check	1.5 (1.5)							
	As Req.			**Stage Totals**	20.0 (12.0)	2.0 (1.0)		5.0 (3.0)	As Req.	16.0		
31.0	As Req.	4.0	As Req.	**Commercial Pilot Course Totals**	40.0 (26.0)	10.0 (9.0)	5.0	15.0 (10.0)	As Req.	25.0	34.0	6.0

NOTE:
1. Stage VI does not contain ground lessons. The total ground training time listed is from Stages IV and V.
2. The individual times shown on the Allocation Tables are for instructor/student guidance only; they are not mandatory for each ground lesson, flight lesson, or stage of training. At the completion of this course, the student must meet the minimum requirements of Part 141 for ground and flight training in order to graduate. Preflight and postflight briefings are as required.
3. In blocks where two times are shown, the first time is for students taking the Commercial Pilot–Airplane Single-Engine Land Practical Test at the end of Stage VI. If the student chooses to complete the second flight time listed (shown in parentheses) for Flight Stages V and VI, the student must also complete the multi-engine flight training time in Stage VII to meet the total time required for commercial pilot certification.

COURSES OVERVIEW

Instrument/Commercial Syllabus

Lesson Time Allocation

Ground Stage VI and Flight Stage VII

Ground Lessons	Pilot Briefings	Stage/Final Exams	Exam Debriefings	Lesson	Dual Day Local	Dual Day Cross-Country	Dual Night	Dual Complex	Dual Instrument	Solo Day Local	Solo Day Cross-Country	Solo Night
2.0				GL 1 – The ME Rating, SRM, and Normal Ops.								
	.5			Briefing – Multi-Engine Operations and Systems								
				FL 1 – Introduction Multi-Engine Airplane and Maneuvers	1.0			1.0	.2			
2.0				GL 2 – Aircraft Systems, Wt. & Balance, & Performance								
	.5			Briefing – ME Performance Considerations								
				FL 2 – Maneuvers – VR/IR	1.0			1.0	.3			
				FL 3 – Short-Field Takeoffs and Landings	1.0			1.0	.2			
1.5				GL 3 – ME/Engine-Out Aerodynamics & Maneuvers								
1.5				GL 4 – Engine-Out Operations								
	.5			Briefing – Engine-Out Operations								
				FL 4 – Engine-Out Operations	1.0			1.0	.2			
				FL 5 – Engine-Out Operations	1.0			1.0	.2			
				FL 6 – Engine-Out Operations Review	1.0			1.0	.2			
2.0				GL 5 – Instrument Flight and Applying SRM								
	.5			Briefing – Multi-Engine Instrument Flight								
				FL 7 – Instrument Procedures	1.0			1.0	.7			
				FL 8 – Multi-Engine Instrument (Day Cross-Country)		3.0		3.0	1.0			
				FL 9 – Multi-Engine Instrument (Night Cross-Country)			3.0	3.0	1.0			
		1.0	1.0	GL 6 – Stage VI Exam								
				Briefing—Multi-Engine Rating Practical Test								
				FL 10 – Stage VII Check	1.0			1.0	.5			
		1.0	1.0	GL 7 – Multi-Engine End-of-Course Exam								
				FL 11 – End-of-Course Flight Check	1.0			1.0	.5			
9.0	2.0	2.0	2.0	Multi-Engine Stage Totals	9.0	3.0	3.0	15.0	5.0			

NOTE: 1. This table covers Ground Stage VI and Flight Stage VII.
2. The individual times shown on the Allocation Tables are for instructor/student guidance only; they are not mandatory for each ground lesson, flight lesson, or stage of training. At the completion of this course, the student must meet the minimum requirements of Part 141 for ground and flight training in order to graduate. Preflight and postflight briefings are as required.
3. The dual instrument flight training time is shown to indicate the recommended portion of the flights that should be devoted to instrument training.

COURSES OVERVIEW

xxviii

Instrument/Commercial Syllabus

Instrument Rating Ground Training Stage I

STAGE OBJECTIVES
During this stage, the student learns about the principles of instrument flight, including the operation, use, and limitations of flight instruments and instrument navigation systems, and how the air traffic control system functions. Stage I also introduces single-pilot resource management (SRM) and human factors concepts related to flight in the IFR environment.

STAGE COMPLETION STANDARDS
The student must pass the Stage I Exam with a minimum score of 80 percent, and review each incorrect response with the instructor to ensure complete understanding before starting Stage II.

GROUND LESSON 1
REFERENCES

Instrument/Commercial Textbook/EBook
Chapter 1 — Building Professional Experience

Instrument Online — Jeppesen Learning Center
GL 1 — Discovering Instrument Flight
GL 2 — Human Factors

NOTE: *Students should read Chapter 1, Sections A and B, prior to Ground Lesson 1.*

OBJECTIVES
- Understand the training requirements for an instrument rating.
- Become familiar with single-pilot resource management (SRM) concepts that apply to flight in the IFR environment.
- Explain aviation physiology factors that apply to flight in the IFR environment.

CONTENT
COURSE OVERVIEW
❏ Course Elements and Materials
❏ Exams and Tests
❏ Policies and Procedures

Instrument/Commercial Syllabus

STAGE I — Instrument Rating Ground Training

❏ Student/Instructor Expectations
❏ Use of a Flight Simulator, FTD, or ATD

SECTION A — INSTRUMENT/COMMERCIAL TRAINING AND OPPORTUNITIES

GL 1 — DISCOVERING INSTRUMENT FLIGHT
❏ Instrument Flight
❏ Instrument/Commercial Training
❏ Commercial Pilot Privileges
❏ Additional Certificates and Ratings

SECTION B — ADVANCED HUMAN FACTORS CONCEPTS

GL 2 — HUMAN FACTORS

SINGLE-PILOT RESOURCE MANAGEMENT
❏ Aeronautical Decision Making
❏ Risk Management
❏ Task Management
❏ Situational Awareness
❏ Controlled Flight Into Terrain Awareness
❏ Automation Management

AVIATION PHYSIOLOGY
❏ Disorientation
❏ Motion Sickness
❏ Hypoxia
❏ Decompression Sickness
❏ Hyperventilation
❏ Fitness for Flight

COMPLETION STANDARDS
Demonstrate understanding of instrument rating training requirements, and SRM and physiology concepts that apply to IFR flight during oral quizzing by the instructor or by completing the online exam for GL 2 with a minimum score of 80 percent.

POSTFLIGHT BRIEFING
❏ Critique maneuvers/procedures and SRM.
❏ Create a plan for skills that need improvement.
❏ Update the record folder and logbook.

STUDY ASSIGNMENT

Instrument/Commercial Textbook/EBook
  Chapter 2 — Principles of Instrument Flight
    Section A — Flight Instrument Systems

Instrument Online — Jeppesen Learning Center
  GL 3 — Analog Flight Instruments
  GL 4 — Digital Flight Instruments

Instrument/Commercial Syllabus

GROUND LESSON 2

REFERENCES

Instrument/Commercial Textbook/EBook
Chapter 2 — Principles of Instrument Flight
Section A — Flight Instrument Systems

Instrument Online — Jeppesen Learning Center
GL 3 — Analog Flight Instruments
GL 4 — Digital Flight Instruments

OBJECTIVES
- Explain the function and operation of the flight instrument systems and components.
- Recognize the limitations and common errors of the flight instrument systems and components.

CONTENT

INSTRUMENTS FOR FLIGHT UNDER IFR
- ❑ FAA Instrument Requirements
- ❑ Inspection Requirements

GYROSCOPIC FLIGHT INSTRUMENTS
- ❑ System Operation
- ❑ System Errors
- ❑ Instrument Check

MAGNETIC COMPASS
- ❑ System Operation
- ❑ System Errors
- ❑ Instrument Check

PITOT-STATIC INSTRUMENTS
- ❑ System Operation
- ❑ System Errors
- ❑ Instrument Check
- ❑ V-Speeds and Color Codes

INTEGRATED DISPLAYS
- ❑ Primary Flight Display (PFD)
- ❑ Attitude and Heading Reference System (AHRS)
- ❑ Attitude Indicator
- ❑ Horizontal Situation Indicator (HSI)
- ❑ Air Data Computer (ADC)
- ❑ Airspeed Indicator
- ❑ Altimeter
- ❑ Vertical Speed Indicator (VSI)
- ❑ PFD Failure

COMPLETION STANDARDS
- Demonstrate understanding of IFR instrument requirements, instrument flight systems, instrument operations, and instrument errors during oral quizzing by the instructor.
- Complete with a minimum score of 80 percent: questions for Chapter 2A or online exams for GL 3 and 4. Review each incorrect response with the instructor to ensure complete understanding before starting Ground Lesson 3.

STUDY ASSIGNMENT
Instrument/Commercial Textbook/EBook
   Chapter 2 — Principles of Instrument Flight
      Section B — Attitude Instrument Flying

Instrument Online — Jeppesen Learning Center
   GL 5 — Attitude Instrument Flying

GROUND LESSON 3

REFERENCES

Instrument/Commercial Textbook/EBook
   Chapter 2 — Principles of Instrument Flight
      Section B — Attitude Instrument Flying

Instrument Online — Jeppesen Learning Center
   GL 5 — Attitude Instrument Flying

OBJECTIVES
- Identify the fundamental procedures related to instrument cross-check, instrument interpretation, and aircraft control.
- Recognize the techniques that apply to attitude instrument flying, including common methods, performing basic maneuvers, managing instrument system failures, partial-panel flying procedures, and unusual attitude recovery.

CONTENT
FUNDAMENTAL SKILLS
- ❏ Instrument Cross-Check
- ❏ Instrument Interpretation
- ❏ Aircraft Control

ATTITUDE INSTRUMENT FLYING METHODS
- ❏ Control and Performance Method
- ❏ Primary and Supporting Method

Instrument/Commercial Syllabus

MANEUVERS
- ❏ Straight-and-Level Flight
- ❏ Standard-Rate Turns
- ❏ Steep Turns
- ❏ Constant Airspeed Climbs
- ❏ Constant Rate Climbs
- ❏ Constant Airspeed Descents
- ❏ Constant Rate Descents
- ❏ Leveloff From Climbs and Descents
- ❏ Climbing and Descending Turns
- ❏ Common Errors

INSTRUMENT FAILURES
- ❏ Partial-Panel Flying
- ❏ Gyroscopic Instrument Failure
- ❏ Compass Turns
- ❏ Timed Turns
- ❏ Pitot-Static Instrument Failures

UNUSUAL ATTITUDE RECOVERY
- ❏ Nose-High Unusual Attitude
- ❏ Nose-Low Unusual Attitude

INTRODUCTION TO THE ATD (OPTION)
- ❏ Orientation and Flight Familiarization
- ❏ Overview of Physical and Virtual Controls
- ❏ Aircraft Systems Related to IFR Operations
- ❏ Instrument and Equipment Cockpit Check
- ❏ Full-Panel Instrument Maneuvers
- ❏ Partial-Panel Instrument Considerations

COMPLETION STANDARDS
- Demonstrate understanding of basic attitude instrument flying, coping with instrument failures, and unusual attitude recovery during oral quizzing by the instructor.
- Complete with a minimum score of 80 percent: questions for Chapter 2B or online exam for GL 5. Review each incorrect response with the instructor to ensure complete understanding before starting Ground Lesson 4.

STUDY ASSIGNMENT
Instrument/Commercial Textbook/EBook
  Chapter 2 — Principles of Instrument Flight
    Section C — Instrument Navigation

Instrument Online — Jeppesen Learning Center
  GL 6 — Instrument Navigation

Instrument/Commercial Syllabus

GROUND LESSON 4

REFERENCES

Instrument/Commercial Textbook/EBook
Chapter 2 — Principles of Instrument Flight
Section C — Instrument Navigation

Instrument Online — Jeppesen Learning Center
GL 6 — Instrument Navigation

OBJECTIVES
- Explain the operation and limitations of VOR, DME, GPS, and ADF equipment.
- Identify how to navigate using VOR, DME, GPS, and ADF equipment.

CONTENT

VOR NAVIGATION
- ❏ Horizontal Situation Indicator
- ❏ Intercepting a Radial
- ❏ Tracking
- ❏ Determining Your Progress
- ❏ Time and Distance to a Station
- ❏ Station Passage
- ❏ VOR Operational Considerations
- ❏ Distance Measuring Equipment
- ❏ DME Arcs

AREA NAVIGATION (RNAV)
- ❏ Required Navigation Performance (RNP)
- ❏ Inertial Navigation System (INS)
- ❏ Flight Management Systems (FMS)

GPS NAVIGATION
- ❏ Wide Area Augmentation System (WAAS)
- ❏ Ground-Based Augmentation System (GBAS)
- ❏ Requirements for IFR GPS Navigation
- ❏ Navigating with GPS

ADF NAVIGATION
- ❏ Radio Magnetic Indicator
- ❏ Intercepting a Bearing
- ❏ Tracking
- ❏ ADF Operational Considerations

ATD (OPTION)
- ❏ VOR Orientation
- ❏ HSI and RMI Orientation
- ❏ Intercepting and Tracking a VOR Radial
- ❏ Intercepting and Tracking DME Arcs
- ❏ GPS Programming

Instrument/Commercial Syllabus

- ❏ Intercepting and Tracking GPS Courses
- ❏ Integrated Display Orientation
- ❏ NDB Orientation
- ❏ Intercepting and Tracking NDB Bearings

COMPLETION STANDARDS
- Demonstrate understanding of the operation and limitations of navigation systems during oral quizzing by the instructor.
- Complete with a minimum score of 80 percent: questions for Chapter 2C or online exam for GL 6. Review each incorrect response with the instructor to ensure complete understanding before starting Ground Lesson 5.

STUDY ASSIGNMENT
FAR/AIM
Instrument FARs

GROUND LESSON 5

REFERENCES

FAR/AIM
Instrument FARs

OBJECTIVES
- Understand the Federal Aviation Regulations related to instrument flight.
- Understand the accident and incident information in NTSB Part 830.

CONTENT
- ❏ FAR Part 1
- ❏ FAR Part 61
- ❏ FAR Part 91
- ❏ NTSB Part 830

COMPLETION STANDARDS
- Demonstrate understanding of the FARs in Parts 1, 61, and 91 related to instrument flight and the accident and incident reporting requirements of NTSB Part 830 during oral quizzing by the instructor before starting Ground Lesson 6.

STUDY ASSIGNMENT
Instrument/Commercial Textbook/EBook
   Chapter 3 — The Flight Environment
      Section A — Airports, Airspace, and Flight Information

Instrument Online — Jeppesen Learning Center
   GL 7 — Airports, Airspace, and Flight Information

GROUND LESSON 6

REFERENCES

Instrument/Commercial Textbook/EBook
Chapter 3 — The Flight Environment
  Section A — Airports, Airspace, and Flight Information

Instrument Online — Jeppesen Learning Center
GL 7 — Airports, Airspace, and Flight Information

OBJECTIVES
- Interpret airport markings, lighting, and signs.
- Identify procedures to avoid runway incursions and to perform land and hold short operations (LAHSO).
- Explain the structure and requirements of the National Airspace System.
- Recognize sources of flight information and how they apply to IFR operations.

CONTENT

AIRPORT ENVIRONMENT
- ❑ Runway and Taxiway Markings and Signs
- ❑ Runway Incursion Avoidance
- ❑ Land and Hold Short Operations (LAHSO)
- ❑ Approach Light System
- ❑ Visual Glide Slope Indicators
- ❑ Runway Lighting
- ❑ Airport Beacons and Obstruction Lights

AIRSPACE
- ❑ Class A, B, C, D, and E Airspace (Controlled)
- ❑ Special VFR
- ❑ Class G Airspace (Uncontrolled)
- ❑ Aircraft Speed Limits
- ❑ Special Use Airspace
- ❑ Other Airspace Areas
- ❑ ADIZ

FLIGHT INFORMATION
- ❑ *Airport/Facility Directory*
- ❑ *Aeronautical Information Manual*
- ❑ *Notices to Airman (NOTAMs)*
- ❑ *International Flight Information Manual*
- ❑ *FAA Advisory Circulars and Handbooks*

COMPLETION STANDARDS
- Demonstrate understanding of the airport environment, airspace, and sources of flight information during oral quizzing by the instructor.
- Complete with a minimum score of 80 percent: questions for Chapter 3A or online exam for GL 7. Review each incorrect response with the instructor to ensure complete understanding before starting Ground Lesson 7.

Instrument/Commercial Syllabus

STUDY ASSIGNMENT
Instrument/Commercial Textbook/EBook
 Chapter 3 — The Flight Environment
  Section B — Air Traffic Control System

Instrument Online — Jeppesen Learning Center
 GL 8 — Air Traffic Control System

GROUND LESSON 7

REFERENCES

Instrument/Commercial Textbook/EBook
 Chapter 3 — The Flight Environment
  Section B — Air Traffic Control System

Instrument Online — Jeppesen Learning Center
 GL 8 — Air Traffic Control System

OBJECTIVES
- Recognize the types of services provided by the air traffic control system.
- Explain the use of enroute and terminal facilities in the IFR environment.

CONTENT

AIR ROUTE TRAFFIC CONTROL CENTER
- ❏ ARTCC Traffic Separation
- ❏ Processing the IFR Flight Plan
- ❏ Air Route Surveillance Radar (ARSR)
- ❏ Separation from VFR Traffic
- ❏ Weather Avoidance
- ❏ Safety Alerts
- ❏ Emergency Assistance

TERMINAL FACILITIES
- ❏ Terminal Radar Approach Control (TRACON)
- ❏ Control Tower
- ❏ ATIS
- ❏ Clearance Delivery

TRAFFIC INFORMATION
- ❏ ADS-B
- ❏ Radar Service for VFR Aircraft
- ❏ Traffic Advisories

COMPLETION STANDARDS
- Demonstrate understanding of enroute and terminal ATC services during oral quizzing by the instructor.

9

Instrument/Commercial Syllabus

- Complete with a minimum score of 80 percent: questions for Chapter 3B or online exam for GL 8. Review each incorrect response with the instructor to ensure complete understanding before starting Ground Lesson 8.

STUDY ASSIGNMENT
Instrument/Commercial Textbook/EBook
   Chapter 3 — The Flight Environment
      Section C — ATC Clearances

Instrument Online — Jeppesen Learning Center
   GL 9 — ATC Clearances

GROUND LESSON 8
REFERENCES

Instrument/Commercial Textbook/EBook
   Chapter 3 — The Flight Environment
      Section C — ATC Clearances

Instrument Online — Jeppesen Learning Center
   GL 9 — ATC Clearances

OBJECTIVES
- Recognize the elements of an IFR clearance.
- Explain ATC clearance procedures in the IFR environment.
- Demonstrate how to write clearance shorthand.

CONTENT

PILOT RESPONSIBILITIES
- ❏ See and Avoid
- ❏ IFR Climb Considerations

IFR FLIGHT PLAN AND ATC CLEARANCE
- ❏ Elements of an IFR Clearance
- ❏ Abbreviated IFR Departure Clearance
- ❏ VFR on Top
- ❏ Approach Clearances
- ❏ VFR Restrictions to an IFR Clearance
- ❏ Composite Flight Plan
- ❏ Tower Enroute Control Clearance
- ❏ Departure Restrictions
- ❏ Clearance Readback
- ❏ Clearance Shorthand

STAGE I ■ Instrument Rating Ground Training

Instrument/Commercial Syllabus

COMPLETION STANDARDS
- Demonstrate understanding of pilot responsibilities and IFR clearance procedures during oral quizzing by the instructor.
- Complete with a minimum score of 80 percent: questions for Chapter 3C or online exam for GL 9. Review each incorrect response with the instructor to ensure complete understanding before starting Ground Lesson 9.

STUDY ASSIGNMENT
Review the content of Ground Lessons 1 – 8 to prepare for the Stage I Exam.

GROUND LESSON 9
STAGE I EXAM

REFERENCES

Ground Lessons 1 – 8

OBJECTIVE
Demonstrate knowledge of the subjects covered in Ground Lessons 1 – 8 by passing the Stage I Exam.

CONTENT
STAGE I EXAM
- ❏ Advanced Human Factors Concepts
- ❏ Flight Instrument Systems
- ❏ Attitude Instrument Flying
- ❏ Instrument Navigation
- ❏ Instrument FARs
- ❏ Airports, Airspace, and Flight Information
- ❏ Air Traffic Control System
- ❏ ATC Clearances

COMPLETION STANDARDS
To complete the lesson and stage, pass the Stage I Exam with a minimum score of 80 percent. Review each incorrect response with the instructor to ensure complete understanding before starting Stage II.

STUDY ASSIGNMENT
Instrument/Commercial Textbook/EBook
  Chapter 4 — Departure

Instrument Online — Jeppesen Learning Center
  GL 11 — Departure Charts and Procedures

Instrument/Commercial Syllabus

STAGE II

STAGE OBJECTIVES
During this stage, the student learns how to interpret instrument charts and explores the procedures for performing IFR departure, enroute, arrival, and approach operations.

STAGE COMPLETION STANDARDS
The student must pass the Stage II Exam with a minimum score of 80 percent, and review each incorrect response with the instructor to ensure complete understanding before starting Stage III.

GROUND LESSON 10

REFERENCES

Instrument/Commercial Textbook/EBook
Chapter 4 — Departure

Instrument Online — Jeppesen Learning Center
GL 11 — Departure Charts and Procedures

OBJECTIVES
- Interpret the information on departure charts.
- Explain how to perform departure procedures.

CONTENT

SECTION A — DEPARTURE CHARTS
GL 11 — DEPARTURE CHARTS AND PROCEDURES
- ❏ Obtaining Charts
- ❏ Departure Standards
- ❏ Instrument Departure Procedures (DPs)
- ❏ Obstacle Departure Procedures (ODPs)
- ❏ Standard Instrument Departures (SIDs)
- ❏ Vector SID
- ❏ Pilot Nav SID

SECTION B — DEPARTURE PROCEDURES
GL 11 — DEPARTURE CHARTS AND PROCEDURES
- ❏ Briefing a Departure
- ❏ Takeoff Minimums
- ❏ Departure Options (SIDs and ODPs)
- ❏ Radar Departures
- ❏ VFR Departures
- ❏ Selecting a Departure Method

Instrument/Commercial Syllabus

COMPLETION STANDARDS
- Demonstrate understanding of interpreting instrument departure charts and following departure procedures during oral quizzing by the instructor.
- Complete with a minimum score of 80 percent: questions for Chapter 4 or online exam for GL 11. Review each incorrect response with the instructor to ensure complete understanding before starting Ground Lesson 11.

STUDY ASSIGNMENT
Instrument/Commercial Textbook/EBook
  Chapter 5 — Enroute
      Section A — Enroute and Area Charts
      Section B — Enroute Procedures

Instrument Online — Jeppesen Learning Center
  GL 12 — Enroute Charts
  GL 13 — Enroute Procedures

GROUND LESSON 11

REFERENCES

Instrument/Commercial Textbook/EBook
  Chapter 5 — Enroute
      Section A — Enroute and Area Charts
      Section B — Enroute Procedures

Instrument Online — Jeppesen Learning Center
  GL 12 — Enroute Charts
  GL 13 — Enroute Procedures

OBJECTIVES
- Interpret the information on IFR enroute and area charts.
- Explain how to perform the proper procedures for the flying enroute in the IFR environment.

CONTENT

SECTION A — ENROUTE AND AREA CHARTS
GL 12 — ENROUTE CHARTS
- ❏ Enroute Charts
- ❏ Front Panel
- ❏ Navigation Aids
- ❏ Victor Airways
- ❏ Communication
- ❏ Airports
- ❏ Airspace
- ❏ Area Charts

SECTION B — ENROUTE PROCEDURES
GL 13 — ENROUTE PROCEDURES
- Enroute Radar Procedures
- Reporting Procedures
- Enroute Navigation Using GPS
- IFR Cruising Altitudes
- Reduced Vertical Separation Minimums
- Descending from the Enroute Segment

COMPLETION STANDARDS
- Demonstrate understanding of IFR enroute charts and enroute procedures in the IFR environment during oral quizzing by the instructor.
- Complete with a minimum score of 80 percent: questions for Chapter 5A and 5B, or online exams for GL 12 and 13. Review each incorrect response with the instructor to ensure complete understanding before starting Ground Lesson 12.

STUDY ASSIGNMENT
Instrument/Commercial Textbook/EBook
  Chapter 5 — Enroute
    Section C — Holding Procedures

Instrument Online — Jeppesen Learning Center
  GL 14 — Holding Procedures

GROUND LESSON 12
REFERENCES

Instrument/Commercial Textbook/EBook
  Chapter 5 — Enroute
    Section C — Holding Procedures

Instrument Online — Jeppesen Learning Center
  GL 14 — Holding Procedures

OBJECTIVE
Describe how to perform holding patterns including entry, timing, and communication.

CONTENT
STANDARD AND NONSTANDARD PATTERN
- Outbound and Inbound Timing
- Crosswind Correction
- Maximum Holding Speed

Instrument/Commercial Syllabus

HOLDING ENTRIES AND ATC INSTRUCTIONS
- ❑ Direct Entry
- ❑ Teardrop Entry
- ❑ Parallel Entry
- ❑ Visualizing Entry Procedures
- ❑ ATC Holding Instructions

ATD (OPTION)
- ❑ Holding Entries
- ❑ VOR, GPS, and NDB Holding
- ❑ Wind Correction and Ground Track

COMPLETION STANDARDS
- Demonstrate understanding of holding pattern procedures, entries, and ATC holding instructions during oral quizzing by the instructor.
- Complete with a minimum score of 80 percent: questions for Chapter 5C or online exam for GL 14. Review each incorrect response with the instructor to ensure complete understanding before starting Ground Lesson 13.

STUDY ASSIGNMENT
Instrument/Commercial Textbook/EBook
  Chapter 6 — Arrival

Instrument Online — Jeppesen Learning Center
  GL 15 — Arrival Charts and Procedures

GROUND LESSON 13

REFERENCES

Instrument/Commercial Textbook/EBook
  Chapter 6 — Arrival

Instrument Online — Jeppesen Learning Center
  GL 15 — Arrival Charts and Procedures

OBJECTIVES
- Interpret the information on arrival charts.
- Explain arrival procedures and methods.

CONTENT

SECTION A — ARRIVAL CHARTS

GL 15 — ARRIVAL CHARTS AND PROCEDURES
- ❑ Standard Terminal Arrival Route
- ❑ Interpreting the STAR
- ❑ Vertical Navigation Planning

Instrument/Commercial Syllabus

SECTION B — ARRIVAL PROCEDURES

GL 15 — ARRIVAL CHARTS AND PROCEDURES
❏ Preparing for the Arrival
❏ Briefing the STAR Procedure

COMPLETION STANDARDS
- Demonstrate understanding of interpreting instrument departure charts and following departure procedures during oral quizzing by the instructor.
- Complete with a minimum score of 80 percent: questions for Chapter 6 or online exams for GL 15. Review each incorrect response with the instructor to ensure complete understanding before starting Ground Lesson 14.

STUDY ASSIGNMENT
Instrument/Commercial Textbook/EBook
   Chapter 7 — Approach
      Section A — Approach Charts

Instrument Online — Jeppesen Learning Center
   GL 16 — Approach Considerations
   GL 17 — Approach Charts

GROUND LESSON 14

REFERENCES

Instrument/Commercial Textbook/EBook
   Chapter 7 — Approach
      Section A — Approach Charts

Instrument Online — Jeppesen Learning Center
   GL 16 — Approach Considerations
   GL 17 — Approach Charts

OBJECTIVES
- Identify approach procedure types and the segments of an instrument approach procedure.
- Interpret and apply information published on instrument approach charts.

CONTENT

SECTION A — APPROACH CHARTS

GL 16 — APPROACH CONSIDERATIONS
❏ Initial Approach Segment
❏ Intermediate Approach Segment
❏ Final Approach Segment
❏ Missed Approach Segment

Instrument/Commercial Syllabus

SECTION A — APPROACH CHARTS
GL 17 — APPROACH CHARTS
- ❏ Heading Section
- ❏ Communications Section
- ❏ Briefing Information
- ❏ Minimum Safe/Sector Altitude
- ❏ Plan View
- ❏ Profile View
- ❏ Descent/Timing Conversion Table and Time and Speed Table
- ❏ Lighting Box
- ❏ Missed Approach Icons
- ❏ Landing Minimums
- ❏ Airport Sketch

AIRPORT CHART AND AIRPORT DIAGRAM
- ❏ Heading and Communications
- ❏ Airport Environment
- ❏ Runway Information
- ❏ Alternate Airports

COMPLETION STANDARDS
- Demonstrate understanding of instrument approach procedure types, segments and chart interpretation during oral quizzing by the instructor.
- Complete with a minimum score of 80 percent: questions for Chapter 7A or online exams for GL 16 and 17. Review each incorrect response with the instructor to ensure complete understanding before starting Ground Lesson 15.

STUDY ASSIGNMENT
Instrument/Commercial Textbook/EBook
  Chapter 7 — Approach
    Section B — Approach Procedures

Instrument Online — Jeppesen Learning Center
  GL 18 — Approach Procedures

GROUND LESSON 15
REFERENCES

Instrument/Commercial Textbook/EBook
  Chapter 7 — Approach
    Section B — Approach Procedures

Instrument Online — Jeppesen Learning Center
  GL 18 — Approach Procedures

Instrument/Commercial Syllabus

OBJECTIVES
- Describe how to prepare for an approach by performing an approach overview and approach briefing.
- Explain how to perform an approach by following the proper procedures depicted on the approach chart.

CONTENT

PREPARING FOR THE APPROACH
- ❏ Approach Overview
- ❏ Approach Briefing
- ❏ Approach Clearance

PERFORMING THE APPROACH
- ❏ Straight-In Landing Vs. Circling Approach
- ❏ Straight-In Approach
- ❏ Use of ATC Radar for Approaches
- ❏ Course Reversals
- ❏ Timed Approaches From a Holding Fix
- ❏ Final Approach
- ❏ Circling Approaches
- ❏ Sidestep Maneuver
- ❏ Missed Approach Procedures
- ❏ Visual and Contact Approaches

COMPLETION STANDARDS
- Demonstrate understanding of how to prepare for and perform an instrument approach procedure during oral quizzing by the instructor.
- Complete with a minimum score of 80 percent: questions for Chapter 7B or online exam for GL 18. Review each incorrect response with the instructor to ensure complete understanding before starting Ground Lesson 16.

STUDY ASSIGNMENT

Instrument/Commercial Textbook/EBook
Chapter 8 — Instrument Approaches
   Section A — VOR and NDB Approaches

Instrument Online — Jeppesen Learning Center
GL 21 — VOR Approach Procedures
GL 22 — NDB Approach Procedures

Instrument/Commercial Syllabus

GROUND LESSON 16

REFERENCES

Instrument/Commercial Textbook/EBook
  Chapter 8 — Instrument Approaches
    Section A — VOR and NDB Approaches

Instrument Online — Jeppesen Learning Center
  GL 21 — VOR Approach Procedures
  GL 22 — NDB Approach Procedures

OBJECTIVES
- Given an instrument approach chart, explain the procedures for performing a VOR approach.
- Given an instrument approach chart, explain the procedures for performing an NDB approach.

CONTENT

SECTION A — VOR AND NDB APPROACHES
GL 21 — VOR APPROACH PROCEDURES
- ❏ Off-Airport and On-Airport Facilities
- ❏ Flying a VOR/DME Approach
- ❏ Approach Briefing
- ❏ Performing the Approach

SECTION A — VOR AND NDB APPROACHES
GL 22 — NDB APPROACH PROCEDURES
- ❏ Flying an NDB Approach
- ❏ Preparing for the Approach
- ❏ Performing the Approach

ATD (OPTION)
- ❏ VOR Approach Procedures
- ❏ NDB Approach Procedures

COMPLETION STANDARDS
- Demonstrate understanding of VOR and NDB approach procedures using instrument approach charts during oral quizzing by the instructor.
- Complete with a minimum score of 80 percent: questions for Chapter 8A or online exams for GL 21 and 22. Review each incorrect response with the instructor to ensure complete understanding before starting Ground Lesson 17.

STUDY ASSIGNMENT

Instrument/Commercial Textbook/EBook
  Chapter 8 — Instrument Approaches
    Section B — ILS Approaches

Instrument Online — Jeppesen Learning Center
  GL 20 — ILS Approach Procedures

STAGE II ■ Instrument Rating Ground Training

Instrument/Commercial Syllabus

GROUND LESSON 17

REFERENCES

Instrument/Commercial Textbook/EBook
Chapter 8 — Instrument Approaches
Section B — ILS Approaches

Instrument Online — Jeppesen Learning Center
GL 20 — ILS Approach Procedures

OBJECTIVE
Given an instrument approach chart, explain the procedures for performing an ILS approach.

CONTENT

ILS CATEGORIES AND COMPONENTS
- Localizer
- Glide Slope
- Range Information

FLYING AN ILS APPROACH
- Flying a Straight-In ILS Approach
- Preparing for the Approach
- Performing the Approach
- ILS Approach with a Course Reversal
- ILS Approaches to Parallel Runways
- Simultaneous Converging Instrument Approach

LOCALIZER, LDA, AND SDF APPROACHES
- Localizer Approach
- Localizer Back Course Approach
- LDA Approach
- SDF Approach

ATD (OPTION)
- ILS Approach Procedures
- Localizer Approach Procedures

COMPLETION STANDARDS
- Demonstrate understanding of ILS and localizer approach procedures using instrument approach charts during oral quizzing by the instructor.
- Complete with a minimum score of 80 percent: questions for Chapter 8B or online exam for GL 20. Review each incorrect response with the instructor to ensure complete understanding before starting Ground Lesson 18.

STUDY ASSIGNMENT
Instrument/Commercial
   Chapter 8 — Instrument Approaches
      Section C — RNAV Approaches

Instrument/Commercial Syllabus

Instrument Online — Jeppesen Learning Center
GL 19 — RNAV Approach Procedures

GROUND LESSON 18

REFERENCES

Instrument/Commercial
Chapter 8 — Instrument Approaches
Section C — RNAV Approaches

Instrument Online — Jeppesen Learning Center
GL 19 — RNAV Approach Procedures

OBJECTIVE
Given an instrument approach chart, explain the procedures for performing an RNAV (GPS) approach.

CONTENT

RNAV (GPS) APPROACH DESIGN AND EQUIPMENT
- ❏ Terminal Arrival Area
- ❏ Waypoints
- ❏ GPS Approach Equipment
- ❏ Landing Minimums
- ❏ LNAV
- ❏ LNAV/VNAV
- ❏ LPV
- ❏ LP
- ❏ RNP Approach
- ❏ RAIM Failure During an Approach

FLYING AN RNAV (GPS) APPROACH
- ❏ Flying an RNAV (GPS) Approach to LPV Minimums
- ❏ Preparing for the Approach
- ❏ Performing the Approach
- ❏ Flying an RNAV (GPS) Approach to LNAV Minimums

COMPLETION STANDARDS
- Demonstrate understanding of RNAV (GPS) approach procedures using instrument approach charts during oral quizzing by the instructor.
- Complete with a minimum score of 80 percent: questions for Chapter 8C or online exams for GL 19. Review each incorrect response with the instructor to ensure complete understanding before starting Ground Lesson 19.

STUDY ASSIGNMENT
Review the content of Ground Lessons 10 – 18 to prepare for the Stage II Exam.

GROUND LESSON 19
STAGE II EXAM

REFERENCES
Ground Lessons 10 – 18

OBJECTIVE
Demonstrate knowledge of the subjects covered in Ground Lessons 10 – 18 by passing the Stage II Exam.

CONTENT
STAGE II EXAM
- Departure Charts and Procedures
- Enroute Charts and Procedures
- Holding Procedures
- Arrival Charts and Procedures
- Approach Charts and Procedures
- VOR and NDB Approaches
- ILS Approaches
- RNAV Approaches

COMPLETION STANDARDS
To complete the lesson and stage, pass the Stage II Exam with a minimum score of 80 percent. Review each incorrect response with the instructor to ensure complete understanding before starting Stage III.

STUDY ASSIGNMENT
Instrument/Commercial Textbook/EBook
  Chapter 9 — Meteorology
    Section A — Weather Factors
    Section B — Weather Hazards

Instrument Online — Jeppesen Learning Center
  GL 24 — Weather Factors and Hazards

Instrument/Commercial Syllabus

Stage III

STAGE OBJECTIVES
During this stage, the student learns to analyze weather information, conditions, and trends while on the ground and in flight. In addition, the student explores IFR flight planning and emergency procedures and develops a greater understanding of how to use single-pilot resource management (SRM) in the IFR environment.

STAGE COMPLETION STANDARDS
The student must pass the Stage III Exam and the Instrument Rating End-of-Course Exam with minimum scores of 80 percent, and review each incorrect response with the instructor to ensure complete understanding.

GROUND LESSON 20
REFERENCES

Instrument/Commercial Textbook/EBook
Chapter 9 — Meteorology
Section A — Weather Factors
Section B — Weather Hazards

Instrument Online — Jeppesen Learning Center
GL 24 — Weather Factors and Hazards

OBJECTIVES
- Recognize the factors that affect weather patterns.
- Identify the causes of and the risks associated with weather hazards that apply to flight operations.

CONTENT

SECTION A — WEATHER FACTORS
GL 24 — WEATHER FACTORS AND HAZARDS
- The Atmosphere
- Atmospheric Circulation
- Moisture, Precipitation, and Stability
- Types of Clouds
- Airmass
- Fronts
- High Altitude Weather

SECTION B — WEATHER HAZARDS
GL 24 — WEATHER FACTORS AND HAZARDS
- Thunderstorms
- Turbulence

- ❏ Wake Turbulence
- ❏ Clear Air Turbulence
- ❏ Mountain Wave Turbulence
- ❏ Reporting Turbulence
- ❏ Wind Shear
- ❏ Low Visibility
- ❏ Volcanic Ash
- ❏ Icing
- ❏ Hydroplaning
- ❏ Cold Weather Operations

COMPLETION STANDARDS
- Demonstrate understanding of weather factors and weather hazards during oral quizzing by the instructor.
- Complete with a minimum score of 80 percent: questions for Chapters 9A and 9B or online exams for GL 24. Review each incorrect response with the instructor to ensure complete understanding before starting Ground Lesson 21.

STUDY ASSIGNMENT
Instrument/Commercial Textbook/EBook
  Chapter 9 — Meteorology
    Section C — Printed Reports and Forecasts

Instrument Online — Jeppesen Learning Center
  GL 25 — Analyzing Weather

GROUND LESSON 21

REFERENCES

Instrument/Commercial Textbook/EBook
  Chapter 9 — Meteorology
    Section C — Printed Reports and Forecasts

Instrument Online — Jeppesen Learning Center
  GL 25 — Analyzing Weather

OBJECTIVE
Recognize how to obtain and interpret printed weather reports and forecasts for flight planning.

CONTENT
PRINTED WEATHER REPORTS
- ❏ Aviation Routine Weather Report (METAR)
- ❏ Radar Weather Reports
- ❏ Pilot Weather Reports

Instrument/Commercial Syllabus

PRINTED WEATHER FORECASTS
- ❑ Terminal Aerodrome Forecast
- ❑ Aviation Area Forecast
- ❑ Winds and Temperatures Aloft Forecast
- ❑ Severe Weather Reports and Forecasts

COMPLETION STANDARDS
- Demonstrate understanding of how to interpret printed reports and forecasts during oral quizzing by the instructor.
- Complete with a minimum score of 80 percent: questions for Chapter 9C. Review each incorrect response with the instructor to ensure complete understanding before starting Ground Lesson 22.

Note: The online exam for GL 25 covers the content contained in Ground Lessons 21, 22, and 23. Complete the online exam after completing Ground Lesson 23.

STUDY ASSIGNMENT
Instrument/Commercial Textbook/EBook
  Chapter 9 — Meteorology
    Section D — Graphic Weather Products

Instrument Online — Jeppesen Learning Center
  GL 25 — Analyzing Weather

GROUND LESSON 22

REFERENCES

Instrument/Commercial Textbook/EBook
  Chapter 9 — Meteorology
    Section D — Graphic Weather Products

Instrument Online — Jeppesen Learning Center
  GL 25 — Analyzing Weather

OBJECTIVE
Recognize how to obtain and interpret graphic weather products for flight planning.

CONTENT

GRAPHIC REPORTS
- ❑ Surface Analysis Chart
- ❑ Weather Depiction Chart
- ❑ Radar Summary Chart
- ❑ Satellite Weather Pictures
- ❑ Composite Moisture Stability Chart
- ❑ Constant Pressure Analysis Chart
- ❑ Observed Winds and Temperatures Aloft Chart

Instrument/Commercial Syllabus

GRAPHIC FORECASTS
- ☐ Low-Level Significant Weather Prog Chart
- ☐ High-Level Significant Weather Prog Chart
- ☐ Convective Outlook Chart
- ☐ Forecast Winds and Temperatures Aloft Chart
- ☐ National Convective Weather Forecast
- ☐ Volcanic Ash Forecast Transport and Dispersion Chart

COMPLETION STANDARDS:
- Demonstrate understanding of how to interpret graphic weather reports and forecasts during oral quizzing by the instructor.
- Complete with a minimum score of 80 percent: questions for Chapter 9D. Review each incorrect response with the instructor to ensure complete understanding before starting Ground Lesson 23.

Note: The online exam for GL 25 covers the content contained in Ground Lessons 21, 22, and 23. Complete the online exam after completing Ground Lesson 23.

STUDY ASSIGNMENT

Instrument/Commercial Textbook/EBook
   Chapter 9 — Meteorology
      Section E — Sources of Weather Information

Instrument Online — Jeppesen Learning Center
   GL 25 — Analyzing Weather

GROUND LESSON 23

REFERENCES

Instrument/Commercial Textbook/EBook
   Chapter 9 — Meteorology
      Section E — Sources of Weather Information

Instrument Online — Jeppesen Learning Center
   GL 25 — Analyzing Weather

OBJECTIVE
Recognize how to obtain preflight and in-flight sources of weather information.

CONTENT

PREFLIGHT WEATHER SOURCES
- ☐ Flight Service Station
- ☐ Preflight Weather Briefing
- ☐ Telephone Information Briefing Service
- ☐ Direct User Access Terminal System
- ☐ Private Industry Sources
- ☐ The Aviation Weather Center

Instrument/Commercial Syllabus

IN-FLIGHT WEATHER SOURCES
- ❏ AIRMETs and SIGMETs
- ❏ Convective SIGMETs
- ❏ Enroute Flight Advisory Service
- ❏ Flight Service
- ❏ Center Weather Advisories
- ❏ Hazardous In-Flight Weather Advisory Service
- ❏ Transcribed Weather Broadcasts (Alaska)
- ❏ Weather Radar Services
- ❏ Automated Surface Observing System (ASOS)
- ❏ Automated Weather Observing System (AWOS)

AIRBORNE WEATHER EQUIPMENT
- ❏ Airborne Weather Radar
- ❏ Other Weather Detection Equipment

COMPLETION STANDARDS
- Demonstrate understanding of how to obtain and use preflight and in-flight weather sources during oral quizzing by the instructor.
- Complete with a minimum score of 80 percent: questions for Chapter 9E or the online exam for GL 25. Review each incorrect response with the instructor to ensure complete understanding before starting Ground Lesson 24.

Note: The online exam for GL 25 covers the content contained in Ground Lessons 21, 22, and 23.

STUDY ASSIGNMENT
Instrument/Commercial Textbook/EBook
   Chapter 10 — IFR Flight Considerations
      Section A — IFR Emergencies

Instrument Online — Jeppesen Learning Center
   GL 28 — IFR Emergencies

GROUND LESSON 24

REFERENCES

Instrument/Commercial Textbook/EBook
   Chapter 10 — IFR Flight Considerations
      Section A — IFR Emergencies

Instrument Online — Jeppesen Learning Center
   GL 28 — IFR Emergencies

Instrument/Commercial Syllabus

OBJECTIVE
Identify emergency situations and recognize the correct procedures to manage emergencies in the IFR environment.

CONTENT
- Declaring an Emergency
- Minimum Fuel
- Gyroscopic Instrument Failure
- Communication Failure
- Emergency Approach Procedures
- Malfunction Reports

COMPLETION STANDARDS
- Demonstrate understanding of how to recognize and respond appropriately to emergency situations during oral quizzing by the instructor.
- Complete with a minimum score of 80 percent: questions for Chapter 10A or online exam for GL 28. Review each incorrect response with the instructor to ensure complete understanding before starting Ground Lesson 25.

STUDY ASSIGNMENT
Instrument/Commercial Textbook/EBook
   Chapter 10 — IFR Flight Considerations
      Section B — IFR Decision Making
      Section C — IFR Flight Planning

Instrument Online — Jeppesen Learning Center
   GL 26 — IFR Single-Pilot Resource Management
   GL 27 — IFR Flight Planning

GROUND LESSON 25

REFERENCES

Instrument/Commercial Textbook/EBook
   Chapter 10 — IFR Flight Considerations
      Section B — IFR Single-Pilot Resource Management
      Section C — IFR Flight Planning

Instrument Online — Jeppesen Learning Center
   GL 26 — IFR Single-Pilot Resource Management
   GL 27 — IFR Flight Planning

OBJECTIVES
- Identify the steps to plan an IFR cross-country flight.
- Describe the skills that apply to effective single-pilot resources management in the IFR environment.
- Explain the factors that affect decision making during IFR operations.

Instrument/Commercial Syllabus

CONTENT

SECTION B — IFR SINGLE-PILOT RESOURCE MANAGEMENT
GL 26 — IFR SINGLE-PILOT RESOURCE MANAGEMENT
- ❑ Aeronautical Decision Making
- ❑ Risk Management
- ❑ Task Management
- ❑ Situational Awareness
- ❑ Controlled Flight Into Terrain
- ❑ Automation Management

SECTION C — IFR FLIGHT PLANNING
GL 27 — IFR FLIGHT PLANNING
- ❑ Flight Overview
- ❑ Route Selection
- ❑ Flight Information Publications
- ❑ Weather Considerations
- ❑ Altitude Selection
- ❑ Completing the Navigation Log
- ❑ Filing the Flight Plan
- ❑ Closing the IFR Flight Plan

COMPLETION STANDARDS
- Demonstrate understanding of IFR flight planning, the factors affecting aeronautical decision making, and single-pilot resource management skills during oral quizzing by the instructor.
- Complete with a minimum score of 80 percent: questions for Chapters 10B and 10C or online exams for GL 26 and 27. Review each incorrect response with the instructor to ensure complete understanding before starting Ground Lesson 26.

STUDY ASSIGNMENT
Review the content of Ground Lessons 20 – 25 to prepare for the Stage III Exam.

GROUND LESSON 26
STAGE III EXAM

REFERENCES
Ground Lessons 20 – 25

OBJECTIVE
Demonstrate knowledge of the subjects covered in Ground Lessons 20 – 25 by passing the Stage III Exam.

Instrument/Commercial Syllabus

CONTENT

STAGE III EXAM
- Weather Factors and Hazards
- Printed Reports and Forecasts
- Graphic Weather Products
- Sources of Weather Information
- IFR Emergencies
- IFR Flight Planning
- IFR Single-Pilot Resource Management

COMPLETION STANDARDS
To complete the lesson and stage, pass the Stage III Exam with a minimum score of 80 percent. Review each incorrect response with the instructor to ensure complete understanding before taking the End-of-Course Exam.

STUDY ASSIGNMENT
Review the content of Ground Lessons 1 – 26 to prepare for the Instrument Rating End-of-Course Exam

GROUND LESSON 27
END-OF-COURSE EXAM

REFERENCES

Ground Lessons 1 – 26

OBJECTIVE
Demonstrate comprehension of the material covered in Ground Lessons 1 – 26 by passing the Instrument Rating End-of-Course Exam to prepare for the FAA Instrument Rating Airman Knowledge Test.

CONTENT
- Instrument Rating End-of-Course Exam

COMPLETION STANDARDS
To complete the lesson and the Instrument Rating Ground Training, pass the Instrument Rating End-of-Course Exam with a minimum score of 80 percent. Review each incorrect response with the instructor to ensure complete understanding before taking the FAA Instrument Rating Airman Knowledge Test.

STUDY ASSIGNMENT
Review the content of Ground Lessons 1 – 27 to prepare for the FAA Instrument Rating Airman Knowledge Test.

Instrument Rating Flight Training Stage I

STAGE OBJECTIVES
During Stage I, the student learns precise airplane attitude control by instrument reference by performing a variety of maneuvers. In addition, the student gains proficiency in VOR, GPS, NDB, and localizer navigation.

STAGE COMPLETION STANDARDS
This stage is complete when the student demonstrates precise airplane attitude control by full-panel and partial-panel instrument reference. In addition, the student must demonstrate proficiency in VOR, GPS, NDB, and localizer navigation by accurately tracking courses and maintaining positional awareness at all times.

NOTE: Completion of the navigation tasks listed in each lesson must be based on the available airplane equipment.

FLIGHT LESSON 1

DUAL — LOCAL

NOTE: As indicated in the Allocation Tables, complete Ground Lessons 1, 2, and 3 prior to this flight.

OBJECTIVES
- Become familiar with the instrument training airplane during the preflight inspection and takeoff and landing procedures.
- Practice attitude instrument flying by performing basic flight maneuvers solely by reference to instruments.

PREFLIGHT DISCUSSION
- ❏ Positive Exchange of Flight Controls
- ❏ Single-Pilot Resource Management (SRM)
- ❏ Crew Resource Management (CRM)

INTRODUCE

FULL-PANEL INSTRUMENT
- ❏ Straight-and-Level Flight
- ❏ Change of Airspeed
- ❏ Standard-Rate Turns
- ❏ Constant Airspeed Climbs
- ❏ Climbing Turns

Instrument/Commercial Syllabus

- [ ] Constant Airspeed Descents
- [ ] Descending Turns
- [ ] Operations in Turbulence

REVIEW

PREFLIGHT PREPARATION
- [ ] Airworthiness Requirements
- [ ] Aircraft Certificates and Documents
- [ ] Aircraft Logbooks
- [ ] Aircraft Weight and Balance
- [ ] Aircraft Performance
- [ ] Operation of Systems

NORMAL PROCEDURES
- [ ] Use of Checklists
- [ ] Engine Starting
- [ ] Normal and Crosswind Taxiing
- [ ] Runway Incursion Avoidance
- [ ] Radio Communications
- [ ] Normal and Crosswind Takeoffs and Landings
- [ ] Situational Awareness
- [ ] Collision Avoidance Procedures
- [ ] Controlled Flight Into Terrain (CFIT) Awareness

COMPLETION STANDARDS
- Perform takeoffs and landings at the private pilot proficiency level.
- Maintain positive aircraft control with altitude ±200 feet, heading ±15°, airspeed ±15 knots, and bank angles ±5° during turns.

POSTFLIGHT DEBRIEFING
- [ ] Critique maneuvers/procedures and SRM.
- [ ] Create a plan for skills that need improvement.
- [ ] Update the record folder and logbook.

FLIGHT LESSON 2

DUAL — LOCAL

OBJECTIVES
- Increase proficiency in attitude instrument flying by performing slow flight, stalls, and steep turns.
- Recover from unusual flight attitudes solely by reference to instruments.
- Become familiar with the aircraft systems, equipment, and preflight checks necessary for IFR flight.

Instrument/Commercial Syllabus

PREFLIGHT DISCUSSION
- ❏ Aircraft Systems Related to IFR Operations
- ❏ Aircraft Flight Instruments and Navigation Equipment
- ❏ Stall/Spin Awareness
- ❏ Single-Pilot Resource Management

INTRODUCE
- ❏ Instrument and Equipment Cockpit Check
- ❏ IFR Takeoff Preparation
- ❏ Postflight Procedures—Checking Instruments and Equipment
    - ◊ Check for proper operation.
    - ◊ Document improper operation or failure.
- ❏ Autopilot Use (if airplane so equipped)

FULL-PANEL INSTRUMENT
- ❏ Maneuvering During Slow Flight
- ❏ Power-Off Stalls
- ❏ Power-On Stalls
- ❏ Steep Turns
- ❏ Recovery From Unusual Flight Attitudes

REVIEW

FULL-PANEL INSTRUMENT
- ❏ Straight-and-Level Flight
- ❏ Change of Airspeed
- ❏ Standard-Rate Turns
- ❏ Constant Airspeed Climbs
- ❏ Climbing Turns
- ❏ Constant Airspeed Descents
- ❏ Descending Turns
- ❏ Operations in Turbulence

COMPLETION STANDARDS
- Demonstrate understanding of the aircraft instrument systems, equipment, and preflight and postflight checks necessary for IFR flight.
- Demonstrate proficiency in full-panel attitude instrument flying while performing basic flight maneuvers.
- Maintain positive aircraft control with altitude ±200 feet, heading ±15°, airspeed ±15 knots, and bank angles ±5° during turns.

POSTFLIGHT DEBRIEFING
- ❏ Critique maneuvers/procedures and SRM.
- ❏ Create a plan for skills that need improvement.
- ❏ Update the record folder and logbook.

STUDY ASSIGNMENT
Ground Lesson 4
  Instrument Navigation

Instrument/Commercial Syllabus

FLIGHT LESSON 3

DUAL — LOCAL

OBJECTIVES
- Perform proper systems and equipment checks.
- Increase proficiency in full-panel attitude instrument flying.

PREFLIGHT DISCUSSION
- ❏ Sensory Illusions in IFR Conditions
- ❏ Automation Management
- ❏ Situational Awareness When Using Automation

REVIEW
- ❏ Aircraft Systems Related to IFR Operations
- ❏ Aircraft Flight Instruments and Navigation Equipment
- ❏ Instrument and Equipment Cockpit Check
- ❏ IFR Takeoff Preparation
- ❏ Postflight Procedures—Checking Instruments and Equipment
- ❏ Autopilot Use (if airplane so equipped)

FULL-PANEL INSTRUMENT
- ❏ Straight-and-Level Flight
- ❏ Change of Airspeed
- ❏ Standard-Rate Turns
- ❏ Constant Airspeed Climbs and Descents
- ❏ Climbing and Descending Turns
- ❏ Maneuvering During Slow Flight
- ❏ Power-Off Stalls
- ❏ Power-On Stalls
- ❏ Steep Turns
- ❏ Recovery From Unusual Flight Attitudes
- ❏ Operations in Turbulence

COMPLETION STANDARDS
- Demonstrate understanding of the aircraft instrument systems, equipment, and preflight and postflight checks necessary for IFR flight.
- Demonstrate proficiency in full-panel attitude instrument flying while performing all flight maneuvers.
- Maintain altitude ±200 feet, heading within ±15°, airspeed within ±15 knots, and bank angles within ±5° during turns.
- Recognize the approach of stalls and perform the correct recovery procedures.
- Recognize unusual flight attitudes and perform the correct recovery procedures.

POSTFLIGHT DEBRIEFING
- ❏ Critique maneuvers/procedures and SRM.
- ❏ Create a plan for skills that need improvement.
- ❏ Update the record folder and logbook.

STAGE I ■ Instrument Rating Flight Training

Instrument/Commercial Syllabus

FLIGHT LESSON 4
DUAL — LOCAL

OBJECTIVES
- Demonstrate proficiency in full-panel attitude instrument flying.
- Perform the proper procedures to manage system and equipment malfunctions.
- Practice partial-panel attitude instrument flying by performing basic flight maneuvers.

PREFLIGHT DISCUSSION
- ❏ Identifying Failed Instruments and Systems
- ❏ Partial-Panel Airplane Control Techniques
- ❏ Emergency Checklist Items
- ❏ Instrument Malfunction Reporting Requirements
- ❏ Task Management
- ❏ Situational Awareness
- ❏ CFIT Awareness

INTRODUCE

SYSTEMS AND EQUIPMENT MALFUNCTIONS
- ❏ Electrical System Failure
- ❏ Vacuum Pump Failure
- ❏ Gyroscopic Instrument Failure
- ❏ Pitot-Static Instrument Failure
- ❏ Loss of Primary Flight Instrument Indications

PARTIAL-PANEL INSTRUMENT
- ❏ Straight-and-Level Flight
- ❏ Standard-Rate Turns
- ❏ Change of Airspeed
- ❏ Constant Airspeed Climbs
- ❏ Constant Airspeed Descents
- ❏ Climbing Turns
- ❏ Descending Turns

REVIEW
- ❏ Aircraft Systems Related to IFR Operations
- ❏ IFR Takeoff Preparation
- ❏ Steep Turns

COMPLETION STANDARDS
- Recognize and understand the effect of instrument systems and equipment malfunctions.
- Recognize the change in instrument cross-check necessary to maintain airplane control while using partial-panel procedures.

STAGE I ■ Instrument Rating Flight Training

Instrument/Commercial Syllabus

POSTFLIGHT DEBRIEFING
- Critique maneuvers/procedures and SRM.
- Create a plan for skills that need improvement.
- Update the record folder and logbook.

STUDY ASSIGNMENT
Ground Lessons 5 and 6
  Instrument FARs
  Airports, Airspace, and Flight Information

FLIGHT LESSON 5

DUAL — LOCAL

OBJECTIVES
- Increase proficiency in full- and partial-panel attitude instrument flying.
- Manage systems and equipment malfunctions.

PREFLIGHT DISCUSSION
- Magnetic Compass Errors
- Timed Turns

INTRODUCE

FULL-PANEL INSTRUMENT
- Constant Rate Climbs
- Constant Rate Descents
- Timed Turns to Magnetic Compass Headings

PARTIAL-PANEL INSTRUMENT
- Recovery From Unusual Flight Attitudes
- Timed Turns to Magnetic Compass Headings
- Magnetic Compass Turns
- Constant Rate Climbs
- Constant Rate Descents

REVIEW

SYSTEMS AND EQUIPMENT MALFUNCTIONS
- Electrical System Failure
- Vacuum Pump Failure
- Gyroscopic Instrument Failure
- Pitot-Static Instrument Failure
- Loss of Primary Flight Instrument Indications

PARTIAL-PANEL INSTRUMENT
- Straight-and-Level Flight
- Standard-Rate Turns
- Change of Airspeed

STAGE I ■ Instrument Rating Flight Training

Instrument/Commercial Syllabus

- ❏ Constant Airspeed Climbs
- ❏ Constant Airspeed Descents

FULL-PANEL INSTRUMENT
- ❏ Steep Turns
- ❏ Maneuvering During Slow Flight
- ❏ Power-Off Stalls
- ❏ Power-On Stalls

COMPLETION STANDARDS
- Demonstrate understanding of IFR systems operation.
- Recognize and manage systems and equipment malfunctions.
- Using partial-panel instrument reference, maintain altitude ±200 feet, heading ±15°, airspeed ±15 knots, and desired climb and descent rates of ±150 feet per minute.

POSTFLIGHT DEBRIEFING
- ❏ Critique maneuvers/procedures and SRM.
- ❏ Create a plan for skills that need improvement.
- ❏ Update the record folder and logbook.

FLIGHT LESSON 6

DUAL — LOCAL

OBJECTIVES
- Gain proficiency in performing slow flight and stalls using partial-panel instrument reference.
- Increase proficiency in full- and partial-panel attitude instrument flying.

PREFLIGHT DISCUSSION
- ❏ Partial-Panel Stall/Spin Awareness

INTRODUCE

PARTIAL-PANEL INSTRUMENT
- ❏ Maneuvering During Slow Flight
- ❏ Power-Off Stalls
- ❏ Power-On Stalls

REVIEW

FULL- AND PARTIAL-PANEL INSTRUMENT
- ❏ Straight-and-Level Flight
- ❏ Constant Rate Climbs and Descents
- ❏ Constant Airspeed Climbs and Descents
- ❏ Timed Turns to Magnetic Compass Headings
- ❏ Magnetic Compass Turns
- ❏ Recovery From Unusual Flight Attitudes

Instrument/Commercial Syllabus

COMPLETION STANDARDS
- Using partial-panel and full-panel instrument reference, recognize the typical indications of stalls and recover without abrupt control usage.
- Perform correct recovery techniques from unusual flight attitudes, using full and partial-panel instrument reference.
- Using partial-panel instrument reference, maintain altitude ±200 feet, heading ±15°, airspeed ±15 knots, and desired climb and descent rates of ±150 feet per minute

POSTFLIGHT DEBRIEFING
❏ Critique maneuvers/procedures and SRM.
❏ Create a plan for skills that need improvement.
❏ Update the record folder and logbook.

STUDY ASSIGNMENT
Ground Lesson 7
   Air Traffic Control Systems

FLIGHT LESSON 7
DUAL — LOCAL

OBJECTIVES
- Increase proficiency in the listed full-panel instrument maneuvers.
- Increase proficiency in partial-panel skills in stall recoveries, slow flight, and unusual attitude recoveries.

PREFLIGHT DISCUSSION
❏ SRM in the IFR Environment
   ◊ Aeronautical Decision Making
   ◊ Risk Management
   ◊ Task Management
   ◊ Situational Awareness
   ◊ CFIT Awareness
   ◊ Automation Management

REVIEW
FULL-PANEL INSTRUMENT
❏ Straight-and-Level Flight
❏ Standard-Rate Turns
❏ Constant Rate Climbs and Descents
❏ Constant Airspeed Climbs and Descents
❏ Power-Off Stalls
❏ Power-On Stalls
❏ Steep Turns
❏ Recovery From Unusual Flight Attitudes

Instrument/Commercial Syllabus

PARTIAL-PANEL INSTRUMENT
- ❑ Maneuvering During Slow Flight
- ❑ Power-Off Stalls
- ❑ Power-On Stalls
- ❑ Recovery From Unusual Flight Attitudes

COMPLETION STANDARDS
- Perform correct recovery techniques from unusual flight attitudes using full- and partial-panel instrument reference.
- Perform correct recovery techniques for stalls using full- and partial-panel instrument reference and positive control techniques with a minimum loss of altitude.
- Using full-panel instrument reference, maintain altitude ±150 feet, heading ±10°, airspeed ±15 knots, and desired descent and climb rate ±100 feet per minute.

POSTFLIGHT DEBRIEFING
- ❑ Critique maneuvers/procedures and SRM.
- ❑ Create a plan for skills that need improvement.
- ❑ Update the record folder and logbook.

STUDY ASSIGNMENT
Ground Lesson 8
 Air Traffic Control Clearances

FLIGHT LESSON 8

DUAL — LOCAL

OBJECTIVES
- Gain proficiency in VOR orientation, radial interception, and tracking.
- Learn how to intercept and track a DME arc.
- Increase proficiency in attitude instrument flying by performing the listed maneuvers.

PREFLIGHT DISCUSSION
- ❑ Identifying the VOR
- ❑ VOR Service Volumes
- ❑ VOR Indicators (Traditional, HSI, RMI)
- ❑ VOR Equipment Check Procedures

INTRODUCE

FULL-PANEL INSTRUMENT
- ❑ VOR Equipment Check
- ❑ VOR Orientation
- ❑ VOR Radial Interception and Tracking
- ❑ Intercepting and Tracking DME Arcs

Instrument/Commercial Syllabus

REVIEW

PARTIAL-PANEL INSTRUMENT
- ❏ Maneuvering During Slow Flight
- ❏ Power-Off Stalls
- ❏ Power-On Stalls

COMPLETION STANDARDS
- Demonstrate understanding of VOR equipment checks, orientation, radial interception, and tracking.
- Demonstrate understanding of intercepting and tracking DME arcs.
- Using full-panel and partial-panel instrument reference, maintain altitude ±100 feet, heading ±10°, airspeed ±15 knots, and desired descent and climb rate ±100 feet per minute.

POSTFLIGHT DEBRIEFING
- ❏ Critique maneuvers/procedures and SRM.
- ❏ Create a plan for skills that need improvement.
- ❏ Update the record folder and logbook.

STUDY ASSIGNMENT
Ground Lesson 9
   Stage I Exam

FLIGHT LESSON 9

DUAL — LOCAL

OBJECTIVES
- Gain proficiency in NDB orientation, homing, bearing interception, and tracking.
- Increase proficiency in VOR orientation, radial interception, and tracking.

PREFLIGHT DISCUSSION
- ❏ Identifying the NDB
- ❏ Frequencies, Classifications, and Effective Range of NDB Stations
- ❏ ADF Indicators (Fixed Card, Moveable Card, RMI)

INTRODUCE
- ❏ NDB Orientation and Homing
- ❏ NDB Bearing Interception and Tracking

REVIEW
- ❏ VOR Equipment Check
- ❏ VOR Orientation
- ❏ VOR Radial Interception and Tracking
- ❏ Intercepting and Tracking DME Arcs

Instrument/Commercial Syllabus

COMPLETION STANDARDS
- Demonstrate increased proficiency in VOR radial interception and tracking
- Demonstrate understanding of ADF equipment and NDB navigation.
- Maintain altitude ±100 feet, heading ±10°, airspeed ±15 knots, and desired descent and climb rate ±100 feet per minute.

POSTFLIGHT DEBRIEFING
- ❏ Critique maneuvers/procedures and SRM.
- ❏ Create a plan for skills that need improvement.
- ❏ Update the record folder and logbook.

FLIGHT LESSON 10

DUAL — LOCAL

OBJECTIVES
- Gain proficiency in performing the GPS preflight check and programming GPS equipment.
- Gain proficiency in GPS orientation, course interception, and course tracking.
- Increase proficiency in NDB navigation.

PREFLIGHT DISCUSSION
- ❏ Requirements for Using GPS Under IFR
- ❏ AFM Supplements to Determine GPS Certification
- ❏ RAIM Availability
- ❏ GPS Database Currency
- ❏ "North Up" and "Track Up" Orientation
- ❏ Basic GPS Programming

INTRODUCE
- ❏ GPS Preflight Check
- ❏ GPS Programming
- ❏ GPS Orientation
- ❏ GPS Course Interception and Tracking

REVIEW
- ❏ NDB Orientation and Homing
- ❏ NDB Bearing Interception and Tracking

COMPLETION STANDARDS
- Demonstrate understanding of the GPS preflight check and programming GPS equipment.
- Demonstrate understanding of GPS orientation, course interception, and course tracking.
- Demonstrate increased proficiency in NDB navigation procedures.

POSTFLIGHT DEBRIEFING
- Critique maneuvers/procedures and SRM.
- Create a plan for skills that need improvement.
- Update the record folder and logbook.

FLIGHT LESSON 11

DUAL — LOCAL

OBJECTIVES
- Increase proficiency in GPS programming, orientation, course interception, and course tracking.
- Interpret the CDI indications associated with the increased sensitivity of the localizer while intercepting and tracking inbound on the front or back course.

PREFLIGHT DISCUSSION
- Localizer Coverage Limits, Sensitivity, Frequencies
- Identifying the Localizer
- Front Course and Back Course Navigation

INTRODUCE
- Localizer Course Interception and Tracking (Front Course)
- Localizer Course Interception and Tracking (Back Course)

REVIEW
- GPS Preflight Check
- GPS Programming
- GPS Orientation
- GPS Course Interception and Tracking

COMPLETION STANDARDS
- Demonstrate understanding of localizer tracking.
- Demonstrate increased proficiency in performing the GPS preflight check and programming GPS equipment.
- Demonstrate increased proficiency in GPS orientation, course interception, and course tracking.
- Maintain heading ±10° and altitude ±100 feet.

POSTFLIGHT DEBRIEFING
- Critique maneuvers/procedures and SRM.
- Create a plan for skills that need improvement.
- Update the record folder and logbook.

Instrument/Commercial Syllabus

FLIGHT LESSON 12

DUAL — LOCAL

OBJECTIVES
- Gain proficiency in VOR, GPS, NDB, and localizer navigation using partial-panel instrument reference.
- Increase proficiency in full- and partial-panel attitude instrument flying by reviewing maneuvers.

PREFLIGHT DISCUSSION
- ❏ Autopilot Capabilities with Loss of Primary Flight Instruments
- ❏ Identifying Failed Instruments and Systems
- ❏ Partial-Panel Navigation Techniques
- ❏ Task Management
- ❏ Situational Awareness

INTRODUCE

PARTIAL-PANEL INSTRUMENT
- ❏ VOR Navigation
- ❏ GPS Navigation
- ❏ NDB Navigation
- ❏ Localizer Navigation

REVIEW

FULL-PANEL INSTRUMENT
- ❏ Localizer Tracking (Front Course)
- ❏ Localizer Tracking (Back Course)

FULL- AND PARTIAL-PANEL INSTRUMENT
- ❏ Straight-and-Level Flight
- ❏ Standard-Rate Turns
- ❏ Timed Turns to Magnetic Compass Headings
- ❏ Magnetic Compass Turns
- ❏ Climbs and Descents
- ❏ Power-Off Stalls
- ❏ Power-On Stalls
- ❏ Recovery From Unusual Flight Attitudes

COMPLETION STANDARDS
- Demonstrate understanding of VOR, GPS, NDB, and localizer navigation using partial-panel instrument reference.
- Demonstrate proficiency in VOR, GPS, NDB, and localizer navigation using full-panel instrument reference.
- Perform correct recovery techniques from unusual flight attitudes using full- and partial-panel instrument reference.
- Apply positive control techniques to recover from stalls with a minimum loss of altitude using full- and partial-panel instrument reference.

STAGE I ■ Instrument Rating Flight Training

Instrument/Commercial Syllabus

- Maintain altitude ±100 feet, heading ±10°, airspeed ±15 knots, and desired descent and climb rate ±100 feet per minute.

POSTFLIGHT DEBRIEFING
- ❏ Critique maneuvers/procedures and SRM.
- ❏ Create a plan for skills that need improvement.
- ❏ Update the record folder and logbook.

STUDY ASSIGNMENT
Stage I Check
  Prepare for the Stage I Check in Flight Lesson 13.

FLIGHT LESSON 13

DUAL — LOCAL
STAGE I CHECK

OBJECTIVE
Demonstrate proficiency in attitude instrument flying and navigation to the chief instructor, assistant chief, or a designated check instructor during the Stage I Check.

PREFLIGHT DISCUSSION
- ❏ Student and Flight Check Instructor Roles and Expectations
- ❏ Questions to Test Student Knowledge

REVIEW
- ❏ Aircraft Systems Related to IFR Operations
- ❏ Aircraft Flight Instruments and Navigation Equipment
- ❏ Instrument and Equipment Cockpit Check
- ❏ IFR Takeoff Preparations

FULL-PANEL INSTRUMENT
- ❏ Steep Turns

FULL- AND PARTIAL-PANEL INSTRUMENT
- ❏ Straight-and-Level Flight
- ❏ Constant Rate Climbs and Descents
- ❏ Constant Airspeed Climbs and Descents
- ❏ Standard-Rate Turns
- ❏ Recovery From Unusual Flight Attitudes
- ❏ Timed Turns to Magnetic Compass Headings
- ❏ Magnetic Compass Turns
- ❏ Maneuvering During Slow Flight
- ❏ Power-Off and Power-On Stalls

Instrument/Commercial Syllabus

FULL- AND PARTIAL-PANEL INSTRUMENT NAVIGATION
- ❏ VOR Navigation
- ❏ GPS Navigation
- ❏ NDB Navigation
- ❏ Localizer Navigation

COMPLETION STANDARDS
- Demonstrate proficiency in VOR, GPS, NDB, and localizer navigation.
- Demonstrate proficiency in recognizing and recovering from unusual flight attitudes using full- and partial-panel instrument reference.
- Demonstrate proficiency in recognizing and recovering from power-off and power-on stalls using full- and partial-panel instrument reference.
- Using full- and partial-panel instrument reference, maintain altitude ±100 feet, heading ±10°, airspeed ±15 knots, and desired descent and climb rate of ±100 feet per minute.
- Demonstrate the ability to use SRM to make effective decisions, maintain situational awareness, prevent CFIT, and manage risk, tasks, and automation.

POSTFLIGHT DEBRIEFING
- ❏ Evaluate maneuvers/procedures and SRM.
- ❏ Plan additional instruction for skills not meeting Stage I completion standards.
- ❏ Update the record folder and logbook.

STUDY ASSIGNMENT
Ground Lessons 10, 11, and 12
 Departure Charts and Departure Procedures
 Enroute Charts and Procedures
 Holding Procedures

Stage II

STAGE OBJECTIVES
During Stage II, the student learns to perform holding patterns and instrument approaches, including circling and missed approach procedures. The student performs VOR, GPS, ILS, and localizer approach procedures using full- and partial-panel instrument reference.

STAGE COMPLETION STANDARDS
This stage is complete when the student can demonstrate proficiency in performing holding patterns and all required instrument approach procedures.

NOTE: Completion of the navigation tasks listed in each lesson must be based on the available airplane equipment.

FLIGHT LESSON 14

DUAL — LOCAL

OBJECTIVES
- Become familiar with VOR, GPS, and NDB standard and nonstandard holding patterns.
- Increase proficiency in instrument systems and equipment malfunctions.

PREFLIGHT DISCUSSION
- ❑ ATC Holding Instructions
- ❑ Recommended Holding Pattern Entries
- ❑ Expect Further Clearance (EFC) Time
- ❑ Airspeed Limitations
- ❑ Fuel Planning Considerations

INTRODUCE

VOR HOLDING
- ❑ Standard Holding
- ❑ Nonstandard Holding

NDB HOLDING
- ❑ Standard Holding
- ❑ Nonstandard Holding

GPS HOLDING
- ❑ Standard Holding
- ❑ Nonstandard Holding

REVIEW
- ❑ Systems and Equipment Malfunctions
- ❑ Full- and Partial-Panel Instrument Flight

Instrument/Commercial Syllabus

COMPLETION STANDARDS
- Demonstrate understanding of performing VOR, GPS, and/or NDB holding pattern procedures.
- Maintain orientation at all times during both standard and nonstandard holding procedures.

POSTFLIGHT DEBRIEFING
- ❑ Critique maneuvers/procedures and SRM.
- ❑ Create a plan for skills that need improvement.
- ❑ Update the record folder and logbook.

FLIGHT LESSON 15

DUAL — LOCAL

OBJECTIVES
- Gain proficiency in performing VOR, GPS, and/or NDB holding patterns.
- Become familiar with standard and nonstandard localizer holding procedures.

PREFLIGHT DISCUSSION
- ❑ Task Management During Holding
- ❑ Situational Awareness During Holding

INTRODUCE
- ❑ Standard and Nonstandard Localizer Holding

REVIEW
- ❑ VOR Holding
- ❑ GPS Holding
- ❑ NDB Holding
- ❑ Localizer Tracking

COMPLETION STANDARDS
- Demonstrate understanding of standard and nonstandard localizer holding patterns using the appropriate entry, timing, and wind correction procedures.
- Given a diagram of a holding pattern and the course from which you are approaching the holding fix, draw the recommended holding pattern entry.
- Demonstrate the ability to perform the correct holding pattern entries and procedures for standard and nonstandard VOR, GPS, and/or NDB holding patterns.
- Maintain altitude ±100 feet, heading ±10°, airspeed ±15 knots, and desired descent and climb rate ±100 feet per minute.

POSTFLIGHT DEBRIEFING
- ❑ Critique maneuvers/procedures and SRM.
- ❑ Create a plan for skills that need improvement.
- ❑ Update the record folder and logbook.

Instrument/Commercial Syllabus

FLIGHT LESSON 16

DUAL — LOCAL

OBJECTIVES
- Become familiar with DME and intersection holding patterns.
- Increase proficiency in VOR, NDB, GPS, and localizer holding procedures.

PREFLIGHT DISCUSSION
- ❏ Task Management During Holding
- ❏ Situational Awareness During Holding

INTRODUCE
- ❏ DME Holding
- ❏ Intersection Holding

REVIEW
- ❏ VOR Holding
- ❏ NDB Holding
- ❏ GPS Holding
- ❏ Localizer Holding

COMPLETION STANDARDS
- Demonstrate understanding of the correct holding pattern entries and procedures for intersection and DME holding patterns.
- Maintain the desired altitude ±100 feet, assigned airspeed ±10 knots and headings ±10°, within 3/4-scale deflection of the CDI during the hold.

POSTFLIGHT DEBRIEFING
- ❏ Critique maneuvers/procedures and SRM.
- ❏ Create a plan for skills that need improvement.
- ❏ Update the record folder and logbook.

STUDY ASSIGNMENT
Ground Lessons 13, 14, 15, and 16
 Arrival Charts and Procedures
 Approach Charts
 Approach Procedures
 VOR and NDB Approaches

Instrument Approaches Briefing

FLIGHT LESSON 17
DUAL — LOCAL

OBJECTIVES
- Become familiar with VOR and VOR/DME approach procedures.
- Become familiar with procedures to terminate an approach: missed approach procedure and straight-in landing.
- Increase proficiency in flying localizer, DME, and intersection holds.

PREFLIGHT DISCUSSION
- Nonprecision Approaches
- Instrument Approach Chart Review
- VOR and VOR/DME Approach Required Equipment
- On- and Off-Airport VORs
- Course Reversals
- Descending Below the MDA
- Transitioning from Instrument to Visual Flight
- When and How to Perform a Missed Approach

INTRODUCE
- VOR and VOR/DME Approaches
- Approach Procedures to Straight-In Landing Minimums
- Missed Approach Procedures

REVIEW
- Holding Procedures

COMPLETION STANDARDS
- Explain and use the information displayed on VOR and VOR/DME approach charts.
- Demonstrate understanding of how to perform several initial and intermediate approach segments to arrive at the final approach fix.
- Demonstrate understanding of how to complete the final approach segment to the missed approach fix.
- Demonstrate understanding of the missed approach procedure as appropriate to the published chart used.

POSTFLIGHT DEBRIEFING
- Critique maneuvers/procedures and SRM.
- Create a plan for skills that need improvement.
- Update the record folder and logbook.

STUDY ASSIGNMENT
Ground Lessons 17 and 18
  ILS Approaches
  RNAV Approaches

Instrument/Commercial Syllabus

FLIGHT LESSONS 18 AND 19
DUAL — LOCAL

OBJECTIVES
- Gain proficiency in RNAV (GPS) and/or NDB approach procedures and missed approach procedures.
- Gain proficiency in performing approaches to straight-in landings.
- Become familiar with performing circling approaches.
- Increase proficiency in VOR and VOR/DME approach procedures.

PREFLIGHT DISCUSSION
- ❏ Approach Procedures with Vertical Guidance (APV)
- ❏ Instrument Approach Chart Review
- ❏ RNAV (GPS) Approach Required Equipment RNAV
- ❏ (GPS) Landing Minimums (LPV, LNAV/VNAV, LNAV, LP)
- ❏ Visual Descent Point (VDP)
- ❏ Land and Hold Short Operations (LAHSO)

INTRODUCE
- ❏ RNAV (GPS) Approaches
- ❏ NDB Approaches
- ❏ Approach Procedures to Circling Landing Minimums
- ❏ Landing From a Straight-In or Circling Approach Procedure

REVIEW
- ❏ VOR and VOR/DME Approaches
- ❏ Approach Procedures to Straight-In Landing Minimums
- ❏ Missed Approach Procedures

COMPLETION STANDARDS
- Maintain altitude ±200 feet on the initial and intermediate approach segments.
- On the final approach segment, maintain heading ±10° and allow less than 3/4-scale deflection of the CDI, airspeed ±10 knots, and altitude that is not more than 100 feet above and 0 feet below the MDA.

POSTFLIGHT DEBRIEFING
- ❏ Critique maneuvers/procedures and SRM.
- ❏ Create a plan for skills that need improvement.
- ❏ Update the record folder and logbook.

Instrument/Commercial Syllabus

FLIGHT LESSON 20

DUAL — LOCAL

OBJECTIVES
- Become familiar with ILS approach procedures.
- Increase proficiency in flying VOR, RNAV (GPS), and NDB approaches.

PREFLIGHT DISCUSSION
- ❏ Precision Approach (PA) Procedures
- ❏ Instrument Approach Chart Review
- ❏ ILS and Localizer Approach Required Equipment
- ❏ DME Arcs to the Approach Course
- ❏ Radar Vectors to the Approach Course
- ❏ Landing Minimums with Inoperative Equipment
- ❏ When to Perform the Missed Approach

INTRODUCE
- ❏ ILS Approaches
- ❏ Front and Back Course Localizer Approaches

REVIEW
- ❏ Intercepting and Tracking DME Arcs
- ❏ RNAV (GPS) and/or NDB Approaches
- ❏ Missed Approach Procedures

COMPLETION STANDARDS
- During ILS approaches, demonstrate understanding of localizer tracking, intercepting and maintaining the glide slope, and using power and attitude changes to control airspeed and descent rates.
- Demonstrate understanding of front and back course localizer approach procedures while maintaining specific descent rates and altitudes.

POSTFLIGHT DEBRIEFING
- ❏ Critique maneuvers/procedures and SRM.
- ❏ Create a plan for skills that need improvement.
- ❏ Update the record folder and logbook.

Instrument/Commercial Syllabus

FLIGHT LESSON 21
DUAL — LOCAL

OBJECTIVES
- Become familiar with flying approach procedures with a loss of the primary flight instrument indicators.
- Become familiar with no-gyro radar vectoring and approach procedures.
- Increase proficiency in full-panel nonprecision, precision, and APV instrument approach procedures.

PREFLIGHT DISCUSSION
- Approaches with Loss of Primary Flight Instrument Indicators
- No-Gyro Radar Vectoring and Approach Procedures
- Instrument and Equipment Malfunction Procedures
- Advising ATC and ATC Assistance
- Task Management During Instrument and Equipment Malfunction
- Situational Awareness During Partial-Panel Approaches

INTRODUCE

APPROACHES WITH LOSS OF PRIMARY FLIGHT INSTRUMENT INDICATORS
- No-Gyro Radar Vectoring and Approach Procedures
- Partial-Panel Approach Procedures
- Partial-Panel Missed Approach Procedures

REVIEW
- VOR Approaches
- RNAV (GPS) Approaches
- NDB Approaches
- ILS Approaches
- Localizer Approaches
- Landing From a Straight-In or Circling Approach Procedure
- Intercepting and Tracking DME Arcs
- Visual Descent Point
- Land and Hold Short Operations

COMPLETION STANDARDS
- Demonstrate understanding of no-gyro radar vectoring and approaches and partial-panel approach and missed approach procedures.
- During ILS approaches, demonstrate accurate localizer and glide slope interception and tracking.
- Maintain the glide slope and localizer course with no more than 3/4-scale needle deflection.
- Maintain altitude ±200 feet on the initial and intermediate approach segments.
- On the final approach segment, maintain heading ±10° and allow less than 3/4-scale deflection of the CDI, airspeed ±10 knots, and altitude that is not more than 100 feet above and 0 feet below the MDA.

STAGE II ■ Instrument Rating Flight Training

52

Instrument/Commercial Syllabus

POSTFLIGHT DEBRIEFING
❏ Critique maneuvers/procedures and SRM.
❏ Create a plan for skills that need improvement.
❏ Update the record folder and logbook.

STUDY ASSIGNMENT
Begin to review for the Stage II Check in Flight Lesson 23.

FLIGHT LESSON 22
DUAL — LOCAL

OBJECTIVES
- Demonstrate proficiency in holding pattern entries and procedures to prepare for the Stage II Check.
- Demonstrate proficiency in instrument approach procedures to prepare for the Stage II Check.

PREFLIGHT DISCUSSION
❏ SRM During Holding and Approach Procedures

REVIEW

HOLDING PROCEDURES
❏ VOR Holding
❏ GPS Holding
❏ NDB Holding
❏ Localizer Holding
❏ DME Holding
❏ Intersection Holding

INSTRUMENT APPROACH PROCEDURES
❏ VOR Approaches
❏ RNAV (GPS) Approaches
❏ NDB Approaches
❏ ILS Approaches
❏ Localizer Approaches
❏ Approach Procedures to Straight-In Landing Minimums
❏ Approach Procedures to Circling Landing Minimums
❏ Landing From a Straight-In or Circling Approach Procedure
❏ Missed Approach Procedures

APPROACHES WITH LOSS OF PRIMARY FLIGHT INSTRUMENT INDICATORS
❏ No-Gyro Radar Vectoring and Approach Procedures
❏ Partial-Panel Approaches

Instrument/Commercial Syllabus

COMPLETION STANDARDS
- Demonstrate proficiency in all holding and approach procedures to prepare for the Stage II Check.
- Maintain altitude ±100 feet, heading ±10°, and airspeed ±10 knots.
- Maintain a stabilized approach to the MDA or DA and allow less than 3/4- scale deflection of the CDI.

POSTFLIGHT DEBRIEFING
- ❏ Critique maneuvers/procedures and SRM.
- ❏ Create a plan for skills that need improvement.
- ❏ Update the record folder and logbook.

STUDY ASSIGNMENT
Ground Lesson 19
  Stage II Exam.

Stage II Check
  Prepare for the Stage II Check in Flight Lesson 23.

FLIGHT LESSON 23
DUAL — LOCAL
STAGE II CHECK

OBJECTIVE
Demonstrate proficiency in holding and instrument approach procedures to the chief instructor, assistant chief, or a designated check instructor during the Stage II Check.

PREFLIGHT DISCUSSION
- ❏ Student and Flight Check Instructor Roles and Expectations
- ❏ Questions to Test Student Knowledge

REVIEW
HOLDING PROCEDURES
- ❏ VOR Holding
- ❏ GPS Holding
- ❏ NDB Holding
- ❏ Localizer Holding
- ❏ DME Holding
- ❏ Intersection Holding

Instrument/Commercial Syllabus

INSTRUMENT APPROACH PROCEDURES
- ❏ VOR Approaches
- ❏ RNAV (GPS) Approaches
- ❏ NDB Approaches
- ❏ ILS Approaches
- ❏ Localizer Approaches
- ❏ Approach Procedures to Straight-In Landing Minimums
- ❏ Approach Procedures to Circling Landing Minimums
- ❏ Landing From a Straight-In or Circling Approach Procedure
- ❏ Missed Approach Procedures

APPROACHES WITH LOSS OF PRIMARY FLIGHT INSTRUMENT INDICATORS
- ❏ No-Gyro Radar Vectoring and Approach Procedures
- ❏ Partial-Panel Approaches

COMPLETION STANDARDS
- Demonstrate proficiency in all instrument procedures at the level required by the Instrument Rating Airman Certification Standards.
- Demonstrate the ability to use SRM to make effective decisions, maintain situational awareness, prevent CFIT, and manage risk, tasks, and automation.

POSTFLIGHT DEBRIEFING
- ❏ Evaluate maneuvers/procedures and SRM. Plan additional instruction for skills not meeting Stage II completion standards.
- ❏ Update the record folder and logbook.

STUDY ASSIGNMENT
Ground Lessons 20 and 21
  Weather Factors and Hazards
  Printed Reports and Forecasts
  IFR Cross-Country Briefing

Instrument/Commercial Syllabus

Stage III

STAGE OBJECTIVES
During Stage III the student learns IFR cross-country procedures and increases proficiency to the level required of an instrument-rated pilot.

STAGE COMPLETION STANDARDS
This stage is complete when the student can demonstrate all IFR maneuvers and procedures at the proficiency level of an instrument-rated pilot, as outlined in the Instrument Rating Airman Certification Standards.

FLIGHT LESSON 24

DUAL — CROSS-COUNTRY

OBJECTIVES
- Gain proficiency in IFR cross-country flight planning and following ATC clearances.
- Gain proficiency in IFR cross-country flight operations by performing an IFR cross-country over 50 nautical miles from the original point of departure.
- Become familiar with the appropriate emergency procedures for enroute IFR operations.

PREFLIGHT DISCUSSION
- ❏ Interpreting Weather Reports and Forecasts
- ❏ Airplane Performance, Limitations, Systems, and Equipment for IFR Flight
- ❏ Review of Enroute, Departure, Arrival, and Approach Charts
- ❏ GPS and RAIM Capability
- ❏ Completing a Navigation Log
- ❏ Alternates and Fuel Considerations
- ❏ IFR Clearances, Clearance Void Times, and Hold-for-Release Times
- ❏ Changes to IFR Clearances

INTRODUCE

IFR CROSS-COUNTRY FLIGHT PLANNING
- ❏ Weather Information Related to IFR Cross-Country Flight
- ❏ Performance and Limitations
- ❏ Estimated Time Enroute
- ❏ Fuel Requirements
- ❏ Weight and Balance
- ❏ SIDs, ODPs, and STARs
- ❏ Navigation Log and Flight Plan
- ❏ Filing an IFR Flight Plan

ATC CLEARANCES AND PROCEDURES
- ❏ Clearance Copying and Readback
- ❏ Compliance with Departure, Enroute, and Arrival Clearances

Instrument/Commercial Syllabus

IFR CROSS-COUNTRY FLIGHT
- ❏ Wake Turbulence Avoidance
- ❏ Use of SIDs and ODPs
- ❏ VOR Enroute Navigation
- ❏ GPS Enroute Navigation
- ❏ Calculating ETEs and ETAs
- ❏ Use of Radar
- ❏ Radio Communications
- ❏ Use of STARs
- ❏ Holding
- ❏ Canceling an IFR Flight Plan
- ❏ Use of Autopilot
- ❏ Single-Pilot Resource Management
- ❏ Aeronautical Decision Making and Judgment

EMERGENCY OPERATIONS (SIMULATED)
- ❏ Loss of Communications
- ❏ Systems and Equipment Malfunctions
- ❏ Loss of Primary Flight Instrument Indicators
- ❏ Partial-Panel Flight
- ❏ Airframe and Powerplant Icing
- ❏ Turbulence
- ❏ Diversion
- ❏ Low Fuel Supply
- ❏ Engine Failure

REVIEW

INSTRUMENT APPROACH PROCEDURES

NOTE: Use specific approach procedures as needed.
- ❏ VOR Approaches
- ❏ RNAV (GPS) Approaches
- ❏ NDB Approaches
- ❏ ILS Approaches
- ❏ Localizer Approaches
- ❏ Missed Approach Procedures
- ❏ Partial-Panel Approaches

COMPLETION STANDARDS
- Demonstrate understanding of the procedures involved in IFR cross-country flight planning, filing IFR flight plans, and obtaining IFR clearances.
- Demonstrate understanding of IFR cross-country operations.
- Demonstrate understanding of emergency procedures in the IFR environment.

POSTFLIGHT DEBRIEFING
- ❏ Critique maneuvers/procedures and SRM.
- ❏ Create a plan for skills that need improvement.
- ❏ Update the record folder and logbook.

STUDY ASSIGNMENT
Ground Lesson 22
  Graphic Weather Products

STAGE III ■ Instrument Rating Flight Training

Instrument/Commercial Syllabus

FLIGHT LESSON 25
DUAL — CROSS-COUNTRY

OBJECTIVES
- Increase proficiency in IFR flight planning and IFR departure, enroute, and arrival procedures by performing an IFR cross-country flight over 50 nautical miles from the original point of departure.
- Increase proficiency in emergency procedures for enroute IFR operations.

PREFLIGHT DISCUSSION
- Alternate Airport Requirements Applying to GPS Approaches
- Emergency and Abnormal Procedures for the Airplane
- Loss of Communications Procedures
- Anti-Icing or Deicing Equipment on the Airplane
- Icing Operational Hazards
- Minimum Fuel
- Declaring an Emergency—Procedures, Frequencies, and Transponder Codes
- Diverting to Another Airport

REVIEW

IFR CROSS-COUNTRY FLIGHT PLANNING
- Weather Information Related to IFR Cross-Country Flight
- Performance and Limitations
- Estimated Time Enroute
- Fuel Requirements
- Weight and Balance
- SIDs, ODPs, and STARs
- Navigation Log and Flight Plan
- Filing an IFR Flight Plan

ATC CLEARANCES AND PROCEDURES
- Clearance Copying and Readback
- Compliance with Departure, Enroute, and Arrival Clearances

IFR CROSS-COUNTRY FLIGHT
- Wake Turbulence Avoidance
- Use of SIDs and ODPs
- VOR Enroute Navigation
- GPS Enroute Navigation
- Calculating ETEs and ETAs
- Use of Radar
- Radio Communications
- Use of STARs
- Holding
- Canceling an IFR Flight Plan
- Use of Autopilot
- Single-Pilot Resource Management
- Aeronautical Decision Making and Judgment

EMERGENCY OPERATIONS (SIMULATED)
- Loss of Communications
- Systems and Equipment Malfunctions

STAGE III ■ Instrument Rating Flight Training

Instrument/Commercial Syllabus

- ❑ Loss of Primary Flight Instrument Indicators
- ❑ Partial-Panel Flight
- ❑ Airframe and Powerplant Icing
- ❑ Turbulence
- ❑ Diversion
- ❑ Low Fuel Supply
- ❑ Engine Failure

COMPLETION STANDARDS
- Demonstrate increased proficiency performing the procedures involved in cross-country flight planning, filing an IFR flight plan, and obtaining IFR clearances.
- Demonstrate increased proficiency in IFR cross-country operations.
- Demonstrate increased proficiency in performing emergency procedures.

POSTFLIGHT DEBRIEFING
- ❑ Critique maneuvers/procedures and SRM.
- ❑ Create a plan for skills that need improvement.
- ❑ Update the record folder and logbook.

STUDY ASSIGNMENT
Ground Lessons 23, 24, and 25
  Sources of Weather Information
  IFR Emergencies
  IFR SRM / IFR Flight Planning

FLIGHT LESSON 26

DUAL — CROSS-COUNTRY

OBJECTIVES
- Increase proficiency in planning and performing an IFR cross-country flight
- Increase proficiency in IFR departure, enroute, and arrival procedures.

NOTE: The flight is designed to meet the cross-country requirements stated in Part 141, Appendix C. The flight must be conducted under IFR in the category and class of airplane for which the course is approved and must be at least 250 nautical miles in length along airways or ATC-directed routing. One leg of the flight must be at least a straight-line distance of 100 nautical miles between airports. The student must perform an instrument approach at each airport and perform a minimum of three different types of approaches using navigation systems.

PREFLIGHT DISCUSSION

SINGLE-PILOT RESOURCE MANAGEMENT (SRM)
- ❑ Aeronautical Decision Making (ADM)
    - ◊ Using the ADM Process
    - ◊ Recognizing Hazardous Attitudes

Instrument/Commercial Syllabus

- ❏ Risk Management
    - ◊ Using a Risk Management Tool (5Ps, PAVE)
    - ◊ Assessing Weather Risk
- ❏ Task Management
    - ◊ Planning and Prioritizing
    - ◊ Checklist Use
- ❏ Situational Awareness
    - ◊ Dangers of Fixating on a Problem
    - ◊ Use of Navigation, Traffic, Terrain, and Weather Displays
- ❏ CFIT Awareness
    - ◊ Flight Planning to Avoid Terrain and Obstacles.
    - ◊ Use of Navigation, Terrain, and TAWS Displays
- ❏ Automation Management
    - ◊ Cross Checking Waypoint and Navaid Locations
    - ◊ Recognizing Mode or Status Changes of the Autopilot/FMS.

REVIEW

IFR CROSS-COUNTRY FLIGHT PLANNING
- ❏ Weather Information Related to IFR Cross-Country Flight
- ❏ Performance and Limitations
- ❏ Estimated Time Enroute
- ❏ Fuel Requirements
- ❏ Weight and Balance
- ❏ SIDs, ODPs, and STARs
- ❏ Navigation Log and Flight Plan
- ❏ Filing an IFR Flight Plan

ATC CLEARANCES AND PROCEDURES
- ❏ Clearance Copying and Readback
- ❏ Compliance with Departure, Enroute, and Arrival Clearances

IFR CROSS-COUNTRY FLIGHT
- ❏ Wake Turbulence Avoidance
- ❏ Use of SIDs and ODPs
- ❏ VOR Enroute Navigation
- ❏ GPS Enroute Navigation
- ❏ Calculating ETEs and ETAs
- ❏ Use of Radar
- ❏ Radio Communications
- ❏ Use of STARs
- ❏ Holding
- ❏ Canceling an IFR Flight Plan
- ❏ Use of Autopilot
- ❏ Single-Pilot Resource Management
- ❏ Aeronautical Decision Making and Judgment

EMERGENCY OPERATIONS (SIMULATED)
- ❏ Loss of Communications
- ❏ Systems and Equipment Malfunctions
- ❏ Loss of Primary Flight Instrument Indicators
- ❏ Partial-Panel Flight
- ❏ Airframe and Powerplant Icing
- ❏ Turbulence

STAGE III ■ Instrument Rating Flight Training

Instrument/Commercial Syllabus

- ❏ Diversion
- ❏ Low Fuel Supply
- ❏ Engine Failure

COMPLETION STANDARDS
- Demonstrate proficiency in the procedures for cross-country flight planning, filing IFR flight plans, and obtaining IFR clearances.
- Demonstrate proficiency in cross-country operations, approach procedures, and emergency operations.
- Demonstrate SRM proficiency by performing IFR operations safely and making effective decisions.

POSTFLIGHT DEBRIEFING
- ❏ Critique maneuvers/procedures and SRM.
- ❏ Create a plan for skills that need improvement.
- ❏ Update the record folder and logbook.

STUDY ASSIGNMENT
Instrument Rating Practical Test Briefing

FLIGHT LESSON 27
DUAL — CROSS-COUNTRY

OBJECTIVES
- Increase proficiency in planning and conducting all phases of the IFR cross-country flight to prepare for the Stage III Check.
- Increase proficiency in managing emergency situations.
- Demonstrate competency in effective SRM skills by making effective decisions during IFR cross-country operations.

PREFLIGHT DISCUSSION
- ❏ SRM in the IFR Environment

REVIEW

IFR CROSS-COUNTRY FLIGHT PLANNING
- ❏ Weather Information Related to IFR Cross-Country Flight
- ❏ Performance and Limitations
- ❏ Estimated Time Enroute
- ❏ Fuel Requirements
- ❏ Weight and Balance
- ❏ SIDs, ODPs, and STARs
- ❏ Navigation Log and Flight Plan
- ❏ Filing an IFR Flight Plan

ATC CLEARANCES AND PROCEDURES
- ❏ Clearance Copying and Readback
- ❏ Compliance with Departure, Enroute, and Arrival Clearances

Instrument/Commercial Syllabus

IFR CROSS-COUNTRY FLIGHT
- ❏ Wake Turbulence Avoidance
- ❏ Use of SIDs and ODPs
- ❏ VOR Enroute Navigation
- ❏ GPS Enroute Navigation
- ❏ Calculating ETEs and ETAs
- ❏ Use of Radar
- ❏ Radio Communications
- ❏ Use of STARs
- ❏ Holding
- ❏ Canceling an IFR Flight Plan
- ❏ Use of Autopilot
- ❏ Single-Pilot Resource Management
- ❏ Aeronautical Decision Making and Judgment

EMERGENCY OPERATIONS (SIMULATED)
- ❏ Loss of Communications
- ❏ Systems and Equipment Malfunctions
- ❏ Loss of Primary Flight Instrument Indicators
- ❏ Partial-Panel Flight
- ❏ Airframe and Powerplant Icing
- ❏ Turbulence
- ❏ Diversion
- ❏ Low Fuel Supply
- ❏ Engine Failure

COMPLETION STANDARDS
Demonstrate instrument pilot knowledge and proficiency in each of the listed tasks at the level required by the Instrument Rating Airman Certification Standards.

POSTFLIGHT DEBRIEFING
- ❏ Critique maneuvers/procedures and SRM.
- ❏ Create a plan for skills that need improvement.
- ❏ Update the record folder and logbook.

STUDY ASSIGNMENT
Ground Lesson 26
Stage III Exam

FLIGHT LESSON 28

DUAL — CROSS COUNTRY
STAGE III CHECK

OBJECTIVE
Demonstrate proficiency in IFR cross-country operations, holding, and instrument approach procedures to the chief instructor, assistant chief, or a designated check instructor during the Stage III Check.

Instrument/Commercial Syllabus

PREFLIGHT DISCUSSION
- ❏ Student and Flight Check Instructor Roles and Expectations
- ❏ Questions to Test Student Knowledge

REVIEW

FR CROSS-COUNTRY FLIGHT PLANNING
- ❏ Weather Information Related to IFR Cross-Country Flight
- ❏ Performance and Limitations
- ❏ Estimated Time Enroute
- ❏ Fuel Requirements
- ❏ Weight and Balance
- ❏ SIDs, ODPs, and STARs
- ❏ Navigation Log and Flight Plan
- ❏ Filing an IFR Flight Plan

ATC CLEARANCES AND PROCEDURES
- ❏ Clearance Copying and Readback
- ❏ Compliance with Departure, Enroute, and Arrival Clearances

IFR CROSS-COUNTRY FLIGHT
- ❏ Wake Turbulence Avoidance
- ❏ Use of SIDs and ODPs
- ❏ VOR Enroute Navigation
- ❏ GPS Enroute Navigation
- ❏ Calculating ETEs and ETAs
- ❏ Use of Radar
- ❏ Radio Communications
- ❏ Use of STARs
- ❏ Holding
- ❏ Canceling an IFR Flight Plan
- ❏ Use of Autopilot
- ❏ Aeronautical Decision Making and Judgment
- ❏ Single-Pilot Resource Management

EMERGENCY OPERATIONS (SIMULATED)
- ❏ Loss of Communications
- ❏ Systems and Equipment Malfunctions
- ❏ Loss of Primary Flight Instrument Indicators
- ❏ Partial-Panel Flight
- ❏ Airframe and Powerplant Icing
- ❏ Turbulence
- ❏ Diversion
- ❏ Low Fuel Supply
- ❏ Engine Failure

COMPLETION STANDARDS
- Demonstrate proficiency in all instrument rating tasks as required by the Instrument Rating Airman Certification Standards.
- Demonstrate the ability to use single-pilot resource management to make effective decisions, maintain situational awareness, prevent CFIT, and manage risk, tasks, and automation.

STAGE III ■ Instrument Rating Flight Training

Instrument/Commercial Syllabus

POSTFLIGHT DEBRIEFING
- Evaluate maneuvers/procedures and SRM.
- Plan additional instruction for skills not meeting Stage III completion standards.
- Update the record folder and logbook.

STUDY ASSIGNMENT
Ground Lesson 27
  Instrument Rating End-of-Course Exam.

FLIGHT LESSON 29

DUAL — LOCAL
END-OF-COURSE FLIGHT CHECK FOR COURSE COMPLETION

OBJECTIVE
Demonstrate proficiency all listed IFR tasks to the chief instructor, assistant chief, or a designated check instructor during the End-of-Course Flight Check. The proficiency level must meet the requirements of the Instrument Rating Airman Certification Standards.

Note: The types of navigation, holding procedures, and approach procedures evaluated will be based on the equipment in the training airplane.

PREFLIGHT DISCUSSION
- Student and Flight Check Instructor Roles and Expectations
- Questions to Test Student Knowledge

REVIEW

FULL-PANEL INSTRUMENT
- Steep Turns

FULL- AND PARTIAL-PANEL INSTRUMENT
- Straight-and-Level Flight
- Constant Rate Climbs and Descents
- Constant Airspeed Climbs and Descents
- Standard-Rate Turns
- Climbing and Descending Turns
- Timed Turns to Magnetic Compass Headings
- Magnetic Compass Turns
- Power-Off Stalls
- Power-On Stalls
- Recovery From Unusual Flight Attitudes

STAGE III ■ Instrument Rating Flight Training

Instrument/Commercial Syllabus

INSTRUMENT NAVIGATION
- ❏ VOR Navigation
- ❏ GPS Navigation
- ❏ NDB Navigation
- ❏ Localizer Navigation

HOLDING
- ❏ VOR Holding
- ❏ GPS Holding
- ❏ NDB Holding)
- ❏ Localizer Holding
- ❏ DME Holding
- ❏ Intersection Holding

IFR CROSS-COUNTRY PROCEDURES
- ❏ IFR Cross-Country Flight Planning
- ❏ ATC Clearances
- ❏ IFR Cross-Country Flight Procedures

APPROACH PROCEDURES
- ❏ VOR and NDB Approaches
- ❏ RNAV (GPS) Approaches
- ❏ ILS Approaches
- ❏ Missed Approach Procedures
- ❏ Partial-Panel Approaches

EMERGENCY OPERATIONS (SIMULATED)
- ❏ Loss of Communications
- ❏ Loss of Primary Flight Instrument Indicators
- ❏ Partial-Panel Flight
- ❏ Systems and Equipment Malfunctions
- ❏ Airframe and Powerplant Icing
- ❏ Turbulence
- ❏ Low Fuel Supply
- ❏ Diversion

COMPLETION STANDARDS
- Demonstrate proficiency in all instrument rating tasks as required by the Instrument Rating Airman Certification Standards.
- Demonstrate the ability to use single-pilot resource management to make effective decisions, maintain situational awareness, prevent CFIT, and manage risk, tasks, and automation.

POSTFLIGHT DEBRIEFING
- ❏ Evaluate maneuvers/procedures and SRM.
- ❏ Plan additional instruction for skills not meeting course completion standards.
- ❏ Update the record folder and logbook.

STAGE III ■ Instrument Rating Flight Training

Instrument/Commercial Syllabus

Commercial Pilot Ground Training Stage IV

STAGE OBJECTIVES
During this stage, the student increases knowledge of airports, airspace, flight information, and meteorology, as well as airplane performance, VFR cross-country flight planning, and navigation. In addition, the student gains a greater understanding of aviation physiology, single-pilot resource management (SRM) and the FARs applicable to commercial pilot operations.

STAGE COMPLETION STANDARDS
The student must pass the Stage IV Exam with a minimum score of 80 percent, and review each incorrect response with the instructor to ensure complete understanding before starting Stage V.

NOTE: Students not enrolled in the combined Instrument/Commercial Course should read Chapter 1, Section A — Instrument/Commercial Training and Opportunities prior to Ground Lesson 28.

GROUND LESSON 28

REFERENCES

Sectional, Terminal, and World Aeronautical Charts

Instrument/Commercial Textbook/EBook
   Chapter 3 — The Flight Environment
      Section A — Airports, Airspace, and Flight Information
   Chapter 9 — Meteorology

Instrument Online — Jeppesen Learning Center
   GL — The Flight Environment
   GL — Weather

NOTE: Students enrolled in the combined Instrument/Commercial Course are not required to accomplish the review of Chapter 3A or Chapter 9 or GL — The Flight Environment and GL — Weather.

OBJECTIVES
- Interpret airport markings, lighting, and signs.

Instrument/Commercial Syllabus

- Identify procedures to avoid runway incursions and to perform land and hold short operations (LAHSO).
- Explain the structure and requirements of the National Airspace System.
- Recognize sources of flight information.
- Interpret aeronautical charts for operations under VFR.
- Explain the weather patterns and hazards related to flight operations.
- Recognize how to obtain and interpret printed weather reports and forecasts, and graphic weather products for flight planning.
- Recognize how to obtain preflight and in-flight sources of weather information.

CONTENT

CHAPTER 3, SECTION A — AIRPORTS, AIRSPACE AND FLIGHT INFORMATION
GL — THE FLIGHT ENVIRONMENT
❏ Runway and Taxiway Markings and Airport Signs
❏ Runway Incursion Avoidance
❏ Land and Hold Short Operations (LAHSO)
❏ Lighting Systems
❏ Airspace
❏ Flight Information

CHAPTER 9 — METEOROLOGY
GL — WEATHER
❏ Weather Factors
❏ Weather Hazards
❏ Printed Reports and Forecasts
❏ Graphic Weather Products
❏ Sources of Weather Information

AERONAUTICAL CHARTS
❏ Sectional Charts
❏ VFR Terminal Area Charts
❏ World Aeronautical Charts
❏ Longitude and Latitude
❏ Airport Symbols and Data
❏ Navigation Aids
❏ Airspace
❏ Topographical Information
❏ Obstructions

COMPLETION STANDARDS

- Demonstrate understanding of the airport environment, airspace, and flight information during oral quizzing by the instructor.
- Demonstrate understanding of weather factors, weather hazards, printed reports and forecasts, graphic weather products, and the sources of weather information during oral quizzing by the instructor.
- Demonstrate understanding of VFR aeronautical charts used for cross-country flight during oral quizzing by the instructor.

Instrument/Commercial Syllabus

- Complete with a minimum score of 80 percent: questions for Chapter 3A and Chapter 9 or online exams for GL — The Flight Environment and GL — Weather. Review each incorrect response with the instructor to ensure complete understanding before starting Ground Lesson 29.

NOTE: Students enrolled in the combined Instrument/Commercial Course are not required to complete the questions for Chapter 3A and Chapter 9 or online exams for GL — The Flight Environment and GL — Weather.

STUDY ASSIGNMENT
Review pilotage and dead reckoning methods for VFR cross-country flight planning and navigation

GROUND LESSON 29

OBJECTIVES
- Increase proficiency in using pilotage and dead reckoning for VFR cross-country flight planning and navigation.
- Increase proficiency in VFR flight planning, including selecting the proper VFR cruising altitudes, creating a route, and lost procedures.

CONTENT
PILOTAGE AND DEAD RECKONING
- ❏ Pilotage
- ❏ Selecting Checkpoints
- ❏ Following a Route
- ❏ Orientation
- ❏ Dead Reckoning
- ❏ Navigation Plotter
- ❏ Flight Planning
- ❏ Navigation Log
- ❏ Flight Plan
- ❏ Flying Over Hazardous Terrain
- ❏ Lost Procedures

COMPLETION STANDARDS
Demonstrate understanding of the pilotage and dead reckoning methods for VFR cross-country flight planning and navigation during oral quizzing by the instructor before starting Ground Lesson 30.

STUDY ASSIGNMENT
Instrument/Commercial Textbook/EBook
   Chapter 1 — Building Professional Experience
      Section B — Advanced Human Factors Concepts

Instrument Online — Jeppesen Learning Center
   GL — Advanced Human Factors

STAGE IV ■ Commercial Pilot Ground Training

Instrument/Commercial Syllabus

GROUND LESSON 30

REFERENCES

Instrument/Commercial Textbook/EBook
  Chapter 1 — Building Professional Experience
    Section B — Advanced Human Factors Concepts

Instrument Online — Jeppesen Learning Center
  GL — Advanced Human Factors

OBJECTIVES
- Explain the causes, symptoms, and prevention of aviation physiology factors, including disorientation, hypoxia, and hyperventilation.
- Explain how aviation physiology factors apply to operations in the commercial flight environment.

CONTENT
AVIATION PHYSIOLOGY
- ❏ Disorientation
- ❏ Spatial Disorientation
- ❏ Vestibular Disorientation
- ❏ Motion Sickness
- ❏ Hypoxia
- ❏ Prevention of Hypoxia
- ❏ Supplemental Oxygen
- ❏ High Altitude Training
- ❏ Decompression Sickness
- ❏ Hyperventilation
- ❏ Stress
- ❏ Fatigue
- ❏ Alcohol and Drugs
- ❏ Fitness for Flight

COMPLETION STANDARDS
Demonstrate knowledge of the causes, symptoms, and prevention of physiological factors affecting flight operations during oral quizzing by the instructor before starting Ground Lesson 31.

STUDY ASSIGNMENT
Instrument/Commercial Textbook/EBook
  Chapter 1 — Building Professional Experience
    Section B — Advanced Human Factors Concepts

Instrument/Commercial Syllabus

GROUND LESSON 31

REFERENCES

Instrument/Commercial Textbook/EBook
Chapter 1 — Building Professional Experience
Section B — Advanced Human Factors Concepts

OBJECTIVES
- Become familiar with the human factors concepts that affect aeronautical decision making and judgment.
- Become familiar with the single-pilot resource management (SRM) techniques that increase flight safety.

CONTENT
SINGLE-PILOT RESOURCE MANAGEMENT
- ❏ Aeronautical Decision Making
- ❏ Risk Management
- ❏ Task Management
- ❏ Situational Awareness
- ❏ CFIT Awareness
- ❏ Automation Management

COMPLETION STANDARDS
- Demonstrate understanding of single-pilot resource management concepts during oral quizzing by the instructor before starting to Ground Lesson 32.

STUDY ASSIGNMENT
FAR/AIM
  Commercial FARs

Instrument Online — Jeppesen Learning Center
  GL — Commercial FARs

Instrument/Commercial Syllabus

GROUND LESSON 32

REFERENCES

FAR/AIM
Commercial FARs

Instrument Online — Jeppesen Learning Center
GL — Commercial FARs

OBJECTIVES
- Recognize the FARs that apply specifically to commercial pilot operations.
- Review NTSB Part 830.

CONTENT
- ❏ FAR Part 1
- ❏ FAR Part 61
- ❏ FAR Part 91
- ❏ FAR Part 119
- ❏ NTSB Part 830

COMPLETION STANDARDS
- Demonstrate understanding of the FARs that apply to commercial operations and NTSB Part 830 during oral quizzing by the instructor.
- Complete with a minimum score of 80 percent: online exams for GL — Commercial FARs. Review each incorrect response with the instructor to ensure complete understanding before taking the Stage IV Exam in Ground Lesson 33.

STUDY ASSIGNMENT
Review the content of Ground Lessons 28 – 32 to prepare for the Stage IV Exam.

GROUND LESSON 33
STAGE IV EXAM

REFERENCES

Ground Lessons 28 – 32

OBJECTIVE
Demonstrate knowledge of the subjects covered in Ground Lessons 28 – 32 by passing the Stage IV Exam.

Instrument/Commercial Syllabus

CONTENT

STAGE IV EXAM
- ❏ Airports, Airspace, and Flight Information
- ❏ Meteorology
- ❏ Aeronautical Charts
- ❏ Pilotage and Dead Reckoning
- ❏ Aviation Physiology
- ❏ Single-Pilot Resource Management
- ❏ Commercial FARs and NTSB Part 830

COMPLETION STANDARDS
To complete the lesson and stage, pass the Stage IV Exam with a minimum score of 80 percent. Review each incorrect response with the instructor to ensure complete understanding before starting Stage V.

STUDY ASSIGNMENT
Instrument/Commercial Textbook/EBook
  Chapter 11 — Advanced Systems
    Section A — High-Performance Powerplants

Instrument Online — Jeppesen Learning Center
  GL — High-Performance Powerplants

Instrument/Commercial Syllabus

Stage V

STAGE OBJECTIVES
During this stage, the student learns about the operation of complex airplane systems, determines airplane performance and weight and balance, and explores advanced aerodynamics concepts. The student increases knowledge of emergency procedures and using single-pilot resource management (SRM) and crew resource management (CRM) skills to help make effective decisions. In addition, the student learns the steps to perform the flight maneuvers required for commercial pilot certification.

STAGE COMPLETION STANDARDS
The student must pass the Stage V Exam and the Commercial Pilot End-of-Course Exam with a minimum score of 80 percent, and review each incorrect response with the instructor to ensure complete understanding.

GROUND LESSON 34

REFERENCES

Instrument/Commercial Textbook/EBook
  Chapter 11 — Advanced Systems
    Section A — High-Performance Powerplants

Instrument Online — Jeppesen Learning Center
  GL — High-Performance Powerplants

OBJECTIVES
- Explain the components and operation of a fuel injection system.
- Describe how a turbocharging system operates.
- Explain the principles of propeller pitch control and the components and operation of a constant-speed propeller.

CONTENT

FUEL INJECTION SYSTEMS
- Operating Procedures
- Normal Starts
- Hot Starts
- Flooded Starts
- Engine Monitoring
- Exhaust Gas Temperature Gauge
- Cylinder Head Temperature Gauge
- Abnormal Combustion
- Induction Icing

Instrument/Commercial Syllabus

TURBOCHARGING SYSTEMS
- ❏ Turbocharging Principles
- ❏ System Operation
- ❏ High Altitude Performance

CONSTANT-SPEED PROPELLERS
- ❏ Propeller Principles
- ❏ Constant-Speed Propeller Operation
- ❏ Power Controls

COMPLETION STANDARDS
- Demonstrate understanding of fuel injection systems, turbocharging systems, and constant-speed propellers during oral quizzing by the instructor.
- Complete with a minimum score of 80 percent: questions for Chapter 11A or online exam for GL — High-Performance Powerplants. Review each incorrect response with the instructor to ensure complete understanding before starting Ground Lesson 35.

STUDY ASSIGNMENT
Instrument/Commercial Textbook/EBook
  Chapter 11 — Advanced Systems
    Section B — Environmental and Ice Control Systems

Instrument Online — Jeppesen Learning Center
  GL — Environmental and Ice Control Systems

GROUND LESSON 35

REFERENCES

Instrument/Commercial Textbook/EBook
  Chapter 11 — Advanced Systems
    Section B — Environmental and Ice Control Systems

Instrument Online — Jeppesen Learning Center
  GL — Environmental and Ice Control Systems

OBJECTIVES
- Explain the components and operation of aircraft oxygen systems.
- Describe the components and operation of cabin pressurization systems.
- Explain the components and operation of ice control systems.

Instrument/Commercial Syllabus

CONTENT

OXYGEN SYSTEMS
- ❏ Continuous-Flow
- ❏ Diluter-Demand
- ❏ Pressure-Demand
- ❏ Pulse-Demand
- ❏ Oxygen Storage
- ❏ Oxygen Servicing

CABIN PRESSURIZATION
- ❏ Pressurization Principles
- ❏ Pressurization Components
- ❏ Pressurization Emergencies

ICE CONTROL SYSTEMS
- ❏ Airfoil Ice Control
- ❏ Windshield Ice Control
- ❏ Propeller Ice Control
- ❏ Other Ice Control Systems

COMPLETION STANDARDS

- Demonstrate understanding of oxygen, cabin pressurization, and ice control systems during oral quizzing by the instructor.
- Complete with a minimum score of 80 percent: questions for Chapter 11B or online exam for GL — Environmental and Ice Control Systems. Review each incorrect response with the instructor to ensure complete understanding before starting Ground Lesson 36.

STUDY ASSIGNMENT

Instrument/Commercial Textbook/EBook
  Chapter 11 — Advanced Systems
    Section C — Retractable Landing Gear

Instrument Online — Jeppesen Learning Center
  GL — Retractable Landing Gear

Instrument/Commercial Syllabus

GROUND LESSON 36

REFERENCES

Instrument/Commercial Textbook/EBook
Chapter 11 — Advanced Systems
Section C — Retractable Landing Gear

Instrument Online — Jeppesen Learning Center
GL — Retractable Landing Gear

OBJECTIVES
- Explain the components and operation of retractable landing gear systems.
- Describe gear system malfunctions and the operation of the emergency gear extension system.

CONTENT

LANDING GEAR SYSTEMS
- ❏ Electrical Gear Systems
- ❏ Hydraulic Gear Systems

GEAR SYSTEM SAFETY
- ❏ Gear Position Indicators
- ❏ Gear Warning Horn
- ❏ Safety Switches
- ❏ Airspeed Limitations

GEAR SYSTEM OPERATION
- ❏ Operating Procedures
- ❏ Gear System Malfunctions
- ❏ Emergency Gear Extension

COMPLETION STANDARDS
- Demonstrate understanding of the components and operation of retractable landing gear systems during oral quizzing by the instructor.
- Complete with a minimum score of 80 percent: questions for Chapter 11C or online exam for GL — Retractable Landing Gear. Review each incorrect response with the instructor to ensure complete understanding before starting Ground Lesson 37.

STUDY ASSIGNMENT
Instrument/Commercial Textbook/EBook
  Chapter 12 — Aerodynamics and Performance Limitations
    Section A — Advanced Aerodynamics
  Chapter 14 — Commercial Maneuvers
    Section A — Accelerated Stalls

Instrument/Commercial Syllabus

Instrument Online — Jeppesen Learning Center
GL — Aerodynamic Principles
GL — Aerodynamic Considerations
ML — Accelerated Stalls

GROUND LESSON 37

REFERENCES

Instrument/Commercial Textbook/EBook
Chapter 12 — Aerodynamics and Performance Limitations
Section A — Advanced Aerodynamics
Chapter 14 — Commercial Maneuvers
Section A — Accelerated Stalls

Instrument Online — Jeppesen Learning Center
GL — Aerodynamic Principles
GL — Aerodynamic Considerations
ML — Accelerated Stalls

OBJECTIVES
- Explain how airplane design and operation affect the forces of lift, weight, thrust, and drag.
- Describe how weight and load factor affect the airplane's flight characteristics.
- Explain how airplane design and operation affect longitudinal, lateral, and directional stability.
- Recognize the aerodynamic characteristics of the airplane in maneuvering flight.
- Identify the causes of and recovery procedures for stalls and spins.
- Recognize the procedures and performance considerations necessary to perform and recover from accelerated stalls.

CONTENT

FOUR FORCES OF FLIGHT
- Lift
- Lift Equation
- Controlling Lift
- High Lift Devices
- Drag
- Induced Drag
- Ground Effect
- Parasite Drag
- High Drag Devices
- Thrust
- Weight and Load Factor
- V-g Diagram

Instrument/Commercial Syllabus

AIRCRAFT STABILITY
- ❏ Static Stability
- ❏ Dynamic Stability
- ❏ Longitudinal Stability
- ❏ Lateral Stability
- ❏ Directional Stability

AERODYNAMICS AND MANEUVERS
- ❏ Straight-and-Level Flight
- ❏ Climbs
- ❏ Glides
- ❏ Turns
- ❏ Stall and Spin Awareness
- ❏ Stall Causes and Types
- ❏ Stall Recognition and Recovery
- ❏ Spin Causes and Phases
- ❏ Spin Recovery

ACCELERATED STALLS
- ❏ Description
- ❏ Procedure

COMPLETION STANDARDS
- Demonstrate understanding of the four forces of flight, aircraft stability, the aerodynamics of flight maneuvers, and stall and spin awareness during oral quizzing by the instructor.
- Complete with a minimum score of 80 percent: questions for Chapter 12A and 14A or online exams for GL — Aerodynamic Principles and GL — Aerodynamic Considerations. Review each incorrect response with the instructor to ensure complete understanding before starting Ground Lesson 38.

STUDY ASSIGNMENT
Instrument/Commercial Textbook/EBook
  Chapter 12 — Aerodynamics and Performance Limitations
    Section B — Predicting Performance

Instrument Online — Jeppesen Learning Center
  GL — Predicting Performance

GROUND LESSON 38

REFERENCES

Instrument/Commercial Textbook/EBook
  Chapter 12 — Aerodynamics and Performance Limitations
    Section B — Predicting Performance

Instrument Online — Jeppesen Learning Center
  GL — Predicting Performance

Instrument/Commercial Syllabus

OBJECTIVES
- Identify the factors that affect airplane performance.
- Determine airplane performance using performance charts in the POH or AFM.

CONTENT

FACTORS AFFECTING PERFORMANCE
- ❏ Density Altitude
- ❏ Surface Winds
- ❏ Weight
- ❏ Runway Conditions

THE PILOT'S OPERATING HANDBOOK
- ❏ Performance Charts
- ❏ Takeoff Charts
- ❏ Climb Performance Charts
- ❏ Cruise Performance Charts
- ❏ Descent Charts
- ❏ Landing Distance Charts
- ❏ Glide Distance
- ❏ Stall Speeds

COMPLETION STANDARDS
- Demonstrate understanding of the factors that affect airplane performance and be able to determine airplane performance using charts during oral quizzing by the instructor.
- Complete with a minimum score of 80 percent: questions for Chapter 12B or online exam for GL — Predicting Performance. Review each incorrect response with the instructor to ensure complete understanding before starting Ground Lesson 39.

STUDY ASSIGNMENT
Instrument/Commercial Textbook/EBook
  Chapter 12 — Aerodynamics and Performance Limitations
    Section C — Controlling Weight and Balance

Instrument Online — Jeppesen Learning Center
  GL — Weight and Balance

Instrument/Commercial Syllabus

GROUND LESSON 39

REFERENCES

Instrument/Commercial Textbook/EBook
Chapter 12 — Aerodynamics and Performance Limitations
Section C — Controlling Weight and Balance

Instrument Online — Jeppesen Learning Center
GL — Weight and Balance

OBJECTIVES
- Recognize how the weight and balance condition affects airplane performance.
- Determine the airplane's weight and balance condition using the computation, graph, and table methods.

CONTENT

LIMITATIONS, DOCUMENTS, AND COMPUTATIONS
- ❏ Maximum Weight Limits
- ❏ Center of Gravity Limits
- ❏ Weight and Balance Documents
- ❏ Weight and Balance Computations

WEIGHT AND BALANCE CONDITION CHECKS
- ❏ Computation Method
- ❏ Graph Method
- ❏ Table Method
- ❏ Weight Shift Computations

COMPLETION STANDARDS
- Demonstrate understanding of how weight and balance affects airplane performance and determine the airplane's weight and balance condition using the computation, graph, and table methods during oral quizzing by the instructor.
- Complete with a minimum score of 80 percent: questions for Chapter 12C or online exam for GL — Weight and Balance. Review each incorrect response with the instructor to ensure complete understanding before starting Ground Lesson 40.

STUDY ASSIGNMENT

Instrument/Commercial Textbook/EBook
  Chapter 14 — Commercial Maneuvers
    Section B — Maximum Performance Takeoffs and Landings

Instrument Online — Jeppesen Learning Center
  ML — Maximum Performance Takeoffs and Landings

Instrument/Commercial Syllabus

GROUND LESSON 40

REFERENCES

Instrument/Commercial Textbook/EBook
Chapter 14 — Commercial Maneuvers
Section B — Maximum Performance Takeoffs and Landings

Instrument Online — Jeppesen Learning Center
ML — Maximum Performance Takeoffs and Landings

OBJECTIVE
Recognize the procedures and performance considerations necessary to perform maximum performance takeoffs and landings.

CONTENT

SOFT FIELD
- ❏ Takeoff and Climb
- ❏ Approach and Landing

SHORT FIELD
- ❏ Takeoff and Maximum Performance Climb
- ❏ Approach and Landing

COMPLETION STANDARDS
- Demonstrate understanding of maximum performance takeoffs and landings during oral quizzing by the instructor.
- Complete the questions for Chapter 14B with a minimum score of 80 percent. Review each incorrect response with the instructor to ensure complete understanding before starting Ground Lesson 41.

STUDY ASSIGNMENT
Instrument/Commercial Textbook/EBook
  Chapter 14 — Commercial Maneuvers
    Section C — Steep Turns
    Section D — Chandelles

Instrument Online — Jeppesen Learning Center
ML — Steep Turns
ML — Chandelles

GROUND LESSON 41

REFERENCES

Instrument/Commercial Textbook/EBook
Chapter 14 — Commercial Maneuvers
  Section C — Steep Turns
  Section D — Chandelles

Instrument Online — Jeppesen Learning Center
ML — Steep Turns
ML — Chandelles

OBJECTIVE
Recognize the procedures and performance considerations necessary to perform steep turns and chandelles.

CONTENT

STEEP TURNS
❏ Description
❏ Procedure

CHANDELLES
❏ Description
❏ Procedure

COMPLETION STANDARDS
- Demonstrate understanding of steep turns and chandelles during oral quizzing by the instructor.
- Complete the questions for Chapter 14, Sections C and D with a minimum score of 80 percent. Review each incorrect response with the instructor to ensure complete understanding before starting Ground Lesson 42.

STUDY ASSIGNMENT

Instrument/Commercial Textbook/EBook
  Chapter 14 — Commercial Maneuvers
    Section E — Lazy Eights
    Section F — Eights-on-Pylons
    Section G — Steep Spirals
    Section H — Power-Off 180° Accuracy Approach and Landing

Instrument Online — Jeppesen Learning Center
  ML — Lazy Eights
  ML — Eights-on-Pylons
  ML — Steep Spirals
  ML — Power-Off 180° Accuracy Approach and Landing

Instrument/Commercial Syllabus

GROUND LESSON 42

REFERENCES

Instrument/Commercial Textbook/EBook
Chapter 14 — Commercial Maneuvers
    Section E — Lazy Eights
    Section F — Eights-on-Pylons
    Section G — Steep Spirals
    Section H — Power-Off 180° Accuracy Approach and Landing

Instrument Online — Jeppesen Learning Center
ML — Lazy Eights
ML — Eights-on-Pylons
ML — Steep Spirals
ML — Power-Off 180° Accuracy Approach and Landing

OBJECTIVES
- Recognize the procedures and performance considerations necessary to perform steep turns lazy eights, eights-on-pylons, and steep spirals.
- Explain how commercial maneuvers develop pilot skill.

CONTENT

LAZY EIGHTS
- ❏ Description
- ❏ Procedure

EIGHTS-ON-PYLONS
- ❏ Description
- ❏ Procedure

STEEP SPIRALS
- ❏ Description
- ❏ Procedure

POWER-OFF 180° ACCURACY APPROACH AND LANDING
- ❏ Description
- ❏ Procedure

COMPLETION STANDARDS
- Demonstrate understanding of lazy eights, eights-on-pylons, steep spirals, and power-off 180° accuracy approaches and landings during oral quizzing by the instructor.
- Complete the questions for Chapter 14, Sections E, F, G, and H with a minimum score of 80 percent. Review each incorrect response with the instructor to ensure complete understanding before starting Ground Lesson 43.

STAGE V ■ Commercial Pilot Ground Training

Instrument/Commercial Syllabus

STUDY ASSIGNMENT
Instrument/Commercial Textbook/EBook
 Chapter 13 — Commercial Flight Considerations
  Section A — Emergency Procedures
 Chapter 14 — Commercial Maneuvers
  Section I — Emergency Descent

Instrument Online — Jeppesen Learning Center
 GL — Emergency Situations

GROUND LESSON 43

REFERENCES

Instrument/Commercial Textbook/EBook
 Chapter 13 — Commercial Flight Considerations
  Section A — Emergency Procedures
 Chapter 14 — Commercial Maneuvers
  Section I — Emergency Descent

Instrument Online — Jeppesen Learning Center
 GL — Emergency Situations

OBJECTIVES
- Explain the procedures used to manage emergencies and systems and equipment malfunctions in the VFR environment.
- Describe forced landing procedures and the items that should be included with emergency equipment and survival gear.

CONTENT
❑ Emergency Descent
❑ Emergency Approach and Landing
❑ In-Flight Fire
❑ Partial Power Loss
❑ Door Opening in Flight
❑ Asymmetrical Flap Extension
❑ Emergency Equipment and Survival Gear

COMPLETION STANDARDS
- Demonstrate understanding of emergency procedures during oral quizzing by the instructor.
- Complete with a minimum score of 80 percent: questions for Chapters 13A and 14I or online exam for GL — Emergency Situations. Review each incorrect response with the instructor to ensure complete understanding before starting Ground Lesson 44.

Instrument/Commercial Syllabus

STUDY ASSIGNMENT
Instrument/Commercial Textbook/EBook
 Chapter 13 — Commercial Flight Considerations
  Section B — Commercial Pilot SRM

Instrument Online — Jeppesen Learning Center
 GL — Commercial Pilot SRM

GROUND LESSON 44

REFERENCES

Instrument/Commercial Textbook/EBook
 Chapter 13 — Commercial Flight Considerations
  Section B — Commercial Pilot SRM

Instrument Online — Jeppesen Learning Center
 GL — Commercial Pilot SRM

OBJECTIVES
- Recognize how single-pilot resources management (SRM) and crew resource management (CRM) skills can enhance flight safety in the commercial flight environment.
- Explain how the to use the aeronautical decision-making process during commercial flight operations.

CONTENT
- ❑ Aeronautical Decision Making
- ❑ Risk Management
- ❑ Task Management
- ❑ Situational Awareness
- ❑ Controlled Flight Into Terrain Awareness
- ❑ Automation Management

COMPLETION STANDARDS
- Demonstrate understanding of using SRM and CRM skills and the ADM process to make effective decisions in the commercial environment during oral quizzing by the instructor.
- Complete with a minimum score of 80 percent: questions for Chapter 13B or online exams for GL — Commercial Pilot SRM. Review each incorrect response with the instructor to ensure complete understanding before starting Ground Lesson 45.

STUDY ASSIGNMENT
Review the content of Ground Lessons 34 – 44 to prepare for the Stage V Exam.

GROUND LESSON 45
STAGE V EXAM

REFERENCES

Ground Lessons 34 – 44

OBJECTIVE
Demonstrate knowledge of the subjects covered in Ground Lessons 34 – 44 by passing the Stage V Exam.

CONTENT
STAGE V EXAM
- ❑ High-Performance Powerplants
- ❑ Environmental and Ice Control Systems
- ❑ Retractable Landing Gear
- ❑ Advanced Aerodynamics
- ❑ Predicting Performance
- ❑ Controlling Weight and Balance
- ❑ Commercial Maneuvers
- ❑ Emergency Procedures
- ❑ Commercial Pilot SRM

COMPLETION STANDARDS
To complete the lesson and stage, pass the Stage V Exam with a minimum score of 80 percent. Review each incorrect response with the instructor to ensure complete understanding before taking the End-of-Course Exam in Ground Lesson 46.

STUDY ASSIGNMENT
Review the references for Ground Lessons 28 – 45 to prepare for the Commercial Pilot End-of-Course Exam.

Instrument/Commercial Syllabus

GROUND LESSON 46

END-OF-COURSE EXAM

REFERENCES
Ground Lessons 28 – 45

OBJECTIVE
Demonstrate comprehension of the material covered in Ground Lessons 28 – 45 by passing the Commercial Pilot End-of-Course Exam to prepare for the FAA Commercial Pilot Airman Knowledge Test.

CONTENT
❑ Commercial Pilot End-of Course Exam

COMPLETION STANDARDS
To complete the lesson and the Commercial Pilot Ground Training, pass the Commercial Pilot End-of-Course Exam with a minimum score of 80 percent. Review each incorrect response with the instructor to ensure complete understanding before taking the FAA Commercial Pilot Airman Knowledge Test.

STUDY ASSIGNMENT
Review the content of Ground Lessons 28 – 46 to prepare for the FAA Commercial Pilot Airman Knowledge Test.

Commercial Pilot Flight Training Stage IV

STAGE OBJECTIVES
During Stage IV, the student increases proficiency in VFR cross-country procedures by planning and performing extended cross-country flights. The student also increases proficiency in performing night operations.

STAGE COMPLETION STANDARDS
This stage is complete when the student can demonstrate proficiency in planning VFR cross-country flights and can safely perform those flights using pilotage, dead reckoning, and navigation systems. In addition, the student must demonstrate proficiency in safe night flight operations.

NOTE: Completion of the instrument navigation tasks listed in each lesson must be based on the available airplane equipment.

FLIGHT LESSON 30
DUAL — CROSS-COUNTRY
NOTE: As indicated in the Allocation Tables, complete Ground Lessons 28 and 29 and the Cross-Country Procedures Briefing prior to this flight.

OBJECTIVES
- Complete a flight of at least two hours in duration that includes a straight-line distance of more than 100 nautical miles from the original departure point.
- Increase proficiency in VFR cross-country skills, including simulated emergency procedures, in preparation for solo cross-country flights.

PREFLIGHT DISCUSSION
- ❏ Positive Exchange of Flight Controls
- ❏ Emergency Procedures
- ❏ Emergency Equipment and Survival Gear
- ❏ Procedures at Unfamiliar Airports
- ❏ Wire Strike Avoidance
- ❏ Aviation Security
- ❏ Runway Incursion Avoidance
- ❏ Risk Management (5Ps, PAVE)
- ❏ Single-Pilot Resource Management (SRM)
- ❏ Crew Resource Management (CRM)

Instrument/Commercial Syllabus

REVIEW

PREFLIGHT PREPARATION
- ❏ Cross-Country Flight Planning
- ❏ Temporary Flight Restrictions (TFRs)
- ❏ Special Use Airspace
- ❏ Airworthiness Requirements
- ❏ Certificates and Documents
- ❏ Performance and Limitations
- ❏ National Airspace System
- ❏ Weather Information
- ❏ Density Altitude Considerations

IN-FLIGHT OPERATIONS
- ❏ Radio Communications and ATC Light Signals
- ❏ Navigation Systems and Radar Services
- ❏ Pilotage and Dead Reckoning
- ❏ VOR, GPS, and/or NDB Navigation
- ❏ Diversion and Lost Procedures
- ❏ Power Settings and Mixture Leaning
- ❏ Radio Facility Shutdown
- ❏ Cockpit Management
- ❏ Low-Level Wind Shear Avoidance
- ❏ Visual Scanning and Collision Avoidance
- ❏ Wake Turbulence Avoidance
- ❏ Runway Incursion Avoidance
- ❏ Land and Hold Short Operations (LAHSO)
- ❏ SRM and CRM

EMERGENCY OPERATIONS (SIMULATED)
- ❏ Systems and Equipment Malfunctions
- ❏ Low Fuel Supply
- ❏ Adverse Weather
- ❏ Airframe and Powerplant Icing
- ❏ Emergency Approach and Landing
- ❏ Emergency Equipment and Survival Gear

UNFAMILIAR AIRPORTS
- ❏ Traffic Patterns
- ❏ Non-Towered Airport
- ❏ Tower-Controlled Airport
- ❏ Operations at Sod or Unimproved Fields
- ❏ CTAF Procedures
- ❏ Airport, Runway, and Taxiway Signs, Markings, and Lighting

FULL-PANEL INSTRUMENT
- ❏ Straight-and-Level Flight
- ❏ Climbs
- ❏ Descents
- ❏ Standard-Rate Turns
- ❏ VOR Navigation
- ❏ GPS Navigation
- ❏ NDB Navigation
- ❏ Use of Radar Vectors

Instrument/Commercial Syllabus

NOTE: The instrument portion of this lesson should be accomplished on an "as required" basis depending on an assessment of the student's capabilities. Students enrolled in the Commercial Pilot Certification Course only must complete 10 hours of instrument training to meet the requirements of Part 141, Appendix D.

COMPLETION STANDARDS
- Demonstrate the ability to make effective decisions as pilot in command on a cross-country flight of at least two hours that includes a straight-line distance of more than 100 nautical miles from the original departure point.
- Maintain positive aircraft control with the appropriate altitude ±100 feet and heading ±10°.
- Arrive at the enroute checkpoints within three minutes of the initial or revised ETA.

POSTFLIGHT DEBRIEFING
- Critique maneuvers/procedures and SRM.
- Create a plan for skills that need improvement.
- Update the record folder and logbook.

STUDY ASSIGNMENT
Ground Lesson 30
  Aviation Physiology

FLIGHT LESSON 31

DUAL — LOCAL, NIGHT

OBJECTIVES
- Increase proficiency in night flying operations and precautions.
- Gain proficiency in performing emergency procedures during night operations.

PREFLIGHT DISCUSSION
- Night Preflight Planning
- Aircraft Lighting and Equipment
- Aeromedical Factors and Physiological Aspects of Night Flight

INTRODUCE
- Night Preflight Preparation
- Engine Starting, Taxiing, Before-Takeoff Check
- Night VFR References
- Lost Procedures
- Night Scanning/Collision Avoidance
- Wake Turbulence Avoidance

REVIEW
- Normal Takeoffs and Climbs
- Normal Approaches and Landings
- Go-Around/Rejected Landing

Instrument/Commercial Syllabus

- ❏ Steep Turns
- ❏ Maneuvering During Slow Flight
- ❏ Recovery from Unusual Attitudes
- ❏ Emergency Operations (Simulated)

COMPLETION STANDARDS
- Demonstrate understanding of the precautions and the procedures appropriate to flying at night.
- Demonstrate the ability to make effective decisions as pilot in command on a night flight.

POSTFLIGHT DEBRIEFING
- ❏ Critique maneuvers/procedures and SRM.
- ❏ Create a plan for skills that need improvement.
- ❏ Update the record folder and logbook.

STUDY ASSIGNMENT
Ground Lesson 31
Single-Pilot Resource Management

FLIGHT LESSON 32

DUAL — CROSS-COUNTRY, NIGHT

OBJECTIVES
- Gain proficiency in night cross-country procedures, including preflight planning, navigation, emergencies, and the use of unfamiliar airports.
- Complete a flight at least two hours in duration that includes a straight-line distance of more than 100 nautical miles from the original departure point.

PREFLIGHT DISCUSSION
- ❏ Night Flight Planning
- ❏ Risk Management (5Ps, PAVE)
- ❏ Aircraft Lighting and Equipment
- ❏ Aeromedical Factors and Physiological Aspects of Night Flight
- ❏ CFIT Awareness

INTRODUCE

NIGHT PREFLIGHT PREPARATION
- ❏ Cross-Country Flight Planning
- ❏ Weather Information
- ❏ Preflight Inspection
- ❏ Cockpit Management
- ❏ Airport, Runway, and Taxiway Signs, Markings, and Lighting
- ❏ Runway Incursion Avoidance
- ❏ Land and Hold Short Operations (LAHSO)
- ❏ SRM and CRM

Instrument/Commercial Syllabus

NIGHT NAVIGATION
- ❏ Night Cross-Country Procedures
- ❏ Navigation Systems and Radar Services
- ❏ Pilotage and Dead Reckoning
- ❏ Diversion and Lost Procedures
- ❏ Use of Unfamiliar Airports

REVIEW

NIGHT OPERATIONS
- ❏ Night Preflight Preparation
- ❏ Engine Starting, Taxiing, Before-Takeoff Check
- ❏ Night VFR References
- ❏ Lost Procedures
- ❏ Night Scanning/Collision Avoidance
- ❏ Wake Turbulence Avoidance

EMERGENCY OPERATIONS (SIMULATED)
- ❏ Systems and Equipment Malfunctions
- ❏ Adverse Weather
- ❏ Low Fuel Supply
- ❏ Airframe and Powerplant Icing

FULL-PANEL INSTRUMENT
- ❏ Straight-and-Level Flight
- ❏ Climbs and Descents
- ❏ Standard-Rate Turns

NOTE: The instrument portion of this lesson should be accomplished on an "as required" basis depending on an assessment of the student's capabilities. Students enrolled in the Commercial Pilot Certification Course only must complete 10 hours of instrument training to meet the requirements of Part 141, Appendix D.

COMPLETION STANDARDS

- Demonstrate the ability to make effective decisions as pilot in command on a night cross-country flight of at least two hours that includes a straight-line distance of more than 100 nautical miles from the original departure point.
- Maintain positive aircraft control with altitude ±100 feet and heading ±10°.
- Arrive at the enroute checkpoints within three minutes of the initial or revised ETA.

POSTFLIGHT DEBRIEFING
- ❏ Critique maneuvers/procedures and SRM.
- ❏ Create a plan for skills that need improvement.
- ❏ Update the record folder and logbook.

STUDY ASSIGNMENT

Ground Lesson 32
  Commercial FARs

Instrument/Commercial Syllabus

FLIGHT LESSONS 33 AND 34
SOLO — LOCAL, NIGHT

OBJECTIVE
Increase proficiency and confidence in performing maneuvers and procedures in the night environment at an airport with an operating control tower.

PREFLIGHT DISCUSSION
❏ Night Flight Operations
❏ Single-Pilot Resource Management

REVIEW
❏ Maneuvering During Slow Flight
❏ Climbs, Descents, and Turns
❏ Takeoffs and Landings (Normal and/or Crosswind)

NOTE: The 10 night takeoffs and landings with each involving flight in the traffic pattern at an airport with an operating control tower are a Part 141 requirement. Five should be completed in Flight Lesson 33 and the other five in Flight Lesson 34. However, this requirement may be accomplished with fewer than five per flight, as long as the total of 10 is completed.

COMPLETION STANDARDS
Successfully complete two night flights with a total of at least 10 takeoffs and landings at an airport with an operating control tower.

POSTFLIGHT DEBRIEFING
❏ Critique maneuvers/procedures and SRM.
❏ Create a plan for skills that need improvement.
❏ Update the record folder and logbook.

FLIGHT LESSON 35
SOLO — CROSS-COUNTRY, NIGHT

NOTE: The night solo training time requirements for this lesson may be completed in more than one flight.

OBJECTIVES
- Increase proficiency and confidence in night operations by planning and performing a night cross-country flight that includes a landing at a point more than 50 nautical miles from the original departure point.
- Increase knowledge of navigation during cross-country flights.

PREFLIGHT DISCUSSION
❏ Night Operational Considerations
❏ Cross-Country Flight Planning
❏ Risk Management (5Ps, PAVE)

STAGE IV ■ Commercial Pilot Flight Training

93

Instrument/Commercial Syllabus

REVIEW
CROSS-COUNTRY FLIGHT ASSIGNED BY THE INSTRUCTOR
NIGHT PREFLIGHT PREPARATION
- ❏ Cross-Country Flight Planning
- ❏ Weather Information
- ❏ Night Preflight Preparation
- ❏ Cockpit Management

NIGHT OPERATIONS
- ❏ Night Cross-Country Procedures
- ❏ Navigation Systems and Radar Services
- ❏ Pilotage and Dead Reckoning
- ❏ VOR, GPS, and/or NDB Navigation
- ❏ Airport, Runway, and Taxiway Signs, Markings, and Lighting
- ❏ Runway Incursion Avoidance
- ❏ Use of Unfamiliar Airports
- ❏ Situational Awareness
- ❏ Automation Management
- ❏ CFIT Awareness
- ❏ Single-Pilot Resource Management

COMPLETION STANDARDS
- Increase skill in cross-country flight planning by selecting optimum cruising altitudes and appropriate checkpoints for a flight with a landing at a point more than 50 nautical miles from the original departure point.
- Demonstrate the ability to accomplish the assigned night cross-country flight.
- During the postflight evaluation, explain the operational and safety considerations associated with night cross-country flying.

POSTFLIGHT DEBRIEFING
- ❏ Critique maneuvers/procedures and SRM.
- ❏ Create a plan for skills that need improvement.
- ❏ Update the record folder and logbook.

STUDY ASSIGNMENT
Ground Lesson 33
  Stage IV Exam

Instrument/Commercial Syllabus

FLIGHT LESSON 36
SOLO (DUAL) — CROSS-COUNTRY

NOTE: This and the following flights are provided to develop the student's cross-country proficiency and confidence. These lessons may also be utilized for additional dual instruction necessary to meet the proficiency requirements for the End-of-Course Flight Check and Commercial Pilot Practical Test.

OBJECTIVES
- Increase proficiency in cross-country operations.
- Increase proficiency in single-pilot resource management (SRM).
- If the lesson is used for dual instruction, demonstrate the ability to meet the proficiency requirements for the End-of-Course Flight Check and Commercial Pilot Practical Test.

PREFLIGHT DISCUSSION
- ❑ Cross-Country Flight Planning
- ❑ Risk Management (5Ps, PAVE)

REVIEW
CROSS-COUNTRY FLIGHT ASSIGNED BY THE INSTRUCTOR
- ❑ Cross-Country Flight Planning
- ❑ Navigation Systems and Radar Services
- ❑ Pilotage and Dead Reckoning
- ❑ VOR, GPS, and/or NDB Navigation
- ❑ Airport, Runway, and Taxiway Signs, Markings, and Lighting
- ❑ Runway Incursion Avoidance
- ❑ Automation Management
- ❑ Single-Pilot Resource Management

COMPLETION STANDARDS
- Demonstrate proficiency in cross-country flight planning by selecting optimum cruising altitudes and appropriate checkpoints for a flight with a landing at a point more than 50 nautical miles from the original departure point.
- Demonstrate fuel planning by accurately calculating fuel burn and provisions for an adequate reserve upon landing.
- If the lesson is used for dual instruction, demonstrate increased proficiency in the listed areas of operation and tasks.

POSTFLIGHT DEBRIEFING
- ❑ Critique maneuvers/procedures and SRM.
- ❑ Create a plan for skills that need improvement.
- ❑ Update the record folder and logbook.

FLIGHT LESSON 37
SOLO (DUAL) — CROSS-COUNTRY

OBJECTIVES
- Increase proficiency in cross-country flights with a focus on pilotage, dead-reckoning, and the use of unfamiliar airports by performing a flight that includes a landing at a point more than 50 nautical miles from the original departure point.
- If the lesson is used for dual instruction, demonstrate the ability to meet the proficiency requirements for the End-of-Course Flight Check and Commercial Pilot Practical Test.

PREFLIGHT DISCUSSION
- ❑ Cross-Country Flight Planning
- ❑ Risk Management (5Ps, PAVE)

REVIEW
CROSS-COUNTRY FLIGHT ASSIGNED BY THE INSTRUCTOR
- ❑ Cross-Country Flight Planning
- ❑ Navigation Systems and Radar Services
- ❑ Pilotage and Dead Reckoning
- ❑ Airport, Runway, and Taxiway Signs, Markings, and Lighting
- ❑ Runway Incursion Avoidance
- ❑ Use of Unfamiliar Airports
- ❑ Situational Awareness
- ❑ Task Management
- ❑ Single-Pilot Resource Management

COMPLETION STANDARDS
- Demonstrate proficiency in cross-country flight planning by selecting optimum cruising altitudes and appropriate checkpoints and accurately calculating fuel burn.
- Complete a flight with a landing at a point more than 50 nautical miles from the original departure point to increase proficiency in cross-country operations, especially pilotage, dead reckoning, and the use of unfamiliar airports.
- If the lesson is used for dual instruction, demonstrate increased proficiency in the listed areas of operation and tasks.

FLIGHT LESSON 38

SOLO (DUAL) — CROSS-COUNTRY

OBJECTIVES
- Increase proficiency in cross-country flights with a focus on VOR, GPS, and/or NDB navigation by performing a flight that includes a landing at a point more than 50 nautical miles from the original departure point.
- If the lesson is used for dual instruction, demonstrate the ability to meet the proficiency requirements for the End-of-Course Flight Check and Commercial Pilot Practical Test.

PREFLIGHT DISCUSSION
- ❏ Cross-Country Flight Planning
- ❏ Risk Management (5Ps, PAVE)

REVIEW

CROSS-COUNTRY FLIGHT ASSIGNED BY THE INSTRUCTOR
- ❏ Preflight Preparation
- ❏ Cross-Country Flight Planning
- ❏ Navigation Systems and Radar Services
- ❏ Pilotage and Dead Reckoning
- ❏ VOR, GPS, and/or NDB Navigation
- ❏ Airport, Runway, and Taxiway Signs, Markings, and Lighting
- ❏ Runway Incursion Avoidance
- ❏ Use of Unfamiliar Airports
- ❏ Automation Management
- ❏ Task Management
- ❏ Single-Pilot Resource Management

COMPLETION STANDARDS
- Demonstrate proficiency in cross-country flight planning by selecting optimum cruising altitudes and appropriate checkpoints and accurately calculating fuel burn.
- Complete a flight with a landing at a point more than 50 nautical miles from the original departure point to increase proficiency in cross-country operations, especially VOR, GPS, and/or NDB navigation.
- If the lesson is used for dual instruction, demonstrate increased proficiency in the listed areas of operation and tasks.

POSTFLIGHT DEBRIEFING
- ❏ Critique maneuvers/procedures and SRM.
- ❏ Create a plan for skills that need improvement.
- ❏ Update the record folder and logbook.

Instrument/Commercial Syllabus

FLIGHT LESSON 39

SOLO (DUAL) — CROSS-COUNTRY

OBJECTIVES
- Increase proficiency in cross-country flights with a focus on using unfamiliar airports by performing a flight that includes a landing at a point more than 50 nautical miles from the original departure point.
- If the lesson is used for dual instruction, demonstrate the ability to meet the proficiency requirements for the End-of-Course Flight Check and Commercial Pilot Practical Test.

PREFLIGHT DISCUSSION
❏ Cross-Country Flight Planning
❏ Risk Management (5Ps, PAVE)

REVIEW
CROSS-COUNTRY FLIGHT ASSIGNED BY THE INSTRUCTOR
❏ Preflight Preparation
❏ Cross-Country Flight Planning
❏ Navigation Systems and Radar Services
❏ Pilotage and Dead Reckoning
❏ VOR, GPS, and/or NDB Navigation
❏ Airport, Runway, and Taxiway Signs, Markings, and Lighting
❏ Runway Incursion Avoidance
❏ Use of Unfamiliar Airports
❏ Single-Pilot Resource Management

COMPLETION STANDARDS
- Demonstrate proficiency in cross-country flight planning by selecting optimum cruising altitudes and appropriate checkpoints and accurately calculating fuel burn.
- Complete a flight with a landing at a point more than 50 nautical miles from the original departure point to increase proficiency in cross-country operations, especially using unfamiliar airports.
- If the lesson is used for dual instruction, demonstrate increased proficiency in the listed areas of operation and tasks.

POSTFLIGHT DEBRIEFING
❏ Critique maneuvers/procedures and SRM.
❏ Create a plan for skills that need improvement.
❏ Update the record folder and logbook.

Instrument/Commercial Syllabus

FLIGHT LESSON 40

SOLO (DUAL) — CROSS-COUNTRY

OBJECTIVES
- Increase proficiency in cross-country flights with a focus on VOR, GPS, and/or NDB navigation by performing a flight that includes a landing at a point more than 50 nautical miles from the original departure point.
- If the lesson is used for dual instruction, demonstrate the ability to meet the proficiency requirements for the End-of-Course Flight Check and Commercial Pilot Practical Test.

PREFLIGHT DISCUSSION
- ❑ Cross-Country Flight Planning
- ❑ Risk Management (5Ps, PAVE)

REVIEW
CROSS-COUNTRY FLIGHT ASSIGNED BY THE INSTRUCTOR
- ❑ Preflight Preparation Cross-Country Flight Planning
- ❑ Navigation Systems and Radar Services
- ❑ Pilotage and Dead Reckoning
- ❑ VOR, GPS, and/or NDB Navigation
- ❑ Airport, Runway, and Taxiway Signs, Markings, and Lighting
- ❑ Runway Incursion Avoidance
- ❑ CFIT Awareness
- ❑ Automation Management
- ❑ Single-Pilot Resource Management

COMPLETION STANDARDS
- Demonstrate proficiency in cross-country flight planning by selecting optimum cruising altitudes and appropriate checkpoints and accurately calculating fuel burn.
- Complete a flight with a landing at a point more than 50 nautical miles from the original departure point to increase proficiency in cross-country operations, especially VOR, GPS, and/or NDB navigation.
- If the lesson is used for dual instruction, demonstrate increased proficiency in the listed areas of operation and tasks.

POSTFLIGHT DEBRIEFING
- ❑ Critique maneuvers/procedures and SRM.
- ❑ Create a plan for skills that need improvement.
- ❑ Update the record folder and logbook.

STAGE IV ■ Commercial Pilot Flight Training

Instrument/Commercial Syllabus

FLIGHT LESSON 41

SOLO (DUAL) — CROSS-COUNTRY

OBJECTIVES
- Increase proficiency in cross-country flights with a focus on pilotage, dead-reckoning, and the use of unfamiliar airports by performing a flight that includes a landing at a point more than 50 nautical miles from the original departure point.
- If the lesson is used for dual instruction, demonstrate the ability to meet the proficiency requirements for the End-of-Course Flight Check and Commercial Pilot Practical Test.

PREFLIGHT DISCUSSION
- ❏ Cross-Country Flight Planning
- ❏ Risk Management (5Ps, PAVE)

REVIEW
CROSS-COUNTRY FLIGHT ASSIGNED BY THE INSTRUCTOR
- ❏ Cross-Country Flight Planning
- ❏ Navigation Systems and Radar Services
- ❏ Pilotage and Dead Reckoning
- ❏ Airport, Runway, and Taxiway Signs, Markings, and Lighting
- ❏ Runway Incursion Avoidance
- ❏ CFIT Awareness
- ❏ Use of Unfamiliar Airports
- ❏ Single-Pilot Resource Management

COMPLETION STANDARDS
- Demonstrate proficiency in cross-country flight planning by selecting optimum cruising altitudes and appropriate checkpoints and accurately calculating fuel burn.
- Complete a flight with a landing at a point more than 50 nautical miles from the original departure point to increase proficiency in cross-country operations, especially pilotage, dead reckoning, and the use of unfamiliar airports.
- The difference between the revised ETA and the ATA at each checkpoint should not be greater than ±5 minutes. The estimate for the destination should be ±10 minutes.
- If the lesson is used for dual instruction, demonstrate increased proficiency in the listed areas of operation and tasks.

POSTFLIGHT DEBRIEFING
- ❏ Critique maneuvers/procedures and SRM.
- ❏ Create a plan for skills that need improvement.
- ❏ Update the record folder and logbook.

STAGE IV ■ Commercial Pilot Flight Training

Instrument/Commercial Syllabus

FLIGHT LESSON 42

DUAL — CROSS-COUNTRY

OBJECTIVES
- Demonstrate proficiency in cross-country flight planning, pilotage, dead reckoning, VOR, GPS, and/or NDB navigation, and using unfamiliar airports.
- Perform a flight that includes a landing at a point more than 50 nautical miles from the original departure point.

PREFLIGHT DISCUSSION
- ❏ Single-Pilot Resource Management (SRM)
- ❏ Crew Resource Management (CRM)
- ❏ Risk Management (5Ps, PAVE)
- ❏ Procedures at Unfamiliar Airports
- ❏ Runway Incursion Avoidance
- ❏ Land and Hold Short Operations (LAHSO)

REVIEW
CROSS-COUNTRY FLIGHT ASSIGNED BY THE INSTRUCTOR
- ❏ Preflight Preparation
- ❏ Cross-Country Flight Planning
- ❏ Navigation Systems and Radar Services
- ❏ Pilotage and Dead Reckoning
- ❏ VOR, GPS, and/or NDB Navigation
- ❏ Airport, Runway, and Taxiway Signs, Markings, and Lighting
- ❏ Runway Incursion Avoidance
- ❏ Use of Unfamiliar Airports
- ❏ Automation Management
- ❏ Single-Pilot Resource Management

COMPLETION STANDARDS
- Demonstrate proficiency in cross-country flight planning by selecting optimum cruising altitudes and appropriate checkpoints and accurately calculating fuel burn.
- Demonstrate proficiency in cross-country operations and SRM as pilot-in-command of a flight with a landing at a point more than 50 nautical miles from the original departure point.
- The difference between the revised ETA and the ATA at each checkpoint should not be greater than ±5 minutes. The estimate for the destination should be ±10 minutes.

POSTFLIGHT DEBRIEFING
- ❏ Critique maneuvers/procedures and SRM.
- ❏ Create a plan for skills that need improvement.
- ❏ Update the record folder and logbook.

STAGE IV ■ Commercial Pilot Flight Training

Instrument/Commercial Syllabus

FLIGHT LESSON 43
SOLO — CROSS-COUNTRY

OBJECTIVES
Gain cross-country experience by completing a flight that meets the long cross-country requirements: landings at a minimum of three points, one of which is at least a straight-line distance of 250 nautical miles from the original departure point. If the flight is conducted in Hawaii, the alternate provisions of FAR 141, Appendix D, apply.

PREFLIGHT DISCUSSION
- Cross-Country Flight Planning
- Risk Management (5Ps, PAVE)

REVIEW
CROSS-COUNTRY FLIGHT ASSIGNED BY THE INSTRUCTOR
- Preflight Preparation
- Cross-Country Flight Planning
- Navigation Systems and Radar Services
- Pilotage and Dead Reckoning
- VOR, GPS, and/or NDB Navigation
- Airport, Runway, and Taxiway Signs, Markings, and Lighting
- Runway Incursion Avoidance
- Use of Unfamiliar Airports
- Situational Awareness
- CFIT Awareness
- Automation Management
- Single-Pilot Resource Management

COMPLETION STANDARDS
- Demonstrate proficiency in cross-country flight planning by selecting optimum cruising altitudes and appropriate checkpoints and accurately calculating fuel burn.
- Complete a solo cross-country with landings at a minimum of three points, one of which is at least a straight-line distance of 250 nautical miles from the original departure point.

POSTFLIGHT DEBRIEFING
- Critique maneuvers/procedures and SRM.
- Create a plan for skills that need improvement.
- Update the record folder and logbook.

Instrument/Commercial Syllabus

FLIGHT LESSON 44
DUAL — CROSS-COUNTRY
STAGE IV CHECK

OBJECTIVE
Demonstrate proficiency in VFR cross-country procedures at the commercial pilot level to the chief instructor, assistant chief, or a designated check instructor during the Stage IV Check.

PREFLIGHT DISCUSSION
- ❏ Student and Flight Check Instructor Roles and Expectations
- ❏ Questions to Test Student Knowledge

REVIEW

PREFLIGHT PREPARATION
- ❏ Cross-Country Flight Planning
- ❏ Airworthiness Requirements
- ❏ Certificates and Documents
- ❏ Performance and Limitations
- ❏ National Airspace System
- ❏ Weather Information
- ❏ Density Altitude Considerations

IN-FLIGHT OPERATIONS
- ❏ Radio Communications and ATC Light Signals
- ❏ Navigation Systems and Radar Services
- ❏ Pilotage and Dead Reckoning
- ❏ VOR, GPS, and/or NDB Navigation
- ❏ Diversion and Lost Procedures
- ❏ Power Settings and Mixture Leaning
- ❏ Radio Facility Shutdown
- ❏ Cockpit Management
- ❏ Low-Level Wind Shear Avoidance
- ❏ Visual Scanning and Collision Avoidance
- ❏ Wake Turbulence Avoidance
- ❏ Runway Incursion Avoidance
- ❏ Single-Pilot Resource Management

EMERGENCY OPERATIONS (SIMULATED)
- ❏ Systems and Equipment Malfunctions
- ❏ Low Fuel Supply
- ❏ Adverse Weather
- ❏ Airframe and Powerplant Icing
- ❏ Emergency Approach and Landing
- ❏ Emergency Equipment and Survival Gear

UNFAMILIAR AIRPORTS
- ❏ Traffic Patterns
- ❏ Non-Towered Airport

Instrument/Commercial Syllabus

- ❑ Tower-Controlled Airport
- ❑ Operations at Sod or Unimproved Fields
- ❑ CTAF Procedures
- ❑ Airport, Runway, and Taxiway Signs, Markings, and Lighting

COMPLETION STANDARDS
- Demonstrate commercial pilot proficiency in each of the listed procedures at the level required by the Commercial Pilot Airman Certification Standards.
- Demonstrate the ability to use single-pilot resource management to make effective decisions, maintain situational awareness, prevent CFIT, and manage risk, tasks, and automation.

POSTFLIGHT DEBRIEFING
- ❑ Evaluate maneuvers/procedures and SRM.
- ❑ Plan additional instruction for skills not meeting Stage IV completion standards.
- ❑ Update the record folder and logbook.

Instrument/Commercial Syllabus

Stage V

STAGE OBJECTIVES
During this stage, the student gains proficiency in operating a complex aircraft. The student learns the procedures to operate the complex airplane's systems and manage equipment malfunctions and failures. In addition, the student gains skills to perform the flight maneuvers required for commercial pilot certification.

STAGE COMPLETION STANDARDS
This stage is complete when the student can demonstrate commercial pilot proficiency in the operation of the complex aircraft and understanding of how to perform commercial maneuvers.

FLIGHT LESSON 45

SOLO — LOCAL

OBJECTIVE
Demonstrate proficiency in performing stalls, slow flight, normal takeoffs and landings, and ground reference maneuvers to enhance coordination and airplane control in preparation for introduction to the complex aircraft.

PREFLIGHT DISCUSSION
- Stall/Spin Awareness
- Situational Awareness

REVIEW
- Maneuvering During Slow Flight
- Power-Off Stalls
- Power-On Stalls
- Normal and Crosswind Takeoffs and Landings
- Private Pilot Ground Reference Maneuvers Assigned by the Instructor

COMPLETION STANDARDS
Demonstrate proficiency in each maneuver to the level required by the Private Pilot Airman Certification Standards.

POSTFLIGHT DEBRIEFING
- Critique maneuvers/procedures and SRM.
- Create a plan for skills that need improvement.
- Update the record folder and logbook.

Instrument/Commercial Syllabus

STUDY ASSIGNMENT
Ground Lessons 34, 35, and 36
  High-Performance Powerplants
  Environmental and Ice Control Systems
  Retractable Landing Gear.

Complex Airplane Transition Briefing

FLIGHT LESSON 46
DUAL — LOCAL, COMPLEX AIRPLANE

OBJECTIVES
- Become familiar with the complex airplane, including systems and basic flight operations.
- Become familiar with the use of high altitude systems, if applicable to the airplane to be used for the practical test.

PREFLIGHT DISCUSSION
- ❏ Pilot's Operating Handbook
- ❏ Complex Airplane Systems and Equipment
- ❏ Aircraft Performance

INTRODUCE

PREFLIGHT PREPARATION AND GROUND OPERATIONS
- ❏ Preflight Inspection
- ❏ Certificates and Documents
- ❏ Airworthiness Requirements
- ❏ Operation of Systems
- ❏ Performance and Limitations
- ❏ Use of Checklists
- ❏ Cockpit Management
- ❏ Engine Starting and Taxiing
- ❏ Before-Takeoff Check

IN-FLIGHT OPERATIONS
- ❏ Normal and Crosswind Takeoffs and Landings
- ❏ Use of Retractable Landing Gear and Flaps
- ❏ Climbs and Descents
- ❏ Go-Around/Rejected Landing
- ❏ Power Settings and Mixture Leaning
- ❏ Use of Constant-Speed Propeller and Effects Upon Airplane Performance

POSTFLIGHT PROCEDURES
- ❏ After Landing
- ❏ Parking and Securing

STAGE V ■ Commercial Pilot Flight Training

Instrument/Commercial Syllabus

HIGH ALTITUDE OPERATIONS (AS REQUIRED)
- ❏ Use of Supplemental Oxygen
- ❏ Use of Pressurization System

NOTE: If high altitude systems are not applicable to the airplane to be used for the practical test, the student must still demonstrate knowledge of high altitude operations sufficient to meet the requirements specified in the FAA Commercial Pilot Airman Certification Standards.

COMPLETION STANDARDS
- Demonstrate understanding of the complex airplane systems and operations.
- Demonstrate proficiency in basic flight operations to the level required by the Private Pilot Airman Certification Standards.

POSTFLIGHT DEBRIEFING
- ❏ Critique maneuvers/procedures and SRM.
- ❏ Create a plan for skills that need improvement.
- ❏ Update the record folder and logbook.

STUDY ASSIGNMENT
Ground Lesson 37
  Advanced Aerodynamics
  Accelerated Stalls

FLIGHT LESSONS 47 AND 48

DUAL — LOCAL, COMPLEX AIRPLANE

OBJECTIVES
- Increase proficiency in basic flight maneuvers and procedures.
- Gain proficiency in recognizing and recovering from power-off, power-on, and accelerated stalls.
- Become familiar with emergency procedures, including landing gear malfunctions and the emergency descent in the complex airplane.
- Become familiar with attitude instrument flying in the complex airplane.
- Become familiar with takeoffs and landings in the complex aircraft.

PREFLIGHT DISCUSSION
- ❏ System and Equipment Malfunctions
- ❏ Emergency Procedures
- ❏ Task Management

Instrument/Commercial Syllabus

INTRODUCE

SLOW FLIGHT AND STALLS
- ❏ Maneuvering During Slow Flight
- ❏ Power-Off Stalls
- ❏ Power-On Stalls
- ❏ Accelerated Stalls
- ❏ Spin Awareness

EMERGENCY OPERATIONS (SIMULATED)
- ❏ Systems and Equipment Malfunctions
- ❏ Landing Gear Malfunctions
- ❏ Fire in Flight
- ❏ Emergency Descent
- ❏ Emergency Approach and Landing

FULL-PANEL INSTRUMENT
- ❏ Straight-and-Level Flight
- ❏ Climbs and Climbing Turns
- ❏ Descents and Descending Turns
- ❏ Standard-Rate Turns
- ❏ Recovery From Unusual Flight Attitudes
- ❏ Maneuvering During Slow Flight

NOTE: The instrument portion of this lesson should be accomplished on an "as required" basis depending on an assessment of the student's capabilities. Students enrolled in the Commercial Pilot Certification Course only must complete 10 hours of instrument training to meet the requirements of Part 141, Appendix D.

REVIEW

PREFLIGHT PREPARATION AND GROUND OPERATIONS
- ❏ Preflight Inspection
- ❏ Certificates and Documents
- ❏ Airworthiness Requirements
- ❏ Operation of Systems
- ❏ Performance and Limitations
- ❏ Use of Checklists
- ❏ Cockpit Management
- ❏ Engine Starting and Taxiing
- ❏ Before-Takeoff Check

IN-FLIGHT OPERATIONS
- ❏ Normal and Crosswind Takeoffs and Landings
- ❏ Use of Retractable Landing Gear and Flaps
- ❏ Climbs and Descents
- ❏ Go-Around/Rejected Landing
- ❏ Power Settings and Mixture Leaning
- ❏ Use of Constant-Speed Propeller and Effects Upon Airplane Performance

HIGH ALTITUDE OPERATIONS (AS REQUIRED)
- ❏ Use of Supplemental Oxygen
- ❏ Use of Pressurization

Instrument/Commercial Syllabus

COMPLETION STANDARDS
- Demonstrate understanding of the flight characteristics, systems, and emergency procedures associated with the complex airplane.
- Demonstrate pilot-in-command proficiency while operating complex airplane systems and performing basic flight procedures.
- Demonstrate proficiency in recognizing and recovering from power-off, power-on, and accelerated stalls.

POSTFLIGHT DEBRIEFING
- ❏ Critique maneuvers/procedures and SRM.
- ❏ Create a plan for skills that need improvement.
- ❏ Update the record folder and logbook.

STUDY ASSIGNMENT
Ground Lessons 38, 39, and 40
  Predicting Performance
  Controlling Weight and Balance
  Maximum Performance Takeoffs and Landings

FLIGHT LESSONS 49 AND 50
DUAL — LOCAL, COMPLEX AIRPLANE

OBJECTIVE
- Gain proficiency in short- and soft-field takeoffs and landings in the complex airplane.
- Increase proficiency in all maneuvers and procedures in the complex airplane.

PREFLIGHT DISCUSSION
- ❏ Airplane Configuration for Short- and Soft-Field Takeoffs and Landings
- ❏ Aeronautical Decision Making and Judgment
- ❏ Risk Management

INTRODUCE

TAKEOFFS AND LANDINGS
- ❏ Short-Field Takeoff and Maximum Performance Climb
- ❏ Short-Field Approach and Landing
- ❏ Soft-Field Takeoff and Climb
- ❏ Soft-Field Approach and Landing

REVIEW
- ❏ Preflight Inspection
- ❏ Power Settings and Mixture Leaning
- ❏ Climbs and Descents
- ❏ Maneuvering During Slow Flight
- ❏ Power-Off and Power-On Stalls

Instrument/Commercial Syllabus

- ❏ Accelerated Stalls
- ❏ Spin Awareness

EMERGENCY OPERATIONS (SIMULATED)
- ❏ Systems and Equipment Malfunctions
- ❏ Landing Gear Malfunctions
- ❏ Fire in Flight
- ❏ Emergency Descent
- ❏ Emergency Approach and Landing

COMPLETION STANDARDS

- Demonstrate proficiency in short- and soft-field takeoff and landing configurations and procedures. During short-field landings, select a point on the runway and land not more than 100 feet beyond the point.

- Demonstrate proficiency at the level required by the Commercial Pilot Airman Certification Standards in all listed maneuvers and procedures in the complex airplane.

- Demonstrate the ability to use single-pilot resource management to make effective decisions as pilot in command of a complex airplane.

POSTFLIGHT DEBRIEFING
- ❏ Critique maneuvers/procedures and SRM.
- ❏ Create a plan for skills that need improvement.
- ❏ Update the record folder and logbook.

FLIGHT LESSON 51

DUAL — LOCAL

OBJECTIVES

- Increase knowledge of the causes and recovery procedures that apply to demonstrated stalls.

- Increase proficiency in recognizing and recovering from power-off, power-on, and accelerated stalls.

- Increase proficiency in short- and soft-field takeoffs and landings.

PREFLIGHT DISCUSSION
- ❏ Stall/Spin Awareness
- ❏ Demonstrated Stalls Causes and Recovery
- ❏ Situational Awareness

INTRODUCE

DEMONSTRATED STALLS
- ❏ Secondary Stall
- ❏ Cross-Control Stall
- ❏ Elevator Trim Stall

NOTE: The demonstrated stalls are not a proficiency requirement for commercial pilot certification. The purpose of the demonstrations is to reinforce private pilot

Instrument/Commercial Syllabus

knowledge of these stalls and help the student recognize, prevent, and if necessary, recover before the stall develops into a spin. These stalls should be practiced with a qualified flight instructor. Some stalls may be prohibited in some airplanes.

REVIEW

SLOW FLIGHT AND STALLS
- ❏ Maneuvering During Slow Flight
- ❏ Power-Off and Power-On Stalls
- ❏ Accelerated Stalls
- ❏ Spin Awareness

TAKEOFFS AND LANDINGS
- ❏ Short-Field Takeoff and Maximum Performance Climb
- ❏ Short-Field Approach and Landing
- ❏ Soft-Field Takeoff and Climb
- ❏ Soft-Field Approach and Landing

COMPLETION STANDARDS
- Demonstrate understanding of stall and spin aerodynamics, including recognition of and recovery procedures for the demonstrated stalls.
- Demonstrate proficiency in recognizing and recovering from power-off, power-on, and accelerated stalls.
- Demonstrate proficiency in short- and soft-field takeoffs and landings.

POSTFLIGHT DEBRIEFING
- ❏ Critique maneuvers/procedures and SRM.
- ❏ Create a plan for skills that need improvement.
- ❏ Update the record folder and logbook.

STUDY ASSIGNMENT
Commercial Maneuvers Briefing

Ground Lesson 41
  Steep Turns
  Chandelles

Instrument/Commercial Syllabus

FLIGHT LESSON 52
DUAL — LOCAL

OBJECTIVES
- Become familiar with the steps to perform steep turns and chandelles.
- Increase proficiency in stall recognition and recovery and spin awareness.
- Increase proficiency in short- and soft-field takeoff and landings.

PREFLIGHT DISCUSSION
- ❑ Steps to Perform Listed Maneuvers
- ❑ Listed Maneuvers – Common Errors

INTRODUCE
MANEUVERS
- ❑ Steep Turns
- ❑ Chandelles

REVIEW
SLOW FLIGHT AND STALLS
- ❑ Maneuvering During Slow Flight
- ❑ Power-Off and Power-On Stalls
- ❑ Accelerated Stalls
- ❑ Spin Awareness

TAKEOFFS AND LANDINGS
- ❑ Short-Field Takeoff and Maximum Performance Climb
- ❑ Short-Field Approach and Landing
- ❑ Soft-Field Takeoff and Climb
- ❑ Soft-Field Approach and Landing

DEMONSTRATED STALLS
- ❑ Secondary Stall
- ❑ Cross-Control Stall
- ❑ Elevator Trim Stall

NOTE: *The demonstrated stalls are not a proficiency requirement for commercial pilot certification. The purpose of the demonstrations is to reinforce private pilot knowledge of these stalls and help the student recognize, prevent, and if necessary, recover before the stall develops into a spin. These stalls should be practiced with a qualified flight instructor. Some stalls may be prohibited in some airplanes.*

COMPLETION STANDARDS
- Demonstrate understanding of the entry, performance, and recovery techniques for steep turns and chandelles.
- Demonstrate increased knowledge of stall and spin recognition and recovery.
- Demonstrate proficiency in short- and soft-field takeoffs and landings.

STAGE V ■ Commercial Pilot Flight Training

Instrument/Commercial Syllabus

POSTFLIGHT DEBRIEFING
- ❑ Critique maneuvers/procedures and SRM.
- ❑ Create a plan for skills that need improvement.
- ❑ Update the record folder and logbook.

STUDY ASSIGNMENT
Ground Lesson 42
  Lazy Eights
  Eights-on-Pylons
  Steep Spirals
  Power-Off 180° Accuracy Approach and Landing

FLIGHT LESSON 53

DUAL — LOCAL

OBJECTIVES
- Become familiar with the steps to perform lazy eights, eights-on-pylons, steep spirals, and power-off 180° accuracy approaches and landings.
- Gain proficiency in performing steep turns and chandelles.

PREFLIGHT DISCUSSION
- ❑ Steps to Perform Listed Maneuvers
- ❑ Listed Maneuvers – Common Errors
- ❑ Single-Pilot Resource Management

INTRODUCE
- ❑ Lazy Eights
- ❑ Eights-On-Pylons
- ❑ Steep Spirals
- ❑ Power-Off 180° Accuracy Approaches and Landings

REVIEW
- ❑ Steep Turns
- ❑ Chandelles

COMPLETION STANDARDS
- Demonstrate an understanding of the steps to perform lazy eights, eights-on-pylons, steep spirals, and power-off 180° accuracy approaches and landings.
- Demonstrate increased proficiency in steep turns and chandelles by performing the correct entry and recovery procedures and displaying increased coordination.

POSTFLIGHT DEBRIEFING
- ❑ Critique maneuvers/procedures and SRM.
- ❑ Create a plan for skills that need improvement.
- ❑ Update the record folder and logbook.

Instrument/Commercial Syllabus

FLIGHT LESSONS 54, 55, AND 56
SOLO — LOCAL

OBJECTIVES
- Gain proficiency in precise airplane control by operating near the performance limits of the airplane during steep turns, chandelles, lazy eights, eights-on-pylons, steep spirals, and power-off 180° accuracy approaches and landings.
- Increase proficiency in performing short- and soft-field takeoffs and landings, slow flight, and stalls.

PREFLIGHT DISCUSSION
- Steps to Perform Listed Maneuvers
- Listed Maneuvers – Common Errors
- Situational Awareness
- Single-Pilot Resource Management

REVIEW

MANEUVERS
- Steep Turns
- Chandelles
- Lazy Eights
- Eights-on-Pylons
- Steep Spirals

TAKEOFFS AND LANDINGS
- Power-Off 180° Accuracy Approaches and Landings
- Short-Field Takeoffs/Maximum Performance Climbs and Landings
- Soft-Field Takeoffs and Landings

SLOW FLIGHT AND STALLS
- Maneuvering During Slow Flight
- Power-Off Stalls and Power-On Stalls
- Accelerated Stalls

COMPLETION STANDARDS
- Increase proficiency in the entry, performance, and recovery techniques for each maneuver.
- Develop precise airplane control by operating near the performance limits of the airplane when performing commercial maneuvers.
- Use single-pilot resource management techniques to make effective decisions during flight operations.

POSTFLIGHT DEBRIEFING
- Critique maneuvers/procedures and SRM.
- Create a plan for skills that need improvement.
- Update the record folder and logbook.

Instrument/Commercial Syllabus

FLIGHT LESSON 57

DUAL — LOCAL

OBJECTIVE
Increase ability to perform each maneuver to the level required by the Commercial Pilot Airman Certification Standards.

PREFLIGHT DISCUSSION
- Maneuver Performance and Aerodynamic Considerations
- Single-Pilot Resource Management

REVIEW

MANEUVERS
- Steep Turns
- Chandelles
- Lazy Eights
- Eights-On-Pylons
- Steep Spirals

SLOW FLIGHT AND STALLS
- Maneuvering During Slow Flight
- Power-Off and Power-On Stalls
- Accelerated Stalls

TAKEOFFS AND LANDINGS
- Power-Off 180° Accuracy Approaches and Landings

FULL- AND PARTIAL-PANEL INSTRUMENT
- Straight-and-Level Flight
- Standard-Rate Turns
- Maneuvering During Slow Flight
- Power-Off and Power-On Stalls
- Recovery From Unusual Flight Attitudes

NOTE: The instrument portion of this lesson should be accomplished on an as required basis depending on an assessment of the student's capabilities. Students enrolled in the Commercial Pilot Certification Course only must complete 10 hours of instrument training to meet the requirements of Part 141, Appendix D.

COMPLETION STANDARDS
- Demonstrate increased proficiency in performing the commercial maneuvers to the level required by the Commercial Pilot Airman Certification Standards.
- Demonstrate proficiency in the instrument maneuvers to the level required by the Instrument Rating Airman Certification Standards.

POSTFLIGHT DEBRIEFING
- Critique maneuvers/procedures and SRM.
- Create a plan for skills that need improvement.
- Update the record folder and logbook.

Instrument/Commercial Syllabus

STUDY ASSIGNMENT
Ground Lesson 43
　Emergency Procedures

FLIGHT LESSON 58
DUAL — LOCAL

OBJECTIVE
Increase ability to perform each maneuver to the level required by the Commercial Pilot Airman Certification Standards.

PREFLIGHT DISCUSSION
❑ Stall/Spin Awareness
❑ Emergency Procedures
❑ Single-Pilot Resource Management

REVIEW

SLOW FLIGHT AND STALLS
❑ Maneuvering During Slow Flight
❑ Power-Off and Power-On Stalls
❑ Accelerated Stalls

TAKEOFFS AND LANDINGS
❑ Short-Field Takeoffs/Maximum Performance Climbs and Landings
❑ Soft-Field Takeoffs and Landings
❑ Power-Off 180° Accuracy Approaches and Landings

FULL- AND PARTIAL-PANEL INSTRUMENT
❑ Straight-and-Level Flight
❑ Standard-Rate Turns
❑ Maneuvering During Slow Flight
❑ Power-Off and Power-On Stalls
❑ Recovery From Unusual Flight Attitudes

NOTE: *The instrument portion of this lesson should be accomplished on an "as required" basis depending on an assessment of the student's capabilities. Students enrolled in the Commercial Pilot Certification Course only must complete 10 hours of instrument training to meet the requirements of Part 141, Appendix D.*

EMERGENCY OPERATIONS (SIMULATED)
❑ Systems and Equipment Malfunctions
❑ Low Fuel Supply
❑ Adverse Weather
❑ Airframe and Powerplant Icing
❑ Fire in Flight
❑ Emergency Descent
❑ Emergency Approach and Landing
❑ Emergency Equipment and Survival Gear

STAGE V ■ Commercial Pilot Flight Training

Instrument/Commercial Syllabus

COMPLETION STANDARDS
- Demonstrate increased proficiency in performing the commercial maneuvers to the level required by the Commercial Pilot Airman Certification Standards.
- Display competency in the instrument maneuvers to the level required by the Instrument Rating Airman Certification Standards.

POSTFLIGHT DEBRIEFING
- ❏ Critique maneuvers/procedures and SRM.
- ❏ Create a plan for skills that need improvement.
- ❏ Update the record folder and logbook.

STUDY ASSIGNMENT
Ground Lesson 44
  Commercial Pilot SRM

FLIGHT LESSONS 59, 60, AND 61

SOLO — LOCAL

OBJECTIVES
- Increase proficiency and confidence in performing commercial maneuvers.
- Increase proficiency in single-pilot resource management and aeronautical decision making skills.
- Increase proficiency in cockpit management skills.

PREFLIGHT DISCUSSION
- ❏ Steps to Perform Listed Maneuvers
- ❏ Listed Maneuvers – Common Errors
- ❏ Single-Pilot Resource Management

REVIEW

MANEUVERS
- ❏ Steep Turns
- ❏ Chandelles
- ❏ Lazy Eights
- ❏ Eights-On-Pylons
- ❏ Steep Spirals

TAKEOFFS AND LANDINGS
- ❏ Power-Off 180° Accuracy Approaches and Landings
- ❏ Short-Field Takeoffs/Maximum Performance Climbs and Landings
- ❏ Soft-Field Takeoffs and Landings

Instrument/Commercial Syllabus

COMPLETION STANDARDS
Gain the ability to use single-pilot resource management, make effective decisions, and manage the cockpit while performing each maneuver to the level required by the Commercial Pilot Airman Certification Standards.

POSTFLIGHT DEBRIEFING
❑ Critique maneuvers/procedures and SRM.
❑ Create a plan for skills that need improvement.
❑ Update the record folder and logbook.

FLIGHT LESSONS 62 AND 63
SOLO — LOCAL

OBJECTIVES
- Increase proficiency and confidence in performing commercial maneuvers, slow flight and stalls, and takeoffs and landings.
- Increase proficiency in single-pilot resource management and aeronautical decision making skills.
- Increase proficiency in cockpit management skills.

NOTE: The instructor may decide to assign additional maneuvers and/or procedures on an "as required" basis.

PREFLIGHT DISCUSSION
❑ Steps to Perform Listed Maneuvers
❑ Listed Maneuvers – Common Errors
❑ Single-Pilot Resource Management

REVIEW

MANEUVERS
❑ Steep Turns
❑ Chandelles
❑ Lazy Eights
❑ Eights-On-Pylons
❑ Steep Spirals

SLOW FLIGHT AND STALLS
❑ Maneuvering During Slow Flight
❑ Power-Off Stalls
❑ Power-On Stalls

TAKEOFFS AND LANDINGS
❑ Power-Off 180° Accuracy Approaches and Landings
❑ Short-Field Takeoffs/Maximum Performance Climbs and Landings
❑ Soft-Field Takeoffs and Landings

COMPLETION STANDARDS:
Be proficient in using single-pilot resource management, making effective decisions, and managing the cockpit while performing each maneuver to the level required by the Commercial Pilot Airman Certification Standards.

Instrument/Commercial Syllabus

POSTFLIGHT DEBRIEFING
❏ Critique maneuvers/procedures and SRM.
❏ Create a plan for skills that need improvement.
❏ Update the record folder and logbook.

FLIGHT LESSONS 64 AND 65
DUAL — LOCAL

OBJECTIVE
Perform the listed maneuvers and procedures to the level required by the Commercial Pilot Airman Certification Standards in preparation for the Stage V Check.

NOTE: The instructor may decide to assign additional maneuvers and/or procedures on an "as required" basis.

PREFLIGHT DISCUSSION
❏ Single-Pilot Resource Management
❏ Commercial Pilot Airman Certification Standards

REVIEW

SLOW FLIGHT AND STALLS
❏ Maneuvering During Slow Flight
❏ Power-Off Stalls and Power-On Stalls

MANEUVERS
❏ Steep Turns
❏ Chandelles
❏ Lazy Eights
❏ Eights-On-Pylons
❏ Steep Spirals

TAKEOFFS AND LANDINGS
❏ Power-Off 180° Accuracy Approaches and Landings
❏ Short-Field Takeoffs/Maximum Performance Climbs and Landings
❏ Soft-Field Takeoffs and Landings

COMPLETION STANDARDS
- Demonstrate proficiency in the listed maneuvers and procedures to the level required by the Commercial Pilot Airman Certification Standards.
- Demonstrate proficiency in using single-pilot resource management to manage risks and make effective decisions.

POSTFLIGHT DEBRIEFING
❏ Critique maneuvers/procedures and SRM.
❏ Create a plan for skills that need improvement.
❏ Update the record folder and logbook.

Instrument/Commercial Syllabus

FLIGHT LESSON 66
DUAL — LOCAL, COMPLEX AIRPLANE

OBJECTIVES
- Increase proficiency in operating the complex airplane by performing slow flight and stalls, commercial maneuvers, and takeoffs and landing.
- Perform the listed maneuvers and procedures to the level required by the Commercial Pilot Airman Certification Standards in preparation for the Stage V Check.

PREFLIGHT DISCUSSION
- ❏ Complex Airplane Systems
- ❏ Single-Pilot Resource Management
- ❏ Commercial Pilot Airman Certification Standards

REVIEW

PREFLIGHT PREPARATION
- ❏ Airworthiness Requirements
- ❏ Certificates and Documents
- ❏ Performance and Limitations
- ❏ National Airspace System
- ❏ Weather Information
- ❏ Density Altitude Considerations

IN-FLIGHT OPERATIONS
- ❏ Power Settings and Mixture Leaning
- ❏ Climbs and Descents
- ❏ Aeronautical Decision Making and Judgment
- ❏ Cockpit Management
- ❏ Single-Pilot Resource Management

SLOW FLIGHT AND STALLS
- ❏ Maneuvering During Slow Flight
- ❏ Power-Off and Power-On Stalls
- ❏ Accelerated Stalls
- ❏ Spin Awareness

MANEUVERS
- ❏ Steep Turns
- ❏ Chandelles
- ❏ Lazy Eights
- ❏ Eights-On-Pylons
- ❏ Steep Spirals

TAKEOFFS AND LANDINGS
- ❏ Power-Off 180° Accuracy Approach and Landing
- ❏ Short-Field Takeoffs/Maximum Performance Climbs and Landings
- ❏ Soft-Field Takeoffs and Landings
- ❏ Go-Around/Rejected Landing

EMERGENCY OPERATIONS (SIMULATED)
- ❏ Systems and Equipment Malfunctions
- ❏ Landing Gear Malfunctions

STAGE V ■ Commercial Pilot Flight Training

Instrument/Commercial Syllabus

- ❏ Low Fuel Supply
- ❏ Adverse Weather
- ❏ Airframe and Powerplant Icing
- ❏ Fire in Flight
- ❏ Emergency Descent
- ❏ Emergency Approach and Landing
- ❏ Emergency Equipment and Survival Gear

HIGH ALTITUDE OPERATIONS (AS REQUIRED)
- ❏ Use of Supplemental Oxygen
- ❏ Use of Pressurization

POSTFLIGHT PROCEDURES
- ❏ After Landing
- ❏ Parking and Securing

COMPLETION STANDARDS
- Demonstrates the ability to safely act as pilot in command of the complex aircraft.
- Perform the listed maneuvers and procedures to the level required by the Commercial Pilot Airman Certification Standards in preparation for the Stage V Check.

POSTFLIGHT DEBRIEFING
- ❏ Critique maneuvers/procedures and SRM.
- ❏ Create a plan for skills that need improvement.
- ❏ Update the record folder and logbook.

STUDY ASSIGNMENT
Ground Lessons 45 and 46
  Stage V Exam
  Commercial Pilot End-Of-Course Exam

FLIGHT LESSON 67
DUAL — LOCAL, COMPLEX AIRPLANE
STAGE V CHECK

OBJECTIVE
Demonstrate proficiency as pilot in command of a complex airplane to the chief instructor, assistant chief, or a designated check instructor during the Stage V Check.

PREFLIGHT DISCUSSION
❏ Student and Flight Check Instructor Roles and Expectations
❏ Questions to Test Student Knowledge

REVIEW

PREFLIGHT PREPARATION
❏ Airworthiness Requirements
❏ Certificates and Documents
❏ Performance and Limitations
❏ National Airspace System
❏ Weather Information
❏ Density Altitude Considerations

IN-FLIGHT OPERATIONS
❏ Power Settings and Mixture Leaning
❏ Climbs and Descents
❏ Aeronautical Decision Making and Judgment
❏ Cockpit Management

SLOW FLIGHT AND STALLS
❏ Maneuvering During Slow Flight
❏ Power-Off and Power-On Stalls
❏ Accelerated Stalls
❏ Spin Awareness

MANEUVERS
❏ Steep Turns
❏ Chandelles
❏ Lazy Eights
❏ Eights-On-Pylons
❏ Steep Spirals

TAKEOFFS AND LANDINGS
❏ Power-Off 180° Accuracy Approach and Landing
❏ Short-Field Takeoffs/Maximum Performance Climbs and Landings
❏ Soft-Field Takeoffs and Landings
❏ Go-Around/Rejected Landing

EMERGENCY OPERATIONS (SIMULATED)
❏ Systems and Equipment Malfunctions
❏ Landing Gear Malfunctions
❏ Low Fuel Supply
❏ Adverse Weather
❏ Airframe and Powerplant Icing

Instrument/Commercial Syllabus

- ❏ Fire in Flight
- ❏ Emergency Descent
- ❏ Emergency Approach and Landing
- ❏ Emergency Equipment and Survival Gear

HIGH ALTITUDE OPERATIONS (AS REQUIRED)
- ❏ Use of Supplemental Oxygen
- ❏ Use of Pressurization

POSTFLIGHT PROCEDURES
- ❏ After Landing
- ❏ Parking and Securing

COMPLETION STANDARDS
- Demonstrate commercial pilot proficiency as pilot in command of a complex airplane as outlined in the Commercial Pilot Airman Certification Standards.
- Demonstrate the ability to use single-pilot resource management to make effective decisions, maintain situational awareness, prevent CFIT, and manage risk, tasks, and automation.

POSTFLIGHT DEBRIEFING
- ❏ Critique maneuvers/procedures and SRM.
- ❏ Create a plan for skills that need improvement.
- ❏ Update the record folder and logbook.

Instrument/Commercial Syllabus

Stage VI

STAGE OBJECTIVES
During this stage, the student performs maneuvers and procedures to attain the proficiency level required of a commercial pilot with an instrument rating.

STAGE COMPLETION STANDARDS
This stage is complete when the student can demonstrate all flight maneuvers and procedures at the level required by the Commercial Pilot Airman Certification Standards for a commercial pilot with an instrument rating. The student also successfully completes the Stage VI and End-of-Course Flight Checks.

NOTE: Completion of the instrument navigation, holding, and approach tasks listed in specific lessons must be based on the available aircraft equipment.

FLIGHT LESSON 68
DUAL — LOCAL

OBJECTIVES
- Increase proficiency in instrument scanning and interpretation while reviewing full-panel instrument maneuvers and procedures.
- Increase proficiency in normal and emergency operations by using the proper procedures and single-pilot resource management.

PREFLIGHT DISCUSSION
❑ Single-Pilot Resource Management

REVIEW
TAKEOFFS AND LANDINGS
❑ Power-Off 180° Accuracy Approach and Landing
❑ Short-Field Takeoffs/Maximum Performance Climbs and Landings
❑ Soft-Field Takeoffs and Landings
❑ Go-Around/Rejected Landing

EMERGENCY OPERATIONS (SIMULATED)
❑ Systems and Equipment Malfunctions
❑ Low Fuel Supply
❑ Adverse Weather
❑ Airframe and Powerplant Icing
❑ Fire in Flight
❑ Emergency Descent
❑ Emergency Approach and Landing
❑ Emergency Equipment and Survival Gear

Instrument/Commercial Syllabus

FULL-PANEL INSTRUMENT
- ❑ Straight-and-Level Flight
- ❑ Standard-Rate Turns
- ❑ Steep Turns
- ❑ Constant Airspeed Climbs and Descents
- ❑ Recovery from Unusual Flight Attitudes

NOTE: The instrument portion of this lesson should be accomplished on an "as required" basis depending on an assessment of the student's capabilities. Students enrolled in the Commercial Pilot Certification Course only must complete 10 hours of instrument training to meet the requirements of Part 141, Appendix D.

COMPLETION STANDARDS
Explain and perform each maneuver and procedure to the level required by the Commercial Pilot Airman Certification Standards.

POSTFLIGHT DEBRIEFING
- ❑ Critique maneuvers/procedures and SRM.
- ❑ Create a plan for skills that need improvement.
- ❑ Update the record folder and logbook.

FLIGHT LESSON 69
DUAL — LOCAL

OBJECTIVES
- Increase proficiency in full- and partial-panel instrument flight, VOR, GPS, and/or NDB navigation, and instrument approaches.
- Increase proficiency in commercial maneuvers.

PREFLIGHT DISCUSSION
- ❑ Instrument Procedures
- ❑ Single-Pilot Resource Management

REVIEW

FULL- AND PARTIAL-PANEL INSTRUMENT
- ❑ Straight-and-Level Flight
- ❑ Climbs and Descents
- ❑ Recovery From Unusual Flight Attitudes
- ❑ VOR, GPS, and/or NDB Navigation
- ❑ VOR Approaches
- ❑ RNAV (GPS) Approaches
- ❑ ILS Approaches
- ❑ NDB Approaches

NOTE: The instrument portion of this lesson should be accomplished on an "as required" basis depending on an assessment of the student's capabilities. Students enrolled in the Commercial Pilot Certification Course only must complete 10 hours of instrument training to meet the requirements of Part 141, Appendix D.

Instrument/Commercial Syllabus

MANEUVERS
- ❏ Steep Turns
- ❏ Chandelles
- ❏ Eights-On-Pylons
- ❏ Steep Spirals

COMPLETION STANDARDS
- Demonstrate proficiency in full- and partial-panel instrument flight, VOR, GPS, and/or NDB navigation, and instrument approaches to the level required by the Instrument Rating Airman Certification Standards.
- Demonstrate proficiency in steep turns, chandelles, eights-on-pylons, and steep spirals to the level required by the Commercial Pilot Airman Certification Standards.

POSTFLIGHT DEBRIEFING
- ❏ Critique maneuvers/procedures and SRM.
- ❏ Create a plan for skills that need improvement.
- ❏ Update the record folder and logbook.

FLIGHT LESSONS 70 AND 71
SOLO — LOCAL

OBJECTIVES
- Increase proficiency in any commercial maneuvers that do not yet meet the requirements of the Commercial Pilot Airman Certification Standards.
- Increase proficiency in using single-pilot resource management techniques to maintain flight safety.

PREFLIGHT DISCUSSION
- ❏ Steps to Perform Listed Maneuvers
- ❏ Listed Maneuvers – Common Errors
- ❏ Single-Pilot Resource Management

REVIEW
MANEUVERS
- ❏ Steep Turns
- ❏ Chandelles
- ❏ Lazy Eights
- ❏ Eights-On-Pylons
- ❏ Steep Spirals

COMPLETION STANDARDS
- Perform the commercial maneuvers with smoothness and coordination to meet the requirements of the Commercial Pilot Airman Certification Standards.
- Use single-pilot resource management techniques to make effective decisions during flight operations.

Instrument/Commercial Syllabus

POSTFLIGHT DEBRIEFING
- ❏ Critique maneuvers/procedures and SRM.
- ❏ Create a plan for skills that need improvement.
- ❏ Update the record folder and logbook.

FLIGHT LESSON 72

DUAL — LOCAL

OBJECTIVES
- Demonstrate proficiency in any commercial maneuvers to meet the requirements of the Commercial Pilot Airman Certification Standards.
- Correct any areas of faulty performance.

PREFLIGHT DISCUSSION
- ❏ Commercial Pilot Airman Certification Standards
- ❏ Single-Pilot Resource Management

REVIEW
- ❏ Steep Turns
- ❏ Chandelles
- ❏ Lazy Eights
- ❏ Eights-On-Pylons
- ❏ Steep Spirals

COMPLETION STANDARDS
- Demonstrate an understanding of the important performance elements of each maneuver including the correct entry, execution, and recovery techniques.
- Demonstrate proficiency in each maneuver at the level required by the Commercial Pilot Airman Certification Standards.
- Use single-pilot resource management techniques to make effective decisions during flight operations.

POSTFLIGHT DEBRIEFING
- ❏ Critique maneuvers/procedures and SRM.
- ❏ Create a plan for skills that need improvement.
- ❏ Update the record folder and logbook.

FLIGHT LESSONS 73, 74, AND 75

SOLO — LOCAL

OBJECTIVES
- Practice each flight maneuver assigned with emphasis on those maneuvers that were poorly or inaccurately performed during the previous dual flight.

STAGE VI ■ Commercial Pilot Flight Training

Instrument/Commercial Syllabus

- Increase proficiency in any commercial maneuvers that do not yet meet the requirements of the Commercial Pilot Airman Certification Standards.
- Increase proficiency in using single-pilot resource management techniques to maintain flight safety.

PREFLIGHT DISCUSSION
- ❏ Steps to Perform Listed Maneuvers
- ❏ Listed Maneuvers – Common Errors
- ❏ Single-Pilot Resource Management

REVIEW

MANEUVERS
- ❏ Steep Turns
- ❏ Chandelles
- ❏ Lazy Eights
- ❏ Eights-On-Pylons
- ❏ Steep Spirals

TAKEOFFS AND LANDINGS
- ❏ Normal Takeoffs and Landings
- ❏ Crosswind Takeoffs and Landings
- ❏ Short-Field Takeoffs/Maximum Performance Climbs and Landings
- ❏ Soft-Field Takeoffs and Landings
- ❏ Power-Off 180° Accuracy Approaches and Landings

COMPLETION STANDARDS
- Perform the commercial maneuvers with smoothness and coordination to meet the requirements of the Commercial Pilot Airman Certification Standards.
- Use single-pilot resource management techniques to make effective decisions during flight operations.

POSTFLIGHT DEBRIEFING
- ❏ Critique maneuvers/procedures and SRM.
- ❏ Create a plan for skills that need improvement.
- ❏ Update the record folder and logbook.

FLIGHT LESSONS 76 AND 77

DUAL — LOCAL

OBJECTIVES
- Increase proficiency in all commercial maneuvers and procedures to identify areas where improved performance is necessary.
- Increase proficiency in instrument procedures on an "as required" basis.

PREFLIGHT DISCUSSION
- ❏ Commercial Pilot Airman Certification Standards
- ❏ Single-Pilot Resource Management

Instrument/Commercial Syllabus

REVIEW

PREFLIGHT PREPARATION AND GROUND OPERATIONS
- ❏ Certificates and Documents
- ❏ Airworthiness Requirements
- ❏ Operation of Systems
- ❏ Performance and Limitations
- ❏ Use of Checklists
- ❏ Cockpit Management
- ❏ Preflight Inspection
- ❏ Engine Starting and Taxiing
- ❏ Before-Takeoff Check

SLOW FLIGHT AND STALLS
- ❏ Maneuvering During Slow Flight
- ❏ Power-Off and Power-On Stalls
- ❏ Accelerated Stalls

MANEUVERS
- ❏ Steep Turns
- ❏ Chandelles
- ❏ Lazy Eights
- ❏ Eights-On-Pylons
- ❏ Steep Spirals

TAKEOFFS AND LANDINGS
- ❏ Normal and Crosswind Takeoff and Landing
- ❏ Short-Field Takeoff/Maximum Performance Climb and Landing
- ❏ Soft-Field Takeoff and Landing
- ❏ Power-Off 180° Accuracy Approach and Landing

EMERGENCY OPERATIONS (SIMULATED)
- ❏ Systems and Equipment Malfunctions
- ❏ Emergency Approach and Landing

INSTRUMENT PROCEDURES (AS REQUIRED)

POSTFLIGHT PROCEDURES
- ❏ After Landing
- ❏ Parking and Securing

COMPLETION STANDARDS
- Demonstrate proficiency in each maneuver at the level required by the Commercial Pilot Airman Certification Standards.
- Use single-pilot resource management techniques to make effective decisions during flight operations.
- Demonstrate proficiency at the level required by the Instrument Rating Airman Certification Standards in all instrument procedures on an "as required" basis.

POSTFLIGHT DEBRIEFING
- ❏ Critique maneuvers/procedures and SRM.
- ❏ Create a plan for skills that need improvement.
- ❏ Update the record folder and logbook.

STAGE VI ■ Commercial Pilot Flight Training

Instrument/Commercial Syllabus

FLIGHT LESSON 78
DUAL — LOCAL, COMPLEX AIRPLANE

PREFLIGHT DISCUSSION
- ❏ Complex Airplane Systems and Equipment
- ❏ Complex Airplane Normal and Emergency Procedures
- ❏ Commercial Pilot Airman Certification Standards
- ❏ Single-Pilot Resource Management

OBJECTIVES
- Increase proficiency in all commercial maneuvers and procedures in the complex airplane to the level required by the Commercial Pilot Airman Certification Standards.
- Operate airplane systems and equipment and perform normal and emergency procedures in the complex airplane to the level required by the Commercial Pilot Airman Certification Standards.

REVIEW

PREFLIGHT PREPARATIONS AND GROUND OPERATIONS
- ❏ Certificates and Documents
- ❏ Airworthiness Requirements
- ❏ Operation of Systems
- ❏ Performance and Limitations
- ❏ Use of Checklists
- ❏ Cockpit Management
- ❏ Preflight Inspection
- ❏ Engine Starting and Taxiing
- ❏ Before-Takeoff Check

SLOW FLIGHT AND STALLS
- ❏ Maneuvering During Slow Flight
- ❏ Power-Off and Power-On Stalls
- ❏ Accelerated Stalls
- ❏ Spin Awareness

MANEUVERS
- ❏ Steep Turns
- ❏ Chandelles
- ❏ Lazy Eights
- ❏ Eights-On-Pylons
- ❏ Steep Spirals

TAKEOFFS AND LANDINGS
- ❏ Normal and Crosswind Takeoff and Landing
- ❏ Short-Field Takeoff/Maximum Performance Climb and Landing
- ❏ Soft-Field Takeoff and Landing
- ❏ Power-Off 180° Accuracy Approach and Landing

EMERGENCY OPERATIONS (SIMULATED)
- ❏ Systems and Equipment Malfunctions
- ❏ Landing Gear Malfunctions
- ❏ Emergency Descent
- ❏ Emergency Approach and Landing

STAGE VI ■ Commercial Pilot Flight Training

Instrument/Commercial Syllabus

POSTFLIGHT PROCEDURES
- After Landing
- Parking and Securing

COMPLETION STANDARDS
- Demonstrate proficiency in all commercial maneuvers and procedures in the complex airplane to the level required by the Commercial Pilot Airman Certification Standards.
- Demonstrate understanding of the complex airplane flight characteristics, systems, equipment, and emergency procedures by performing all operations to the level required by the Commercial Pilot Airman Certification Standards.

POSTFLIGHT DEBRIEFING
- Critique maneuvers/procedures and SRM.
- Create a plan for skills that need improvement.
- Update the record folder and logbook.

FLIGHT LESSONS 79, 80, AND 81
SOLO — LOCAL

OBJECTIVE
Practice slow flight and stalls, commercial maneuvers, and takeoffs and landings to correct any faulty performance areas from the previous dual flight.

PREFLIGHT DISCUSSION
- Steps to Perform Listed Maneuvers
- Listed Maneuvers – Common Errors
- Single-Pilot Resource Management

REVIEW

MANEUVERS
- Steep Turns
- Chandelles
- Lazy Eights
- Eights-On-Pylons
- Steep Spirals

SLOW FLIGHT AND STALLS
- Maneuvering During Slow Flight
- Power-Off and Power-On Stalls
- Accelerated Stalls

TAKEOFFS AND LANDINGS
- Short-Field Takeoffs/Maximum Performance Climbs and Landings
- Soft-Field Takeoffs and Landings
- Power-Off 180° Accuracy Approaches and Landings

Instrument/Commercial Syllabus

COMPLETION STANDARDS
Perform all commercial maneuvers and procedures to the level required by the Commercial Pilot Airman Certification Standards by correcting any areas of faulty performance.

POSTFLIGHT DEBRIEFING
❑ Critique maneuvers/procedures and SRM.
❑ Create a plan for skills that need improvement.
❑ Update the record folder and logbook.

FLIGHT LESSON 82

DUAL — CROSS-COUNTRY, COMPLEX AIRPLANE

OBJECTIVES
- Increase proficiency cross-country flight planning and flight operations in a complex airplane by performing a cross-country flight over 50 nautical miles from the original point of departure.
- Increase proficiency in using single-pilot resources management skills to make effective decisions during a cross-country flight in a complex airplane.

PREFLIGHT DISCUSSION
❑ Cross-Country Flight Planning
❑ Wire Strike Avoidance
❑ Aviation Security
❑ Risk Management (5Ps, PAVE)

REVIEW

PREFLIGHT PREPARATION
❑ Cross-Country Flight Planning
❑ Temporary Flight Restrictions (TFRs)
❑ Special Use Airspace
❑ Airworthiness Requirements
❑ Certificates and Documents
❑ Performance and Limitations
❑ National Airspace System
❑ Weather Information
❑ Density Altitude Considerations

IN-FLIGHT OPERATIONS
❑ Radio Communications and ATC Light Signals
❑ Navigation Systems and Radar Services
❑ Pilotage and Dead Reckoning
❑ VOR, GPS, and/or NDB Navigation
❑ Diversion and Lost Procedures
❑ Power Settings and Mixture Leaning
❑ Radio Facility Shutdown
❑ Cockpit Management
❑ Low-Level Wind Shear Avoidance
❑ Visual Scanning and Collision Avoidance
❑ Wake Turbulence Avoidance

Instrument/Commercial Syllabus

- Runway Incursion Avoidance
- Land and Hold Short Operations (LAHSO)
- SRM and CRM

EMERGENCY OPERATIONS (SIMULATED)
- Systems and Equipment Malfunctions
- Landing Gear Malfunctions
- Low Fuel Supply
- Adverse Weather
- Airframe and Powerplant Icing
- Fire in Flight
- Emergency Descent
- Emergency Approach and Landing
- Emergency Equipment and Survival Gear

UNFAMILIAR AIRPORTS
- Traffic Patterns
- Non-Towered Airport
- Tower-Controlled Airport
- Operations at Sod or Unimproved Fields
- CTAF Procedures
- Airport, Runway, and Taxiway Signs, Markings, and Lighting

FULL-PANEL INSTRUMENT
- Climbs and Descents
- Standard-Rate Turns
- Climbing and Descending Turns
- Recovery From Unusual Flight Attitudes
- VOR Navigation
- GPS Navigation
- NDB Navigation
- Use of Radar Vectors
- Radio Facility Shutdown

NOTE: The instrument portion of this lesson should be accomplished on an "as required" basis depending on an assessment of the student's capabilities. Students enrolled in the Commercial Pilot Certification Course only must complete 10 hours of instrument training to meet the requirements of Part 141, Appendix D.

COMPLETION STANDARDS
- Demonstrate the ability to safely act as pilot in command of the complex airplane during cross-country flights.
- Demonstrate proficiency in managing systems and equipment malfunctions and performing emergency procedures in a complex airplane during a cross-country flight.

POSTFLIGHT DEBRIEFING
- Critique maneuvers/procedures and SRM.
- Create a plan for skills that need improvement.
- Update the record folder and logbook.

STUDY ASSIGNMENT
Prepare for the Stage VI Check in Flight Lesson 86.

Instrument/Commercial Syllabus

FLIGHT LESSON 83
DUAL — LOCAL, COMPLEX AIRPLANE

OBJECTIVE
Perform all maneuvers and procedures at the level required in the Commercial Pilot Airman Certification Standards in preparation for the Stage VI Flight Check and the FAA Commercial Pilot Practical Test.

PREFLIGHT DISCUSSION
- ❏ Complex Airplane Systems and Equipment
- ❏ Commercial Pilot Airman Certification Standards
- ❏ Single-Pilot Resource Management

REVIEW

PREFLIGHT PREPARATION AND GROUND OPERATIONS
- ❏ Use of Checklists
- ❏ Postflight Procedures

MANEUVERS
- ❏ Steep Turns
- ❏ Chandelles
- ❏ Lazy Eights
- ❏ Eights-On-Pylons
- ❏ Steep Spirals

SLOW FLIGHT AND STALLS
- ❏ Maneuvering During Slow Flight
- ❏ Power-On and Power-Off Stalls
- ❏ Accelerated Stalls
- ❏ Spin Awareness

TAKEOFFS AND LANDINGS
- ❏ Short-Field Takeoffs/Maximum Performance Climbs and Landings
- ❏ Soft-Field Takeoffs and Landings
- ❏ Power-Off 180° Accuracy Approaches and Landings
- ❏ Go-Around/Rejected Landing

EMERGENCY OPERATIONS (SIMULATED)
- ❏ Systems and Equipment Malfunctions
- ❏ Landing Gear Malfunctions
- ❏ Emergency Descent
- ❏ Emergency Approach and Landing

COMPLETION STANDARDS
Demonstrate proficiency in performing each of the listed maneuvers and procedures to the level required by the Commercial Pilot Airman Certification Standards.

POSTFLIGHT DEBRIEFING
- ❏ Critique maneuvers/procedures and SRM.
- ❏ Create a plan for skills that need improvement.
- ❏ Update the record folder and logbook.

STAGE VI ■ Commercial Pilot Flight Training

Instrument/Commercial Syllabus

STUDY ASSIGNMENT
Commercial Pilot Practical Test Briefing

FLIGHT LESSONS 84 AND 85
DUAL — LOCAL

OBJECTIVE
Perform all maneuvers and procedures at the level required in the Commercial Pilot Airman Certification Standards in preparation for the Stage VI Flight Check and the FAA Commercial Pilot Practical Test.

PREFLIGHT DISCUSSION
- ❑ Commercial Pilot Airman Certification Standards
- ❑ Single-Pilot Resource Management

REVIEW
MANEUVERS
- ❑ Steep Turns
- ❑ Chandelles
- ❑ Lazy Eights
- ❑ Eights-On-Pylons Steep Spirals

SLOW FLIGHT AND STALLS
- ❑ Maneuvering During Slow Flight
- ❑ Power-Off and Power-On Stalls
- ❑ Accelerated Stalls
- ❑ Spin Awareness

TAKEOFFS AND LANDINGS
- ❑ Short-Field Takeoff/Maximum Performance Climb and Landing
- ❑ Soft-Field Takeoff and Landing
- ❑ Crosswind Takeoff and Landing
- ❑ Power-Off 180° Accuracy Approach and Landing

COMPLETION STANDARDS
- Demonstrate proficiency and competence required for commercial pilot certification by performing the outlined maneuvers with smoothness and coordination and using single-pilot resource management to manage risk and make effective decisions.
- Demonstrate the ability to meet or exceed the performance tolerances listed in the Commercial Pilot Airman Certification Standards.
- Demonstrate the ability to use single-pilot resource management to make effective decisions, maintain situational awareness, prevent CFIT, and manage risk, tasks, and automation.

POSTFLIGHT DEBRIEFING
- ❏ Critique maneuvers/procedures and SRM.
- ❏ Create a plan for skills that need improvement.
- ❏ Update the record folder and logbook.

STUDY ASSIGNMENT
Prepare for the Stage VI Check in Flight Lesson 86 and the End-of-Course Flight Check in Flight Lesson 87.

FLIGHT LESSON 86
DUAL — LOCAL
STAGE VI CHECK

OBJECTIVES
- Demonstrate proficiency in performing commercial maneuvers to the chief instructor, assistant chief, or a designated check instructor during the Stage VI Check.
- Demonstrate proficiency in all IFR tasks listed to the chief instructor, assistant chief, or a designated check instructor during the Stage VI Check.

NOTE: The instrument competency portion of this stage check will be conducted on an "as required" basis. This part of the flight applies to students who are enrolled, in the Instrument/Commercial Course concurrently and have not completed the FAA Instrument Rating Practical Test.

PREFLIGHT DISCUSSION
- ❏ Student and Flight Check Instructor Roles and Expectations
- ❏ Questions to Test Student Knowledge

REVIEW

MANEUVERS
- ❏ Steep Turns
- ❏ Chandelles
- ❏ Lazy Eights
- ❏ Eights-On-Pylons
- ❏ Steep Spirals

SLOW FLIGHT AND STALLS
- ❏ Maneuvering During Slow Flight
- ❏ Power-Off and Power-On Stalls
- ❏ Accelerated Stalls
- ❏ Spin Awareness

TAKEOFFS AND LANDINGS
- ❏ Normal and Crosswind Takeoffs and Landings
- ❏ Short-Field Takeoffs/Maximum Performance Climbs and Landings
- ❏ Soft-Field Takeoffs and Landings

Instrument/Commercial Syllabus

- ❏ Power-Off 180° Accuracy Approaches and Landings
- ❏ Go-Around/Rejected Landing

INSTRUMENT PROCEDURES
- ❏ VOR, GPS, and NDB Navigation
- ❏ Holding Procedures

APPROACH PROCEDURES
- ❏ VOR and NDB Approaches
- ❏ RNAV (GPS) Approaches
- ❏ ILS Approaches
- ❏ Localizer Approaches
- ❏ Partial-Panel Approaches
- ❏ Missed Approach Procedures

EMERGENCY OPERATIONS (SIMULATED)
- ❏ Systems and Equipment Malfunctions
- ❏ Emergency Descent
- ❏ Emergency Approach and Landing

POSTFLIGHT PROCEDURES
- ❏ After Landing
- ❏ Parking and Securing

COMPLETION STANDARDS
- Demonstrate proficiency in all commercial pilot tasks as required by the Commercial Pilot Airman Certification Standards.
- Demonstrate proficiency in all instrument rating tasks as required by the Instrument Rating Airman Certification Standards.
- Demonstrate the ability to use single-pilot resource management to make effective decisions, maintain situational awareness, prevent CFIT, and manage risk, tasks, and automation.

POSTFLIGHT DEBRIEFING
- ❏ Critique maneuvers/procedures and SRM.
- ❏ Create a plan for skills that need improvement.
- ❏ Update the record folder and logbook.

STUDY ASSIGNMENT
Prepare for the End-of-Course Flight Check in Flight Lesson 87.

Instrument/Commercial Syllabus

FLIGHT LESSON 87

DUAL — LOCAL
END-OF-COURSE FLIGHT CHECK
FOR COURSE COMPLETION

OBJECTIVES

- Demonstrate proficiency in all listed IFR tasks to the chief instructor, assistant chief, or a designated check instructor during the End-of-Course Flight Check. The proficiency level must meet the requirements of the Instrument Rating Airman Certification Standards.

- Demonstrate proficiency in all listed commercial tasks to the chief instructor, assistant chief, or a designated check instructor during the End-of-Course Flight Check. The proficiency level must meet the requirements of the Commercial Pilot Airman Certification Standards.

NOTE: *The instrument competency portion of this stage check will be conducted on an "as required" basis. This part of the flight applies to students who are enrolled, in the Instrument/Commercial Course concurrently and have not completed the FAA practical test for the instrument rating.*

Note: *The types of navigation, holding procedures, and approach procedures evaluated will be based on the equipment in the training aircraft.*

PREFLIGHT DISCUSSION
❑ Student and Flight Check Instructor Roles and Expectations
❑ Questions to Test Student Knowledge

REVIEW

FULL-PANEL INSTRUMENT
❑ Steep Turns

FULL- AND PARTIAL-PANEL INSTRUMENT
❑ Straight-and-Level Flight
❑ Climbs and Descents
❑ Standard-Rate Turns
❑ Climbing and Descending Turns
❑ Timed Turns to Magnetic Compass Headings
❑ Magnetic Compass Turns
❑ Power-Off and Power-On Stalls
❑ Recovery From Unusual Flight Attitudes

INSTRUMENT PROCEDURES
❑ Clearance Copying and Readback
❑ VOR, GPS, and NDB Navigation
❑ Holding Procedures
❑ Use of SIDs and ODPs

Instrument/Commercial Syllabus

APPROACH PROCEDURES
- VOR and NDB Approaches
- RNAV (GPS) Approaches
- ILS Approaches
- Localizer Approaches
- Partial-Panel Approaches Missed Approach Procedures

IFR CROSS-COUNTRY FLIGHT PLANNING
- Weather Information Related to IFR Cross-Country Flight
- Aircraft Performance, Limitations, and Systems Related to IFR Cross Country
- Enroute Chart Interpretation
- Navigation Log and Flight Plan Completion
- Filing an IFR Flight Plan

IFR CROSS-COUNTRY PROCEDURES
- IFR Cross-Country Flight Planning
- ATC Clearances
- IFR Cross-Country Flight Procedures

EMERGENCY OPERATIONS (SIMULATED)
- Systems and Equipment Malfunctions
- Loss of Communications
- Low Fuel Supply
- Diversion
- Adverse Weather
- Airframe and Powerplant Icing
- Fire in Flight
- Emergency Descent
- Emergency Approach and Landing
- Emergency Equipment and Survival Gear

MANEUVERS
- Steep Turns
- Chandelles
- Lazy Eights
- Eights-On-Pylons
- Steep Spirals

SLOW FLIGHT AND STALLS
- Maneuvering During Slow Flight
- Power-Off and Power-On Stalls
- Accelerated Stalls
- Spin Awareness

TAKEOFFS AND LANDINGS
- Normal and Crosswind Takeoffs and Landings
- Short-Field Takeoffs/Maximum Performance Climbs and Landings
- Soft-Field Takeoffs and Landings
- Power-Off 180° Accuracy Approaches and Landings
- Go-Around/Rejected Landing

POSTFLIGHT PROCEDURES
- After Landing
- Parking and Securing

STAGE VI ■ Commercial Pilot Flight Training

Instrument/Commercial Syllabus

SINGLE-PILOT RESOURCE MANAGEMENT
- ❏ Aeronautical Decision Making
- ❏ Risk Management
- ❏ Task Management
- ❏ Situational Awareness
- ❏ Controlled Flight Into Terrain Awareness
- ❏ Automation Management

COMPLETION STANDARDS
- Demonstrate proficiency in all commercial pilot tasks as required by the Commercial Pilot Airman Certification Standards.
- Demonstrate proficiency in all instrument rating tasks as required by the Instrument Rating Airman Certification Standards.
- Demonstrate the ability to use single-pilot resource management to make effective decisions, maintain situational awareness, prevent CFIT, and manage risk, tasks, and automation.

NOTE: If the student has not taken the FAA Instrument Rating Practical Test, the Instrument Rating Practical Test Briefing also should be used during this Flight Lesson.

POSTFLIGHT DEBRIEFING
- ❏ Evaluate maneuvers/procedures and SRM.
- ❏ Plan additional instruction for skills not meeting course completion standards.
- ❏ Update the record folder and logbook.

Instrument/Commercial Syllabus

Multi-Engine Rating Ground Training Stage VI

STAGE OBJECTIVES
During this stage, the student learns multi-engine aerodynamics, operating procedures, systems, and performance considerations. The student learns to accurately use performance charts and compute weight and balance data for the multi-engine airplane. In addition, the student explores the principles, techniques, and procedures that apply to engine-out and instrument flight in the multi-engine airplane.

STAGE COMPLETION STANDARDS
The student must pass the Stage VI Exam and the Multi-Engine End-of-Course Exam with a minimum score of 80 percent, and review each incorrect response with the instructor to ensure complete understanding.

GROUND LESSON 1

REFERENCES

Multi-Engine Textbook/EBook
  Chapter 1 — Exploring the Multi-Engine Rating
  Chapter 4 — Performing Maneuvers and Procedures
    Section A — Normal Operations

Instrument Online — Jeppesen Learning Center
  Multi-Engine Maneuvers Lessons
    ML — Normal Takeoff and Climb
    ML — Normal Approach and Landing
    ML — Short-Field Takeoff
    ML — Short Field Landing

OBJECTIVES
- Become familiar with the training program and applicable regulations.
- Become familiar with single-pilot resource management (SRM) concepts that apply to multi-engine airplane operations.
- Describe normal operations in the multi-engine airplane, including the preflight, ground operations, and normal and short-field takeoff and landing procedures.

Instrument/Commercial Syllabus

CONTENT

CHAPTER 1A — SEEKING A NEW EXPERIENCE
- ❏ Why a Multi-Engine Rating?
- ❏ The Training Path

CHAPTER 1B — CONSIDERING SRM
- ❏ Multi-Engine Safety
- ❏ Aeronautical Decision Making
- ❏ Risk Management
- ❏ Task Management
- ❏ Situational Awareness
- ❏ Controlled Flight Into Terrain Awareness
- ❏ Automation Management

CHAPTER 4A — NORMAL OPERATIONS
MULTI-ENGINE MANEUVERS LESSONS
- ❏ Using Checklists
- ❏ Preflight Inspection (Including Airworthiness Requirements)
- ❏ Ground Operations
  - Engine Starting
  - Taxiing
  - Before-Takeoff Check
- ❏ Takeoff and Climb
- ❏ Propeller Synchronization
- ❏ Short-Field Takeoff and Maximum Performance Climb
- ❏ Cruise and Descent
- ❏ Approach and Landing
- ❏ Short-Field Approach and Landing
- ❏ Go-Around

COMPLETION STANDARDS
- Demonstrate understanding of the multi-engine training program and the single-pilot resource management (SRM) concepts that apply to flight in a multi-engine airplane during oral quizzing by the instructor.
- Demonstrate understanding of normal operations in the multi-engine airplane during oral quizzing by the instructor.
- Complete the questions for Chapter 4A with a minimum score of 80 percent. Review each incorrect response with the instructor to ensure complete understanding before starting Ground Lesson 2.

STUDY ASSIGNMENT
Multi-Engine Textbook/EBook
 Chapter 2 — Understanding Your Airplane

Instrument Online — Jeppesen Learning Center
 GL — Light Twin System Differences
 GL — Light Twin Performance

STAGE VI ■ Multi-Engine Rating Ground Training

Instrument/Commercial Syllabus

GROUND LESSON 2

REFERENCES

Multi-Engine Textbook/EBook
Chapter 2 — Understanding Your Airplane

Instrument Online — Jeppesen Learning Center
GL — Light Twin System Differences
GL — Light Twin Performance

OBJECTIVES
- Describe multi-engine systems and equipment including, powerplant, propeller, and retractable landing gear systems.
- Explain weight and balance considerations for multi-engine airplanes and calculate weight and balance for multi-engine airplanes.
- Determine performance for light twin airplanes operating on both engines and with an inoperative engine.
- Explain how the loss of an engine affects performance on a light twin.

CONTENT

SECTION A — EXAMINING SYSTEMS
GL — LIGHT TWIN SYSTEM DIFFERENCES

RECIPROCATING-ENGINE-POWERED OPERATIONS
- ❏ Fuel Metering Systems
- ❏ Ignition and Starting Systems
- ❏ Lubrication Systems
- ❏ Induction Systems
- ❏ Cooling And Exhaust Systems
- ❏ Engine Indicating Systems
- ❏ Engine Accessory Systems
- ❏ Diesel Engines

CONSTANT-SPEED PROPELLER OPERATION
- ❏ Power Control
- ❏ Full Authority Digital Engine Control (FADEC)
- ❏ Propeller Synchronization
- ❏ Governor Checks
- ❏ Feathering
- ❏ Restarting

ELECTRICAL SYSTEMS
- ❏ Generation
- ❏ Storage And External Power
- ❏ Distribution Buses

Instrument/Commercial Syllabus

FUEL SYSTEMS
- ❏ Fuel Pumps
- ❏ Fuel Selector Controls
- ❏ Cross Feeding
- ❏ Auxiliary Fuel Tanks

LANDING GEAR SYSTEMS
- ❏ Electrohydraulic Landing Gear
- ❏ Electric Landing Gear
- ❏ Gear Position Lights
- ❏ Gear Warning Horn
- ❏ Safety Switches
- ❏ Emergency Landing Gear Extension

ICE CONTROL SYSTEMS
- ❏ Propeller Anti-Ice System
- ❏ Wing and Tail Surface Deice Systems
- ❏ Windshield Anti-Ice Systems

CABIN ENVIRONMENTAL SYSTEMS
- ❏ Cabin Heating
- ❏ Oxygen Systems
- ❏ Cabin Pressurization Systems

SECTION B — CALCULATING WEIGHT AND BALANCE
GL — LIGHT TWIN PERFORMANCE

WEIGHT AND BALANCE TERMS
- ❏ Maximum Zero Fuel Weight
- ❏ Maneuvering Speed
- ❏ Center of Gravity

FINDING WEIGHT AND CG LOCATION
- ❏ Center of Gravity Limits
- ❏ Using the Weight Shift Formula

SECTION C — DETERMINING PERFORMANCE
GL — LIGHT TWIN PERFORMANCE

PERFORMANCE DEFINITIONS
- ❏ Power Required
- ❏ The Engine-Out Performance Penalty

USING PERFORMANCE DATA
- ❏ The Associated Conditions
- ❏ V-Speeds
- ❏ Takeoff and Climb
    - ◊ Accelerate-Stop Distance
    - ◊ Accelerate-Go Distance
    - ◊ Climb – Two Engine
    - ◊ Climb – One Engine Inoperative
- ❏ Cruise Flight
- ❏ Single-Engine Ceilings
- ❏ Descent Performance

Instrument/Commercial Syllabus

- ❏ Landing Performance
- ❏ Engine-Out Go-Around

COMPLETION STANDARDS

- Demonstrate understanding of multi-engine airplane systems, including high-performance powerplants, constant-speed propellers, retractable landing gear, environmental systems, and ice control systems during oral quizzing by the instructor.
- Demonstrate understanding of weight and balance considerations for a multi-engine airplane during oral quizzing by the instructor.
- Demonstrate understanding of light twin performance with both engines operating and with an inoperative engine during oral quizzing by the instructor.
- Correctly compute the weight and balance and performance for the training airplane based on at least two different loading conditions with the airport and environmental conditions as specified by the instructor.
- Complete with a minimum score of 80 percent: questions for Chapter 2 or online exams for GL — Light Twin System Differences and GL — Light Twin Performance. Review each incorrect response with the instructor to ensure complete understanding before starting Ground Lesson 3.

STUDY ASSIGNMENT

Multi-Engine Textbook/EBook
  Chapter 3 — Discovering Aerodynamics
  Chapter 4 — Performing Maneuvers and Procedures
    Section B — Maneuvers

Instrument Online — Jeppesen Learning Center
  GL — Light Twin Aerodynamics
  Multi-Engine Maneuvers Lessons
    ML — Maneuvering During Slow Flight
    ML — Power-Off Stalls
    ML — Power-On Stalls

GROUND LESSON 3

REFERENCES

Multi-Engine Textbook/EBook
  Chapter 3 — Discovering Aerodynamics
  Chapter 4 — Performing Maneuvers and Procedures
    Section B — Maneuvers

Instrument Online — Jeppesen Learning Center
  GL — Light Twin Aerodynamics
  Multi-Engine Maneuvers Lessons
    ML — Maneuvering During Slow Flight
    ML — Power-Off Stalls
    ML — Power-On Stalls

Instrument/Commercial Syllabus

OBJECTIVES
- Explain multi-engine aerodynamics, including the characteristics of the boundary layer, induced flow, and high-speed flight.
- Describe the aerodynamic forces acting on a multi-engine airplane when an engine fails and how to counteract yaw and roll toward the inoperative engine and reduce drag when flying with an inoperative engine.
- Identify the steps and techniques to perform steep turns, slow flight, stalls, and emergency descents in the multi-engine airplane.
- Develop stall/spin awareness and a clear understanding of the causes and recovery procedures that apply to stalls and spins in multi-engine airplanes.

CONTENT

CHAPTER 3A — INTRODUCING MULTI-ENGINE AERODYNAMICS
GL — LIGHT TWIN AERODYNAMICS
- ❏ Boundary Layer
- ❏ Induced Flow
- ❏ Turning Tendencies
- ❏ High-Speed Flight

CHAPTER 3B — MASTERING ENGINE-OUT AERODYNAMICS
GL — LIGHT TWIN AERODYNAMICS
- ❏ Engine Failure
- ❏ Yaw and Roll
- ❏ Critical Engine
- ❏ Cure for Yaw and Roll
- ❏ V_{MC}
- ❏ Windmilling Propeller
- ❏ Feathering
- ❏ Sideslip
- ❏ Zero Sideslip
- ❏ Controllability vs. Performance
  - ◊ Weight
  - ◊ Center of Gravity
  - ◊ Power

CHAPTER 4B — MANEUVERS
MULTI-ENGINE MANEUVERS LESSONS
- ❏ Steep Turns
- ❏ Slow Flight
- ❏ Stalls (Power-On and Power-Off)
- ❏ Spin Awareness
- ❏ Emergency Descent

COMPLETION STANDARDS
- Demonstrate understanding of aerodynamics, including the characteristics of the boundary layer, induced flow, and high-speed flight, during oral quizzing by the instructor.

STAGE VI ■ Multi-Engine Rating Ground Training

- Demonstrate understanding of engine-out aerodynamics and how to counteract the effects of a failed engine during oral quizzing by the instructor.
- Demonstrate understanding of the steps and techniques to perform steep turns, slow flight, stalls, and emergency descents in the multi-engine airplane.
- Demonstrate stall/spin awareness and a clear understanding of the causes and recovery procedures that apply to stalls and spins in multi-engine airplanes during oral quizzing by the instructor.
- Complete with a minimum score of 80 percent: questions for Chapter 3 and Chapter 4B or online exams for GL — Light Twin Aerodynamics. Review each incorrect response with the instructor to ensure complete understanding before starting Ground Lesson 5.

STUDY ASSIGNMENT
Multi-Engine Textbook/EBook
    Chapter 5 — Mastering Engine-Out Operations
        Section A — When an Engine Fails
        Section B — Engine-Out Maneuvers

Instrument Online — Jeppesen Learning Center
    Multi-Engine Maneuvers Lessons
        ML — Engine Failure During Takeoff Before V_{MC}
        ML — V_{MC} Demonstration

GROUND LESSON 4

REFERENCES

Multi-Engine Textbook/EBook
    Chapter 5 — Mastering Engine-Out Operations
        Section A — When an Engine Fails
        Section B — Engine-Out Maneuvers

Instrument Online — Jeppesen Learning Center
    Multi-Engine Maneuvers Lessons
        ML — Engine Failure During Takeoff Before V_{MC}
        ML — V_{MC} Demonstration

OBJECTIVES
- Explain the steps to take to manage an engine failure, including identifying the failed engine, maintaining control of the airplane, and securing the inoperative engine.
- Describe how to manage an engine failure during takeoff, climb, enroute, and landing.
- Identify the steps to perform the V_{MC} demonstration and drag demonstration.

Instrument/Commercial Syllabus

CONTENT

SECTION A — WHEN AN ENGINE FAILS
- Taking Action
  - Pitch
  - Power
  - Drag
  - Identify
  - Verify
  - Troubleshoot
- Feathering
  - After Actual Engine Failure
  - During Training
  - Restarting the Engine
- Establishing a Bank
- Securing the Inoperative Engine
- Monitoring the Operating Engine

SECTION B — ENGINE-OUT MANEUVERS
MULTI-ENGINE MANEUVERS LESSONS
- Engine Failure During Takeoff and Climb
  - Engine Failure During Takeoff Before V_{MC}
  - Engine Failure After Liftoff
  - Takeoff Briefing
- Enroute
- V_{MC} Demonstration
- Drag Demonstration
- Landing
- Engine-Out Go-Around

COMPLETION STANDARDS
- Demonstrate understanding of taking the proper steps to manage an engine failure in different phases of flight and making appropriate decisions about the continuation of flight during oral quizzing by the instructor.
- Demonstrate understanding of the steps to perform the V_{MC} demonstration and drag demonstration during oral quizzing by the instructor.
- Complete with a minimum score of 80 percent: questions for Chapter 5A and 5B. Review each incorrect response with the instructor to ensure complete understanding before starting Ground Lesson 6.

STUDY ASSIGNMENT
Multi-Engine Textbook/EBook
  Chapter 5 — Mastering Engine-Out Operations
    Section C — Operating on Instruments
  Chapter 6 — Applying SRM

Instrument/Commercial Syllabus

GROUND LESSON 5

REFERENCES

Multi-Engine Textbook/EBook
Chapter 5 — Mastering Engine-Out Operations
   Section C — Operating on Instruments
Chapter 6 — Applying SRM

OBJECTIVES
- Recognize how to perform instrument procedures in the multi-engine airplane with both engines operating and with one engine inoperative.
- Explain how to use single-pilot resource management skills to make effective decisions as pilot in command of a multi-engine airplane.

CONTENT

CHAPTER 5C — OPERATING ON INSTRUMENTS
- ❏ Attitude Instrument Flying
- ❏ Departure
- ❏ Enroute
- ❏ Engine-Out Instrument Approach

CHAPTER 6 — APPLYING SRM
- ❏ Poor Judgment Chain
- ❏ Aeronautical Decision Making
- ❏ Risk Management
- ❏ Task Management
- ❏ Situational Awareness
- ❏ Controlled Flight Into Terrain Awareness
- ❏ Automation Management

COMPLETION STANDARDS
- Demonstrate understanding of performing instrument procedures in the multi-engine airplane with both engines operating and with one engine inoperative during oral quizzing by the instructor.
- Demonstrate understanding of how to use single-pilot resource management to make effective decisions, maintain situational awareness, prevent CFIT, and manage risk, tasks, and automation.
- Complete with a minimum score of 80 percent: questions for Chapters 5C and Chapter 6. Review each incorrect response with the instructor to ensure complete understanding before taking the Stage VI Exam in Ground Lesson 7.

STUDY ASSIGNMENT
Review the content of Multi-Engine Ground Lessons 1 – 5 to prepare for the Stage VI Exam.

GROUND LESSON 6
STAGE VI EXAM

REFERENCES

Ground Lessons 1 – 5

OBJECTIVE
Demonstrate knowledge of the subjects covered in Multi-Engine Ground Lessons 1 – 5 by passing the Stage VI Exam.

CONTENT
STAGE VI EXAM
- ❏ Multi-Engine Operation and Systems
- ❏ Calculating Weight and Balance
- ❏ Determining Performance
- ❏ Multi-Engine Aerodynamics
- ❏ Engine-Out Aerodynamics
- ❏ Maneuvers and Procedures
- ❏ Engine-Out Operations
- ❏ Multi-Engine Instrument Flight
- ❏ Applying SRM

COMPLETION STANDARDS
To complete the lesson and stage, pass the Stage VI Exam with a minimum score of 80 percent. Review each incorrect response with the instructor to ensure complete understanding before taking the Multi-Engine End-of-Course Exam.

STUDY ASSIGNMENT
Review the content of Multi-Engine Ground Lessons 1 – 6 to prepare for the Mult-Engine End-of-Course Exam.

Instrument/Commercial Syllabus

GROUND LESSON 7

END-OF-COURSE EXAM

REFERENCES

Ground Lessons 1-7

OBJECTIVE
Demonstrate comprehension of the material covered in Multi-Engine Ground Lessons 1 – 6 by passing the Multi-Engine End-of-Course Exam.

CONTENT
❑ Multi-Engine End-of-Course Exam

COMPLETION STANDARDS
To complete the lesson and the Multi-Engine Ground Training, pass the Multi-Engine End-of-Course Exam with a minimum score of 80 percent. Review each incorrect response with the instructor to ensure complete understanding.

Instrument/Commercial Syllabus

Multi-Engine Rating Flight Training Stage VII

STAGE OBJECTIVES
During Stage VII, the student learns to fly the multi-engine airplane with both engines operating and in engine-out situations. The student learns to identify and manage an engine failure and perform engine-out maneuvers and procedures. Additionally, the student gains proficiency in IFR operations in the multi-engine airplane and learns to use single-pilot resource management (SRM) skills to make effective decisions in the multi-engine airplane.

STAGE COMPLETION STANDARDS
This stage is complete when the student demonstrates all multi-engine flight maneuvers and procedures at the proficiency level of a commercial pilot with an instrument rating as outlined in the multi-engine land sections of the Commercial Pilot Airman Certification Standards.

NOTE: Completion of the navigation and instrument approach tasks listed in specific lessons must be based on the available aircraft equipment.

FLIGHT LESSON 1

DUAL — LOCAL

NOTE: Prior to this flight, complete Ground Lesson 1 and the Multi-Engine Operations and Systems Briefing.

OBJECTIVES
- Become familiar with the multi-engine training airplane.
- Become familiar with the attitudes, power settings, and configurations required for the performance of the listed maneuvers and procedures using visual references (VR) and instrument references (IR).

PREFLIGHT DISCUSSION
- ❑ Multi-Engine Training Airplane Systems and Equipment
- ❑ Task Management

INTRODUCE

PREFLIGHT PREPARATION
- ❑ Certificates and Documents
- ❑ Airworthiness Requirements
- ❑ Multi-Engine Operation of Systems

Instrument/Commercial Syllabus

- ❏ Multi-Engine Performance and Limitations
- ❏ Review of V-Speeds

PREFLIGHT PROCEDURES
- ❏ Preflight Inspection
- ❏ Cockpit Management
- ❏ Engine Starting
- ❏ Normal and Crosswind Taxiing
- ❏ Before-Takeoff Check

SAFETY-RELATED OPERATIONS AND PROCEDURES
- ❏ Use of Checklists
- ❏ Positive Exchange of Flight Controls
- ❏ Wake Turbulence Avoidance
- ❏ Low-Level Wind Shear Avoidance
- ❏ Visual Scanning and Collision Avoidance
- ❏ Runway Incursion Avoidance
- ❏ Land and Hold Short Operations (LAHSO)
- ❏ Crew Resource Management
- ❏ Single-Pilot Resource Management

MANEUVERS (VR) (IR)
- ❏ Straight-and-Level Flight
- ❏ Constant Altitude Change of Airspeed
- ❏ Constant Airspeed Climbs and Descents
- ❏ Turns to Headings

TAKEOFFS AND LANDINGS
- ❏ Normal and Crosswind Takeoffs and Climbs
- ❏ Traffic Patterns
- ❏ Normal and Crosswind Approaches and Landings

POSTFLIGHT PROCEDURES
- ❏ After Landing
- ❏ Parking and Securing

COMPLETION STANDARDS
- Perform the listed ground operations with a minimum of instructor assistance.
- Demonstrate understanding of the attitudes and configurations necessary to perform the listed maneuvers and procedures by maintaining positive aircraft control with altitude ±200 feet, heading ±10°, and airspeed ±10 knots.

POSTFLIGHT DEBRIEFING
- ❏ Critique maneuvers/procedures and SRM.
- ❏ Create a plan for skills that need improvement.
- ❏ Update the record folder and logbook.

STUDY ASSIGNMENT
Ground Lesson 2
  Aircraft Systems, Weight and Balance, and Performance
Multi-Engine Performance Considerations Briefing

STAGE VII ■ Multi-Engine Rating Flight Training

Instrument/Commercial Syllabus

FLIGHT LESSON 2
DUAL — LOCAL

OBJECTIVES
- Become familiar with the flight characteristics of the multi-engine airplane by performing slow flight stalls, and steep turns, and emergency operations.
- Gain proficiency in performing preflight procedures, basic maneuvers, takeoffs, and landings.
- Gain proficiency in full- and partial-panel attitude instrument flying and recovery from unusual attitudes.

PREFLIGHT DISCUSSION
❏ Multi-Engine Training Airplane Systems and Equipment
❏ Emergency Procedures
❏ Stall/Spin Awareness
❏ Single-Pilot Resource Management

INTRODUCE
MANEUVERS
❏ Steep Turns

SLOW FLIGHT AND STALLS
❏ Maneuvering During Slow Flight
❏ Power-Off Stalls
❏ Power-On Stalls
❏ Accelerated Stalls
❏ Spin Awareness

FULL- AND PARTIAL-PANEL INSTRUMENT
❏ Straight-and-Level Flight
❏ Constant Rate Climbs and Descents
❏ Constant Airspeed Climbs and Descents
❏ Standard-Rate Turns
❏ Climbing and Descending Turns
❏ Timed Turns to Magnetic Compass Headings
❏ Magnetic Compass Turns
❏ Recovery From Unusual Flight Attitudes

EMERGENCY OPERATIONS
❏ Emergency Descent
❏ Systems and Equipment Malfunctions
❏ Emergency Equipment and Survival Gear

REVIEW
PREFLIGHT PREPARATION
❏ Certificates and Documents
❏ Airworthiness Requirements
❏ Multi-Engine Operation of Systems
❏ Multi-Engine Performance and Limitations

STAGE VII ■ Multi-Engine Rating Flight Training

Instrument/Commercial Syllabus

PREFLIGHT PROCEDURES
- ❏ Preflight Inspection
- ❏ Cockpit Management
- ❏ Engine Starting
- ❏ Normal and Crosswind Taxiing
- ❏ Before-Takeoff Check

SAFETY-RELATED OPERATIONS AND PROCEDURES
- ❏ Use of Checklists
- ❏ Positive Exchange of Flight Controls
- ❏ Wake Turbulence Avoidance
- ❏ Low-Level Wind Shear Avoidance
- ❏ Visual Scanning and Collision Avoidance
- ❏ Runway Incursion Avoidance
- ❏ Land and Hold Short Operations (LAHSO)
- ❏ Crew Resource Management
- ❏ Single-Pilot Resource Management

MANEUVERS (VR) (IR)
- ❏ Straight-and-Level Flight
- ❏ Constant Altitude Change of Airspeed
- ❏ Constant Airspeed Climbs and Descents
- ❏ Turns to Headings

TAKEOFFS AND LANDINGS
- ❏ Normal Takeoff and Climb
- ❏ Crosswind Takeoff and Climb
- ❏ Traffic Patterns
- ❏ Normal Approach and Landing
- ❏ Crosswind Approach and Landing

POSTFLIGHT PROCEDURES
- ❏ After Landing
- ❏ Parking and Securing

COMPLETION STANDARDS

- Demonstrate proficiency in ground operations by performing procedures without instructor assistance.

- During takeoff and landing, demonstrate directional control and maintain liftoff, climb, approach, and touchdown airspeed within ±10 knots. Perform straight-and-level flight, climbs, and descents while maintaining assigned airspeed ±10 knots, rollouts from turns ±10° of assigned heading, and specified altitude ±150 feet.

- Demonstrate the correct flight procedures for maneuvering during slow flight, steep turns, emergency descents, and the correct entry and recovery procedures for stalls. Complete slow flight and stalls no lower than 3,000 feet AGL or the manufacturer's recommended altitude, whichever is higher.

- Demonstrate the correct technique for full- and partial-panel attitude instrument flying while performing basic flight maneuvers.

- Demonstrate the correct procedures for recognizing and recovering from unusual flight attitudes.

Instrument/Commercial Syllabus

POSTFLIGHT DEBRIEFING
❑ Critique maneuvers/procedures and SRM.
❑ Create a plan for skills that need improvement.
❑ Update the record folder and logbook.

FLIGHT LESSON 3
DUAL — LOCAL

OBJECTIVES
- Become familiar with short-field takeoffs and maximum performance climbs, short-field approaches and landings, go-arounds, and high altitude operations.
- Gain proficiency in performing slow flight stalls, steep turns, and emergency operations.
- Increase proficiency in preflight procedures, basic maneuvers, takeoffs, and landings and full- and partial-panel attitude instrument flying.

PREFLIGHT DISCUSSION
❑ High Altitude Operations
❑ Risk Management

INTRODUCE

TAKEOFFS AND LANDINGS
❑ Short-Field Takeoff and Maximum Performance Climb
❑ Short-Field Approach and Landing
❑ Go-Around/Rejected Landing

HIGH ALTITUDE OPERATIONS (AS REQUIRED)
❑ Use of Supplemental Oxygen
❑ Use of Pressurization

REVIEW
❑ Preflight Preparation
❑ Preflight Procedures

TAKEOFFS AND LANDINGS
❑ Normal and Crosswind Takeoffs and Climbs
❑ Normal and Crosswind Approaches and Landings

MANEUVERS
❑ Steep Turns

SLOW FLIGHT AND STALLS
❑ Maneuvering During Slow Flight
❑ Power-Off and Power-On Stalls
❑ Accelerated Stalls
❑ Spin Awareness

Instrument/Commercial Syllabus

SAFETY-RELATED OPERATIONS AND PROCEDURES
- ❑ Use of Checklists
- ❑ Crew Resource Management
- ❑ Positive Exchange of Flight Controls
- ❑ Wake Turbulence Avoidance
- ❑ Low-Level Wind Shear Avoidance
- ❑ Visual Scanning and Collision Avoidance
- ❑ Runway Incursion Avoidance
- ❑ Land and Hold Short Operations (LAHSO)
- ❑ Single-Pilot Resource Management

FULL- AND PARTIAL-PANEL INSTRUMENT
- ❑ Straight-and-Level Flight
- ❑ Constant Rate Climbs and Descents
- ❑ Constant Airspeed Climbs and Descents
- ❑ Standard-Rate Turns
- ❑ Climbing and Descending Turns
- ❑ Timed Turns to Magnetic Compass Headings
- ❑ Magnetic Compass Turns
- ❑ Recovery From Unusual Flight Attitudes

EMERGENCY OPERATIONS
- ❑ Emergency Descent
- ❑ Systems and Equipment Malfunctions
- ❑ Emergency Equipment and Survival Gear

POSTFLIGHT PROCEDURES
- ❑ After Landing
- ❑ Parking and Securing

COMPLETION STANDARDS
- Demonstrate understanding of short-field takeoffs and landings and high altitude operations using the correct procedures and maintaining positive control of the airplane.
- Demonstrate proficiency in all the maneuvers and procedures listed for review at the level required by multi-engine land sections of the Commercial Pilot Airman Certification Standards.

POSTFLIGHT DEBRIEFING
- ❑ Critique maneuvers/procedures and SRM.
- ❑ Create a plan for skills that need improvement.
- ❑ Update the record folder and logbook.

STUDY ASSIGNMENT
Ground Lessons 3 and 4
  Multi-Engine/Engine-Out Aerodynamics and Maneuvers
  Engine-Out Operations

Engine-Out Operations Briefing

FLIGHT LESSON 4

DUAL — LOCAL

OBJECTIVES
- Become familiar with engine-out procedures and how to identify the inoperative engine, initiate appropriate corrective procedures, and maneuver the airplane with one engine inoperative.
- Become familiar with V_{MC} characteristics and the significance of the relationship of V_{MC} to stall speed as the instructor performs the V_{MC} demonstration.
- Increase proficiency in the listed review tasks.

PREFLIGHT DISCUSSION
- ❑ Engine-Out Procedures
- ❑ Engine-Out Aerodynamics
- ❑ Engine-Out Performance
- ❑ Situational Awareness
- ❑ Single-Pilot Resource Management

INTRODUCE

ENGINE-OUT OPERATIONS
- ❑ Flight Principles — Engine-Inoperative
- ❑ Engine Failure During Cruise
- ❑ Identification of Inoperative Engine
- ❑ Procedures for Shutdown and Feathering
- ❑ Use of Controls to Counteract Yaw and Roll
- ❑ V_{MC} Demonstration (by Instructor)

NOTE: The V_{MC} demonstration must be completed no lower than 3,000 feet AGL or the manufacturer's recommended altitude, whichever is higher. In addition, it is imperative that instructors observe precautions applicable to the airplane being flown, particularly limitations associated with high density altitude conditions. In some high density altitude situations, the demonstration might not be practical and should not be attempted.

MANEUVERING WITH ONE ENGINE INOPERATIVE
- ❑ Straight-and-Level Flight
- ❑ Turns in Both Directions
- ❑ Climbs and Descents to Assigned Altitudes
- ❑ Effects of Various Airspeeds and Configurations on Engine-Out Performance

REVIEW
- ❑ Preflight Preparation
- ❑ Preflight Procedures
- ❑ Postflight Procedures

TAKEOFFS AND LANDINGS
- ❑ Normal and Crosswind Takeoffs and Landings
- ❑ Short-Field Takeoffs/Maximum Performance Climbs and Landings
- ❑ Go-Arounds/Rejected Landings

Instrument/Commercial Syllabus

MANEUVERS AND PROCEDURES
- ❏ Safety-Related Operations and Procedures
- ❏ Steep Turns
- ❏ Full- and Partial-Panel Attitude Instrument Flying

SLOW FLIGHT AND STALLS
- ❏ Maneuvering During Slow Flight
- ❏ Power-Off and Power-On Stalls
- ❏ Accelerated Stalls
- ❏ Spin Awareness

HIGH ALTITUDE OPERATIONS (AS REQUIRED)
- ❏ Use of Supplemental Oxygen
- ❏ Use of Pressurization

COMPLETION STANDARDS
- Identify the inoperative engine during cruise and use the correct control inputs to maintain straight flight.
- Demonstrate knowledge of the cause, effect, and significance of engine-out minimum control speed (V_{MC}) and recognize the imminent loss of control.
- Demonstrate understanding of how to maneuver with one engine inoperative and the effects of various airspeeds and configurations on engine-out performance.
- Demonstrate proficiency in slow flight and stalls, steep turns, full- and partial-panel attitude instrument flying and short field takeoffs/maximum performance climbs and landings.

POSTFLIGHT DEBRIEFING
- ❏ Critique maneuvers/procedures and SRM.
- ❏ Create a plan for skills that need improvement.
- ❏ Update the record folder and logbook.

FLIGHT LESSON 5

DUAL — LOCAL

OBJECTIVES
- Become familiar with managing engine failure on takeoff and initial climb.
- Become familiar with performing approaches and landings with an inoperative engine.
- Perform the V_{MC} demonstration and the proper recovery.
- Increase proficiency in the review maneuvers and procedures.

PREFLIGHT DISCUSSION
- ❏ Engine Failure on Takeoff and Initial Climb
- ❏ Factors Affecting V_{MC}

Instrument/Commercial Syllabus

INTRODUCE

ENGINE-OUT OPERATIONS
- Engine Failure During Takeoff Before V_{MC} (Simulated)
- Engine Failure After Liftoff (Simulated)
- V_{MC} Demonstration
- Full Feather and In-Flight Restart
- Approach and Landing with an Inoperative Engine (Simulated)

NOTE: The V_{MC} demonstration must be completed no lower than 3,000 feet AGL or the manufacturer's recommended altitude, whichever is higher. In addition, it is imperative that instructors observe precautions applicable to the airplane being flown, particularly limitations associated with high density altitude conditions. In some high density altitude situations, the demonstration might not be practical and should not be attempted.

REVIEW

ENGINE-OUT OPERATIONS
- Flight Principles — Engine-Inoperative
- Engine Failure During Cruise
- Identification of Inoperative Engine
- Procedures for Shutdown and Feathering
- Use of Controls to Counteract Yaw and Roll

MANEUVERING WITH ONE ENGINE INOPERATIVE
- Straight-and-Level Flight
- Turns in Both Directions
- Climbs and Descents to Assigned Altitudes
- Effects of Various Airspeeds and Configurations on Engine Inoperative Performance

MANEUVERS AND PROCEDURES
- Safety-Related Operations and Procedures
- Steep Turns
- Full- and Partial-Panel Attitude Instrument Flying

COMPLETION STANDARDS
- Maneuver the airplane during level flight with one engine inoperative, while maintaining altitude ±150 feet and heading ±15°.
- During engine-out climbs, maintain airspeed within 5 knots of, but never below, that recommended by the manufacturer.
- Promptly identify the inoperative engine and demonstrate correct shutdown and feathering procedures during simulated engine failures.
- Demonstrate understanding of the cause, effect, and significance of engine-out minimum control speed (V_{MC}) and demonstrate the correct procedure for engine failure on takeoff before and after liftoff.
- Demonstrate understanding of the procedures to manage an engine failure during takeoff before V_{MC}, an engine failure after liftoff, and an approach and landing with an inoperative engine.
- Demonstrate understanding of the procedures to feather the propeller and restart an engine in flight.

Instrument/Commercial Syllabus

POSTFLIGHT DEBRIEFING
- ❏ Critique maneuvers/procedures and SRM.
- ❏ Create a plan for skills that need improvement.
- ❏ Update the record folder and logbook.

FLIGHT LESSON 6

DUAL — LOCAL

OBJECTIVE
- Become familiar with identifying an inoperative engine and performing engine-out procedures solely by reference to instruments.
- Increase proficiency in engine-out operations.

PREFLIGHT DISCUSSION
- ❏ Engine-Out Instrument Procedures
- ❏ Situational Awareness
- ❏ Single-Pilot Resource Management

INTRODUCE

ENGINE-OUT OPERATIONS (IR)
- ❏ Identification of Inoperative Engine
- ❏ Procedures for Shutdown and Feathering
- ❏ Engine Failure During Climbs
- ❏ Engine Failure During Straight-and-Level Flight and Turns
- ❏ Engine Failure During Descents

REVIEW

TAKEOFFS AND LANDINGS
- ❏ Short-Field Takeoff and Maximum Performance Climb
- ❏ Short-Field Approach and Landing

ENGINE-OUT OPERATIONS
- ❏ Engine Failure During Takeoff Before V_{MC} (Simulated)
- ❏ Engine Failure After Liftoff (Simulated)
- ❏ Flight Principles – Engine Inoperative
- ❏ Maneuvering with One Engine Inoperative
- ❏ V_{MC} Demonstration (by Student)
- ❏ Full Feather and In-Flight Restart
- ❏ Approach and Landing with an Inoperative Engine (Simulated)

COMPLETION STANDARDS
- Demonstrate proficiency in correctly identifying the inoperative engine during cruise and using the proper control inputs to maintain straight-and-level flight using instrument and visual references.
- Demonstrate understanding of performing engine-out maneuvers and procedures solely by reference to instruments

- Demonstrate understanding of the cause, effect, and significance of engine-out minimum control speed (V_{MC}) and recognize the imminent loss of control when performing the V_{MC} demonstration.
- Demonstrate proficiency in performing all engine-out maneuvers and procedures with positive aircraft control.

POSTFLIGHT DEBRIEFING
❏ Critique maneuvers/procedures and SRM.
❏ Create a plan for skills that need improvement.
❏ Update the record folder and logbook.

STUDY ASSIGNMENT
Ground Lesson 5
 Multi-Engine Instrument Flight and Decision Making
Multi-Engine Instrument Flight Briefing

FLIGHT LESSON 7
DUAL — LOCAL

OBJECTIVES
- Gain proficiency in performing instrument approaches, missed approach procedures, and holding with both engines operating.
- Increase proficiency in engine-out operations.

PREFLIGHT DISCUSSION
❏ Instrument Approach Chart Review
❏ Single-Pilot Resource Management

INTRODUCE

INSTRUMENT PROCEDURES
❏ VOR Holding
❏ GPS Holding
❏ NDB Holding
❏ Intercepting and Tracking a Course Using Navigational Systems
❏ Intercepting and Tracking DME Arcs (based on airplane equipment)

INSTRUMENT APPROACHES — ALL ENGINES OPERATING
❏ VOR Approaches
❏ RNAV (GPS) Approaches
❏ NDB Approaches
❏ ILS Approaches
❏ Localizer Approaches
❏ Approach Procedures to Straight-In Minimums
❏ Approach Procedures to Circling Minimums
❏ Missed Approach Procedures

Instrument/Commercial Syllabus

REVIEW

ENGINE-OUT OPERATIONS
- ❏ Engine Failure During Takeoff Before (V_{MC}) (Simulated)
- ❏ Engine Failure After Liftoff (Simulated)
- ❏ Flight Principles — Engine Inoperative
- ❏ Maneuvering with One Engine Inoperative
- ❏ V_{MC} Demonstration (by Student)
- ❏ Full Feather and In-Flight Restart
- ❏ Approach and Landing with an Inoperative Engine (Simulated)

ENGINE-OUT OPERATIONS (IR)
- ❏ Identification of Inoperative Engine
- ❏ Procedures for Shutdown and Feathering
- ❏ Engine Failure During Climbs
- ❏ Engine Failure During Straight-and-Level Flight and Turns
- ❏ Engine Failure During Descents

COMPLETION STANDARDS
- Perform holding and instrument approaches using the correct procedures and positive aircraft control.
- Demonstrate the ability to identify the inoperative engine during cruise and use the correct control inputs to maintain heading ±10° at all times.
- Demonstrate understanding of the cause, effect, and significance of engine-out minimum control speed (V_{MC}) and recognize the imminent loss of control while maintaining airspeed within 5 knots of, but never below, the assigned speed during the V_{MC} demonstration.
- Demonstrate proficiency in using the proper control inputs, flap and landing gear cleanup procedures, accurate engine shutdown, and correct feathering procedures.

POSTFLIGHT DEBRIEFING
- ❏ Critique maneuvers/procedures and SRM.
- ❏ Create a plan for skills that need improvement.
- ❏ Update the record folder and logbook.

FLIGHT LESSON 8

DUAL — CROSS-COUNTRY, VFR CONDITIONS

OBJECTIVES
- Increase proficiency in basic instrument flight operations during a planned cross-country flight to at least one point more than 100 nautical miles straight-line distance from the departure point.
- Become familiar with engine-out approach procedures solely by reference to instruments.

PREFLIGHT DISCUSSION
- ❏ Cross-Country Flight Planning
- ❏ Instrument Approach Chart Review

Instrument/Commercial Syllabus

STAGE VII ■ Multi-Engine Rating Flight Training

- ❏ Engine Failure Considerations During Cross-Country Flight
- ❏ Risk Management (5Ps, PAVE)

INTRODUCE

CROSS-COUNTRY FLIGHT
- ❏ Cross-Country Flight Planning
- ❏ National Airspace System
- ❏ Weather Information
- ❏ Radio Communications and ATC Light Signals
- ❏ Navigation Systems and Radar Services
- ❏ Pilotage and Dead Reckoning
- ❏ VOR, GPS, and/or NDB Navigation
- ❏ Lost Procedures
- ❏ Diversion
- ❏ Single-Pilot Resource Management

REVIEW

INSTRUMENT PROCEDURES
- ❏ VOR Holding
- ❏ GPS Holding
- ❏ NDB Holding
- ❏ Intercepting and Tracking a Course Using Navigational Systems
- ❏ Intercepting and Tracking DME Arcs (based on airplane equipment)

ENGINE-OUT OPERATIONS (IR)
- ❏ Identification of Inoperative Engine
- ❏ Procedures for Shutdown and Feathering
- ❏ Engine Failure During Climbs
- ❏ Engine Failure During Straight-and-Level Flight and Turns
- ❏ Engine Failure During Descents

INSTRUMENT APPROACHES – ONE ENGINE INOPERATIVE
- ❏ VOR Approaches
- ❏ RNAV (GPS) Approaches
- ❏ NDB Approaches
- ❏ ILS Approaches
- ❏ Localizer Approaches
- ❏ Approach Procedure to Straight-In Minimums
- ❏ Approach Procedure to Circling Minimums
- ❏ Missed Approach

COMPLETION STANDARDS
- Demonstrate the ability to identify the inoperative engine during cruise, use the correct control inputs to maintain straight and level flight, and be able to make decisions concerning the continued safety of the flight.
- Demonstrate proficiency in performing one-engine inoperative instrument approach procedures.

POSTFLIGHT DEBRIEFING
- ❏ Critique maneuvers/procedures and SRM.
- ❏ Create a plan for skills that need improvement.
- ❏ Update the record folder and logbook.

FLIGHT LESSON 9

DUAL — CROSS-COUNTRY, NIGHT

OBJECTIVES
- Increase proficiency in flying instrument approaches, missed approach procedures, and holding with all engines operating and in engine-out situations.
- Gain proficiency in basic cross-country and instrument flight operations at night by planning and performing a cross-country flight to a point more than 100 nautical miles straight-line distance from the departure point.

PREFLIGHT DISCUSSION
- ❏ Cross-Country Flight Planning
- ❏ Risk Management (5Ps, PAVE)
- ❏ Instrument Approach Chart Review
- ❏ Night Flying Considerations

REVIEW

CROSS-COUNTRY FLIGHT
- ❏ Cross-Country Flight Planning
- ❏ National Airspace System
- ❏ Weather Information
- ❏ Radio Communications and ATC Light Signals
- ❏ Navigation Systems and Radar Services
- ❏ Pilotage and Dead Reckoning
- ❏ VOR, GPS, and/or NDB Navigation
- ❏ Lost Procedures
- ❏ Diversion
- ❏ Lighting and Equipment for Night Flight
- ❏ Physiological Aspects of Night Flight
- ❏ Single-Pilot Resource Management

INSTRUMENT PROCEDURES
- ❏ VOR Holding
- ❏ GPS Holding
- ❏ NDB Holding
- ❏ Intercepting and Tracking a Course Using Navigational Systems
- ❏ Intercepting and Tracking DME Arcs (based on airplane equipment)

INSTRUMENT APPROACHES — ALL ENGINES OPERATING
- ❏ VOR Approaches
- ❏ RNAV (GPS) Approaches
- ❏ NDB Approaches
- ❏ ILS Approaches
- ❏ Localizer Approaches
- ❏ Approach Procedures to Straight-In Minimums
- ❏ Approach Procedures to Circling Minimums
- ❏ Missed Approach Procedures

ENGINE-OUT OPERATIONS (IR)
- ❏ Identification of Inoperative Engine
- ❏ Procedures for Shutdown and Feathering

Instrument/Commercial Syllabus

- ❏ Engine Failure During Climbs
- ❏ Engine Failure During Straight-and-Level Flight and Turns
- ❏ Engine Failure During Descents

INSTRUMENT APPROACHES — ONE ENGINE INOPERATIVE
- ❏ VOR Approaches
- ❏ RNAV (GPS) Approaches
- ❏ NDB Approaches
- ❏ ILS Approaches
- ❏ Localizer Approaches
- ❏ Approach Procedures to Straight-In Minimums
- ❏ Approach Procedures to Circling Minimums
- ❏ Missed Approach Procedures

COMPLETION STANDARDS
- Demonstrate the ability to identify the inoperative engine during cruise, use the correct control inputs to maintain straight and level flight, and be able to make decisions concerning the continued safety of the flight.
- Demonstrate proficiency in one-engine inoperative instrument approach procedures using correct operating techniques, coordination, smoothness, and understanding.

POSTFLIGHT DEBRIEFING
- ❏ Critique maneuvers/procedures and SRM.
- ❏ Create a plan for skills that need improvement.
- ❏ Update the record folder and logbook.

STUDY ASSIGNMENT
Ground Lesson 6
  Stage VI Exam
Multi-Engine Rating Practical Test Briefing
Stage VII Check
  Prepare for the Stage VII Check in Flight Lesson 10.

FLIGHT LESSON 10

DUAL — LOCAL
STAGE VII CHECK

OBJECTIVE
Demonstrate proficiency in multi-engine and engine out operations to the chief instructor, assistant chief, or a designated check instructor during the Stage VII Check.

PREFLIGHT DISCUSSION
- ❏ Student and Flight Check Instructor Roles and Expectations
- ❏ Questions to Test Student Knowledge

Instrument/Commercial Syllabus

REVIEW

PREFLIGHT PREPARATION
- ❑ Certificates and Documents
- ❑ Airworthiness Requirements
- ❑ Multi-Engine Operations of Systems
- ❑ Multi-Engine Performance and Limitations

MANEUVERS AND PROCEDURES
- ❑ Safety-Related Operations and Procedures
- ❑ Steep Turns
- ❑ Full- and Partial-Panel Attitude Instrument Flying

TAKEOFFS AND LANDINGS
- ❑ Traffic Pattern
- ❑ Normal and Crosswind Takeoffs and Landings
- ❑ Short-Field Takeoff/Maximum Performance Climbs and Landings
- ❑ Go-Around/Rejected Landing
- ❑ Maneuvering During Slow Flight
- ❑ Power-Off and Power-On Stalls
- ❑ Accelerated Stalls
- ❑ Spin Awareness

ENGINE-OUT OPERATIONS
- ❑ Engine-Inoperative Flight Principles
- ❑ Maneuvering With One Engine Inoperative
- ❑ Engine Failure During Cruise
- ❑ Identification of Inoperative Engine
- ❑ Procedures for Shutdown and Feathering
- ❑ Use of Controls to Counteract Yaw and Roll
- ❑ V_{MC} Demonstration

INSTRUMENT APPROACHES — ALL ENGINES OPERATING
- ❑ VOR Approaches
- ❑ RNAV (GPS) Approaches
- ❑ NDB Approaches
- ❑ ILS Approaches
- ❑ Localizer Approaches
- ❑ Approach Procedures to Straight-In Minimums
- ❑ Approach Procedures to Circling Minimums Missed Approach Procedures

INSTRUMENT APPROACHES — ONE ENGINE INOPERATIVE
- ❑ VOR Approaches
- ❑ RNAV (GPS) Approaches
- ❑ NDB Approaches
- ❑ ILS Approaches
- ❑ Localizer Approaches
- ❑ Approach Procedures to Straight-In Minimums
- ❑ Approach Procedures to Circling Minimums

EMERGENCY PROCEDURES
- ❑ Emergency Descent
- ❑ Systems and Equipment Malfunction
- ❑ Emergency Equipment and Survival Gear

STAGE VII ■ Multi-Engine Rating Flight Training

Instrument/Commercial Syllabus

POSTFLIGHT PROCEDURES
- After Landing
- Parking and Securing

COMPLETION STANDARDS
- Demonstrate proficiency in all the maneuvers and procedures listed for review at the level required by multi-engine land sections of the Commercial Pilot Airman Certification Standards.
- Demonstrate the ability to use single-pilot resource management to make effective decisions, maintain situational awareness, prevent CFIT, and manage risk, tasks, and automation.

POSTFLIGHT DEBRIEFING
- Evaluate maneuvers/procedures and SRM.
- Plan additional instruction for skills not meeting course completion standards.
- Update the record folder and logbook.

STUDY ASSIGNMENT
Ground Lesson 7
 Multi-Engine Rating End-of-Course Exam

Flight Lesson 11
 Prepare for the End-of-Course Flight Check.

FLIGHT LESSON 11

DUAL — LOCAL
END-OF-COURSE FLIGHT CHECK FOR COURSE COMPLETION

OBJECTIVE
Demonstrate proficiency all listed tasks to the chief instructor, assistant chief, or a designated check instructor during the End-of-Course Flight Check. The proficiency level must meet the requirements of the multi-engine land sections of the Commercial Pilot Airman Certification Standards.

PREFLIGHT DISCUSSION
- Student and Flight Check Instructor Roles and Expectations
- Questions to Test Student Knowledge

REVIEW

PREFLIGHT DISCUSSION
- Student and Flight Check Instructor Roles and Expectations
- Questions to Test Student Knowledge

Instrument/Commercial Syllabus

REVIEW

PREFLIGHT PREPARATION
- ❏ Certificates and Documents
- ❏ Airworthiness Requirements
- ❏ Multi-Engine Operations of Systems
- ❏ Multi-Engine Performance and Limitations

MANEUVERS AND PROCEDURES
- ❏ Safety-Related Operations and Procedures
- ❏ Steep Turns
- ❏ Full- and Partial-Panel Attitude Instrument Flying

TAKEOFFS AND LANDINGS
- ❏ Traffic Pattern
- ❏ Normal and Crosswind Takeoffs and Landings
- ❏ Short-Field Takeoff/Maximum Performance Climbs and Landings
- ❏ Go-Around/Rejected Landing
- ❏ Maneuvering During Slow Flight
- ❏ Power-Off and Power-On Stalls
- ❏ Accelerated Stalls
- ❏ Spin Awareness

ENGINE-OUT OPERATIONS
- ❏ Engine-Inoperative Flight Principles
- ❏ Maneuvering With One Engine Inoperative
- ❏ Engine Failure During Cruise
- ❏ Identification of Inoperative Engine
- ❏ Procedures for Shutdown and Feathering
- ❏ Use of Controls to Counteract Yaw and Roll
- ❏ V_{MC} Demonstration

INSTRUMENT APPROACHES — ALL ENGINES OPERATING
- ❏ VOR Approaches
- ❏ RNAV (GPS) Approaches
- ❏ NDB Approaches
- ❏ ILS Approaches
- ❏ Localizer Approaches
- ❏ Approach Procedures to Straight-In Minimums
- ❏ Approach Procedures to Circling Minimums
- ❏ Missed Approach Procedures

INSTRUMENT APPROACHES — ONE ENGINE INOPERATIVE
- ❏ VOR Approaches
- ❏ RNAV (GPS) Approaches
- ❏ NDB Approaches
- ❏ ILS Approaches
- ❏ Localizer Approaches
- ❏ Approach Procedures to Straight-In Minimums
- ❏ Approach Procedures to Circling Minimums

EMERGENCY PROCEDURES
- ❏ Emergency Descent
- ❏ Systems and Equipment Malfunction
- ❏ Emergency Equipment and Survival Gear

STAGE VII ■ Multi-Engine Rating Flight Training

Instrument/Commercial Syllabus

POSTFLIGHT PROCEDURES
- ❏ After Landing
- ❏ Parking and Securing

COMPLETION STANDARDS
- Demonstrate proficiency in all the maneuvers and procedures listed at the level required by multi-engine land sections of the Commercial Pilot Airman Certification Standards.
- Demonstrate the ability to use single-pilot resource management to make effective decisions, maintain situational awareness, prevent CFIT, and manage risk, tasks, and automation.

POSTFLIGHT DEBRIEFING
- ❏ Evaluate maneuvers/procedures and SRM.
- ❏ Plan additional instruction for skills not meeting course completion standards.
- ❏ Update the record folder and logbook.

Appendix — Pilot Briefing Questions

Instrument Rating Course Briefings

INSTRUMENT APPROACHES BRIEFING

These questions help prepare the student for flying instrument approach procedures. The student should demonstrate understanding of these questions and any additional questions that develop during the briefing before practicing instrument approach procedures.

1. Describe the segments of a typical instrument approach and the purpose of each segment.
2. What does the notation "NoPT" on an approach chart mean?
3. If a standard procedure turn symbol is shown, what type of course reversals are authorized? If a teardrop or holding pattern is shown? If no procedure turn symbol is shown?
4. What does the phrase "...cleared for straight-in approach" mean?
5. What determines the aircraft approach category?
6. If you fly a Category A airplane at an approach speed appropriate to Category B, which minimums should you use and why?
7. At what point during a circling approach may you begin descent from the MDA?
8. How should you initiate a missed approach if you lose visual contact during a circling approach?
9. What does the term "...cleared approach" mean?
10. What requirements must you meet to descend below the DA/MDA?
11. Is it permissible to land a civil aircraft when the visibility is below minimums if you have the runway environment in sight?
12. If one or more approach components are inoperative, unusable, or not utilized, how do you determine the adjustments required in approach minimums?
13. What is RVR? If both RVR and prevailing visibility are reported, which takes precedence?
14. Where is the MAP on a precision approach? on an APV? on a nonprecision approach?
15. What is the lowest possible DA and visibility for a Category I ILS approach?
16. What is the CDI sensitivity of a localizer signal compared to a VOR signal?
17. Do you ever use an ILS glide slope with a back course approach?
18. How do you determine the allowable uses for the specific GPS installation in your airplane?

171

Instrument/Commercial Syllabus

19. Describe the characteristics of a terminal arrival area (TAA).
20. What airplane equipment do you need to fly an RNAV (GPS) approach to LNAV minimums? LNAV/VNAV minimums? LPV minimums?
21. What are the characteristics of an RNAV (GPS) approach to LP minimums?
22. If RAIM is not available when you set up an RNAV (GPS) approach, what should you do?
23. What is the minimum navigation equipment required for a VOR/DME approach?
24. Given an approach chart, brief the approach.
25. Compare and contrast visual and contact approaches.

IFR CROSS-COUNTRY BRIEFING

These questions help prepare the student for IFR cross-country flight operations. The student should demonstrate understanding of these questions and any additional questions that develop during the briefing before performing IFR cross-country flight operations.

1. If you plan to fly a SID or a STAR, how do you indicate this on your flight plan? How do you indicate that you do not wish to use SIDs or STARs?
2. What aircraft equipment code do you indicate on your IFR flight plans?
3. What standard takeoff minimums apply to flights conducted under Part 91 as compared to commercial operators?
4. When are you required to have an alternate airport for a flight under IFR?
5. What are the IFR fuel requirements?
6. List the items of an IFR clearance in the normal sequence.
7. After receiving a takeoff clearance from the tower, when do you contact departure control?
8. What reports should you make to ATC without request when operating in a radar environment?
9. What additional reports should you make to ATC in a nonradar environment? Where must you make position reports?
10. On a direct route segment, what points are considered to be compulsory reporting points?
11. Give an example of a position report.
12. Explain a VFR-on-top clearance.
13. Explain a clearance to climb to VFR on top.
14. What does flight at or above an MEA guarantee? At or above the MOCA?
15. What is the significance of an MRA? Of an MCA?
16. What altimeter setting should you use during IFR flight below 18,000 feet? For flight at or above 18,000 feet?
17. What are the appropriate IFR cruising altitudes below and above 18,000 feet?
18. What procedures should you follow if you lose two-way radio communications under IFR?
19. How can you obtain weather information enroute on an IFR flight?
20. What temperature range normally is conducive to structural icing when you are operating in visible moisture?
21. If you encounter icing conditions in flight, what actions should you take?

Instrument/Commercial Syllabus

22. You are being radar vectored with your last assigned altitude as 9,000 feet. ATC then issues your approach clearance. At what point during the approach can you descend to a lower altitude?

INSTRUMENT RATING PRACTICAL TEST BRIEFING

These questions help prepare the student for the FAA Instrument Rating Practical Test. The student should demonstrate understanding of these questions and any additional questions that develop during the briefing before taking the End-of-Course Flight Check and FAA Instrument Rating Practical Test.

These sample questions are examples of the types of questions that the examiner might ask during the oral and flight portions of the practical test. The examiner may ask questions at any time to determine if the student's knowledge of a subject area is adequate. Preparation for the practical test should include a review of FAR Parts 61, 91, and NTSB 830, with emphasis on the rules that apply to instrument pilots. In addition, thoroughly discuss each FAA question incorrectly answered on the knowledge test because the examiner might emphasize these areas.

AIRPLANE REQUIREMENTS

1. What equipment, in addition to that required for a VFR flight, must the airplane have for a flight under IFR?
2. What airplane and equipment inspections are required for flight under IFR, how often are they required, and where can you find the appropriate logbook entries? Locate each entry for the training airplane.
3. How often must the VOR equipment be operationally checked when you use VORs for a flight conducted under IFR?
4. What are the acceptable methods of checking the airplane's VOR equipment, and what are the allowable errors for each method?
5. Under what conditions must you have a transponder for flight under VFR or IFR?
6. What are the differences in aircraft equipment requirements for flight under IFR in controlled and uncontrolled airspace?
7. How do you determine that the required instruments are working properly prior to flight?

PILOT REQUIREMENTS

1. What recency of experience requirements must you meet to act as pilot in command of a flight under IFR? How much time and how many approaches may you conduct in an approved FTD or simulator?
2. Assume your instrument currency expires on June 1. What is the latest date that you can regain your currency without having to pass an instrument proficiency check?
3. What are the differences in pilot requirements to act as pilot in command of an airplane flying IFR in controlled and uncontrolled airspace?

APPENDIX ■ Instrument Rating Course Briefings

173

Instrument/Commercial Syllabus

APPROACH CHARTS AND PROCEDURES

To answer questions 1 through 15, use an ILS approach chart from the local area.
1. What is the approach category of your airplane?
2. What is the DA and visibility requirements for the ILS approach with all components operating? If the approach lighting systems are inoperative?
3. What is the localizer frequency and identifier?
4. Can you use DME for this approach? Is DME required?
5. What is the minimum procedure turn altitude?
6. What is the minimum glide slope intercept altitude?
7. Where does the final approach segment begin?
8. What is the final approach course?
9. How is the missed approach point determined for this approach?
10. What is the height of the electronic glide slope at the runway threshold?
11. Are there any limitations noted for the straight-in or circle-to-land procedures?
12. What is the elevation of the touchdown zone?
13. What are the landing minimum requirements if the glide slope is inoperative?
14. During a localizer approach, where does the final approach segment begin and how do you determine the missed approach point?
15. If applicable, what is the MSA to the east? What does flight at or above an MSA guarantee and when can you use an MSA?

To answer questions 16 through 34, use an RNAV (GPS) approach chart from the local area.
16. How will you obtain the latest weather observation at this airport before you begin the approach?
17. At which IAFs must you perform a course reversal? At which IAFs is no procedure turn authorized?
18. Where does the final approach segment begin?
19. At what point may you begin a descent from the procedure turn altitude?
20. What is the final approach course?
21. What requirements must your airplane's GPS equipment meet for you to fly the approach to LNAV minimums? To LNAV/VNAV minimums? To LPV minimums?
22. What are the ceiling and visibility requirements when flying the approach to LNAV minimums? To LNAV/VNAV minimums? To LPV minimums?
23. Where is the missed approach point?
24. What is the missed approach procedure?

To answer questions 25 through 33, use a VOR approach chart from the local area.
25. What is the frequency and identification of the primary facility?
26. What is the minimum procedure turn altitude for the approach?
27. What types of course reversal(s) may you use for the procedure turn?
28. Where does the final approach segment begin?
29. At what point may you begin a descent from the procedure turn altitude?
30. What is the final approach course?
31. What are the landing minimum requirements for a Category C aircraft?

174

Instrument/Commercial Syllabus

32. Where is the missed approach point?
33. Assume you are flying a Category A aircraft at an approach speed of 100 knots during a circle-to-land maneuver. Which minimums should you use and why?

AIR TRAFFIC CONTROL
1. When may you deviate from a clearance?
2. When may you cancel IFR?
3. Assume you have been issued a clearance to climb from 5,000 feet to 8,000 feet. What rate(s) of climb does ATC expect you to maintain?
4. If you reach a clearance limit before you receive a further clearance, what action should you take?
5. What does the phrase *"...radar service terminated"* mean?
6. What does the phrase *"...resume own navigation"* mean?
7. What is the maximum indicated airspeed you can use in any civil aircraft in a holding pattern below 6,000 feet MSL?
8. What are the requirements for a visual approach, and who may initiate the procedure?
9. What are the requirements for a contact approach, and who may initiate the procedure?
10. How is your IFR flight plan closed at an airport served by an operating control tower? At an airport not served by a control tower?
11. How is your flight plan closed at an airport not served by a control tower or flight service station?
12. What procedures should you follow if you are unable to contact ATC on an assigned frequency?

Instrument/Commercial Syllabus

Commercial Pilot Course Briefings

CROSS-COUNTRY PROCEDURES BRIEFING

These questions help review VFR cross-country flight planning and flight operations. The student should demonstrate understanding of these questions and any additional questions that develop during the briefing before performing VFR cross-country flight operations.

1. Explain what weather product you would use to obtain the most current weather condition at your destination.
2. What is the meaning of code "9900" found on a winds aloft forecast?

To answer questions 3 through 8, use the appropriate pilot's operating handbook.

3. Based on the following conditions, determine the distance required to take off and clear a 50-foot obstacle, assuming maximum takeoff weight and a 10-knot headwind.
   - Field elevation..4,000 ft
   - Temperature..24°C
   - Altimeter setting..30.00
4. Determine the time, fuel, and distance needed to climb from a field elevation of 2,000 feet to a cruising altitude of 7,500 feet. Assume standard conditions and calm wind.
5. Based on a cruise altitude of 7,500 feet and standard conditions, determine the true airspeed and fuel flow at approximately 65% power. What is the airplane's maximum range with full fuel?
6. Based on the following conditions, determine the distance required to land over a 50-foot obstacle with a calm wind.
   - Field elevation......................................3,000 ft
   - Temperature...24°C
   - Altimeter Setting.....................................29.92
7. What are the standard service volumes of the three classes of VORs? What basic restriction affects VOR signal reception? How can you verify that a VOR is usable?
8. What are the different methods for conducting a VOR check?
9. Using a sectional chart, identify how each class of airspace is depicted. What are the basic VFR weather minimums and pilot and equipment requirements to operate in each class?
10. What is a special VFR clearance? Can you request it at night? What visibility and cloud clearances apply?
11. Name the various types of special use airspace and explain the restrictions they impose.
12. How can you tell when a part-time control tower is operating?

Instrument/Commercial Syllabus

13. If your route takes you through Class C airspace and you have established two-way radio contact with the approach controller but have not received a clearance to enter Class C airspace yet, what should you do? What if the airspace is Class B?
14. What if ATC issues a clearance that would cause you to enter a cloud in Class C or Class B airspace. Should you comply with the clearance? Explain.
15. If ATIS indicates the ceiling is 800 feet overcast and the visibility is two miles, can you land under VFR at an airport with Class C airspace?
16. Assume the same weather as in the previous question and clear skies above the ceiling. Can you legally operate above the cloud ceiling in Class C airspace without obtaining a special VFR clearance?
17. What minimum weather conditions must exist for you to enter Class D, C or B airspace without requesting special VFR?

COMPLEX AIRPLANE TRANSITION BRIEFING

These questions help prepare the student for flying a complex airplane. Because a wide variety of complex training airplanes exist, determine the questions appropriate to the specific training airplane. The student should demonstrate understanding of these questions and any additional questions that develop during the briefing before operating the complex airplane.

ELECTRICAL SYSTEM

1. What equipment provides the electrical power?
2. How are the electrical system components protected?
3. What is the voltage of the electrical system when the alternator is operating and when it is off?
4. What is the difference between an ammeter and a loadmeter? How is an alternator failure indicated on an ammeter or on a loadmeter? Which is installed in your airplane?
5. What should you expect if the alternator fails?
6. What is the correct procedure for resetting a popped circuit breaker?
7. What should you do in the case of an electrical fire?

FUEL SYSTEM

1. Is your airplane equipped with a carburetor or a fuel injection system?
2. How many fuel tanks does your airplane have? What is the total amount of usable fuel?
3. What is the minimum allowable grade of fuel that you can use with your airplane? What color is it?
4. Describe the recommended fuel management procedures in the POH.
5. When should you switch fuel tanks during a flight? What is the procedure for switching fuel tanks?
6. What is the purpose of the fuel pump, if appropriate, on your airplane? When should you use it?
7. Where are the fuel tank vents located and what is their purpose?

Instrument/Commercial Syllabus

8. Where are the fuel drains located on your airplane? When should you use them?
9. Some fuel tanks have a tab located within them that is visible with the fuel cap removed. What is its purpose?

LANDING GEAR SYSTEM
1. Explain how the landing gear system operates.
2. At what point during the takeoff should you retract the landing gear?
3. When approaching to land, where do you normally extend the landing gear?
4. Explain the procedure for manually extending the landing gear if the primary power source fails.
5. After extending the landing gear manually as a training procedure, is it advisable or possible to retract it normally? Is it possible to retract the landing gear manually?
6. What airspeed limitations exist during landing gear extension and retraction? Is there an additional limitation when the gear is down and locked?
7. Explain the purpose of each annunciator light of the landing gear system.
8. What procedure should you follow if a gear-down annunciator light fails to illuminate?
9. Explain the operation of the landing gear warning system.

COWL FLAPS
1. What is the purpose of the cowl flaps and how are they controlled?
2. What gauge/instrument helps you determine how to position the cowl flaps?
3. Generally, how should you position the cowl flaps for takeoff, during climb, in cruise flight, during descent, approach, and after landing?

CONSTANT-SPEED PROPELLERS
1. Explain the advantages and disadvantages of constant-speed and fixed-pitch propellers.
2. Explain how a constant-speed propeller operates.
3. Explain how you should set the propeller control or takeoff, climb, cruise, and landing. What gauge/instrument do you use to set the propeller?
4. When you apply power by using the throttle, what gauge/instrument indicates the increase in power?
5. What does the manifold pressure gauge indicate when the airplane is sitting on the ramp after the engine is shut down? Why?
6. What gauge/instrument do you use to set the propeller?
7. As a general rule, when decreasing power, do you move the throttle or the propeller control first? Which do you move first to increase power?
8. If the oil pressure to the propeller governor is cut off, what pitch setting does the propeller go to in most single-engine airplanes?
9. Why do you check the oil pressure when cycling the propeller during engine runup?
10. What should you do if you are ready for takeoff before the oil temperature is in the normal operating range?

Instrument/Commercial Syllabus

WEIGHT AND BALANCE
1. What is the basic empty weight for your airplane?
2. Compute the weight and balance of your airplane as you typically operate it during training with full fuel. What is the airplane's maximum payload? How must you distribute the weight to keep the airplane in balance?
3. Compute a weight and balance problem, assuming yourself and three 170-pound passengers, each with 20 pounds of baggage. How much fuel can the airplane carry? With that fuel load, how must you load the baggage to keep the airplane in balance?

GENERAL CONSIDERATIONS
1. List the following airspeeds for your airplane and, where applicable, the corresponding airspeed indicator color codes.
   - Stalling speed in the landing configuration
   - Stalling speed in a specified configuration
   - Best angle-of-climb speed
   - Best rate-of-climb speed
   - Normal approach speed
   - Approach speed with the flaps retracted
   - Short-field landing approach speed
   - Maximum flap extension speed(s)
   - Maximum landing gear extended speed
   - Maximum landing gear operating speed
   - Design maneuvering speed
   - Maximum structural cruising speed
   - Never-exceed speed
2. Where is the ELT located?
3. Explain the proper procedures for leaning the mixture for your airplane.
4. Where is the alternate static source and how do you use it?
5. Explain the procedures for dealing with an engine fire during flight.
6. What configuration and airspeed provides the greatest glide distance?

COMMERCIAL FLIGHT MANEUVERS BRIEFING
These questions help prepare the student for flying commercial flight maneuvers and expand the student's understanding of the aerodynamics of these maneuvers. Consult the current FAA Commercial Pilot Airman Certification Standards for the required maneuvers.

SHORT-FIELD AND SOFT-FIELD TAKEOFFS AND LANDINGS
1. What flap setting should you use for a short-field takeoff? For a soft-field takeoff?
2. During a short-field approach and landing over a 50-foot obstacle, why is it necessary to establish a constant angle of descent over the obstacle?

APPENDIX ■ Commercial Pilot Course Briefings

179

Instrument/Commercial Syllabus

3. Explain the effects of torque and P-factor on airplane control during short-field takeoffs.
4. What climb speed should you use during the initial portion of the short-field takeoff?
5. During a short-field approach and landing, how accurately must you land the airplane relative to a selected touchdown point?
6. How can you increase braking effectiveness during the landing roll after a short-field approach and landing?
7. At approximately what airspeed will the airplane become airborne during a soft-field takeoff?
8. At what point during the soft-field takeoff do you begin a climb? At what point during the soft-field takeoff do you retract the flaps?
9. Explain how you use power during the landing flare and touchdown during a soft-field landing.
10. Explain how to position the controls during crosswind takeoffs and landings.
11. What is the maximum demonstrated crosswind component for your airplane? Is this a limitation? Explain.
12. What effect does flap extension have on approach speed and descent angle?
13. If the airplane is low and slow on final approach, what corrective action should you take?
14. What is the significance of the key position during a landing?
15. Explain the procedures for performing a go-around.

STALL/SPIN AWARENESS

1. When practicing stall recognition and recovery, at what point should you initiate the recovery maneuver?
2. What is an accelerated stall? Explain how to perform and recover from an accelerated stall.
3. Are the manufacturer's spin recovery techniques included in the POH proven for the airplane and, if not, why not?
4. Describe the conditions required for a spin, the indications of an incipient spin and a full spin, and the spin recovery techniques for your airplane.

STEEP TURNS, CHANDELLES, AND STEEP SPIRALS

1. At what altitude and airspeed should you enter steep turns and chandelles?
2. How do you perform a steep turn? What bank angle should you use?
3. If an airplane weighs 2,500 pounds, how much weight must the wings support during a level turn with a 60° bank?
4. Explain the changes in elevator (or stabilator) pressure necessary to maintain level flight during the roll from a steep turn in one direction to a turn in the opposite direction.
5. What is the maximum recommended angle of bank for the chandelle?
6. Explain how you adjust the power during a chandelle.
7. What should your airspeed be at the completion of the chandelle?
8. Describe the differences in control pressures between the rollout from a chandelle to the right and one to the left. Where is the rudder pressure greatest?
9. Explain how you should recover from a chandelle. Why is altitude gain not the basis for judging the quality of a chandelle?
10. Describe the steps to perform a steep spiral.

Instrument/Commercial Syllabus

LAZY EIGHTS AND EIGHTS-ON-PYLONS
1. What altitude and airspeed should you use to enter lazy eights?
2. What reference points do you use during lazy eights?
3. Where do the highest and lowest altitudes occur during lazy eights?
4. Do you use pitch or power to control the altitude and symmetry of the loops during lazy eights? Explain.
5. At what point during lazy eights do you use the greatest control pressures?
6. Compare and contrast turns around a point and eights-on-pylons.
7. How does wind direction affect the entry for eights-on-pylons?
8. At what altitude should you enter eights-on-pylons? How do you determine the pivotal altitude?
9. What is the maximum angle of bank that you should use during eights-on-pylons? Where does this bank angle occur?
10. Describe how you make changes in altitude during eights-on-pylons to hold the pylon position relative to the wing. Where do the highest and lowest altitudes occur?

POWER-OFF 180° ACCURACY APPROACHES AND LANDINGS
1. What is the objective of power-off accuracy landings?
2. What is the key position and why is it important?
3. What are some techniques to conserve or dissipate altitude?
4. Name the advantages and disadvantages of flaps and slips.
5. In which direction should you perform a slip when a crosswind exists?

COMMERCIAL PILOT PRACTICAL TEST BRIEFING

These questions help prepare the student for the FAA Commercial Pilot Practical Test. The student should demonstrate understanding of these questions and any additional questions that develop during the briefing before taking the End-of Course Flight Check and the FAA Commercial Pilot Practical Test.

These sample questions are examples of the types of questions that the examiner might ask during the oral and flight portions of the practical test. The examiner may ask questions at any time to determine if the student's knowledge of a subject area is adequate. Preparation for the practical test should include a review of FAR Parts 61, 91, and NTSB 830, with emphasis on the rules that apply to commercial pilots. Ensure the student knows what regulations apply to agricultural operations (Part 137), external load operations (Part 133), and air transportation of hazardous materials (HMR 175). In addition, thoroughly discuss each FAA question incorrectly answered on the knowledge test because the examiner might emphasize these areas.

AIRPLANE REQUIREMENTS
1. What certificates and documents must you have on board the airplane?
2. Locate the following inspections, as appropriate, in the airframe and engine logbooks: annual, 100-hour, pitot-static, altimeter, and transponder.

Instrument/Commercial Syllabus

3. What equipment, in addition to that required for flight during the day, must you have for night operations?
4. When is an electric landing light required?
5. Must all airplanes be equipped with an ELT? If your airplane requires an ELT to be installed, when may you fly without one?

PILOT REQUIREMENTS
1. What recency of experience requirements must you meet to act as a pilot in command of an aircraft carrying passengers during the day? At night?
2. Can the holder of a commercial pilot certificate rent an airplane (with a recent 100-hour inspection) from a fixed-base operator and use it to carry passengers for hire?
3. What minimum class of medical certificate must you hold when exercising commercial privileges? How long is the appropriate medical certificate valid for operations that require a commercial pilot certificate?
4. Define the term "commercial operator."

THE FLIGHT ENVIRONMENT
1. What is the significance of 14,500 feet MSL in relation to Class E airspace?
2. What are the prerequisites for flight within Class A airspace?
3. Explain the vertical limit for Class D airspace.
4. Explain the pilot and equipment requirements within Class B and C airspace.
5. What is the maximum authorized airspeed below 10,000 feet MSL within a Class D airspace area below the floor of associated Class B airspace?
6. What are the minimum visibility and cloud clearance requirements for VFR flight in both controlled and uncontrolled airspace?
7. Explain when you may operate within the following areas: prohibited, restricted, warning, alert, and MOA.
8. Under what conditions must you file a VFR flight plan?
9. What are the pilot and passenger oxygen requirements?
10. Explain the meaning of ATC light gun signals to aircraft on the ground and in flight.

AVIATION PHYSIOLOGY
1. Explain the four types of hypoxia.
2. Discuss the similarities and differences between the conditions of hypoxia and hyperventilation. What are the symptoms and effects for each condition, and what corrective actions should you take in each case?
3. If a passenger exhibits symptoms that could be attributed to more than one condition, what should you do?
4. What are the rules concerning alcohol use and the operation of an airplane?
5. Name several common medications that you should not take before or during a flight.
6. What is spatial disorientation, when is it most likely to occur, and what corrective action should you take if you become spatially disoriented?
7. What are the effects of fatigue on a pilot?
8. What are the effects of nitrogen on a SCUBA diver, and what precautions need to be observed prior to flight?

Instrument/Commercial Syllabus

AIRPLANE EQUIPMENT AND SYSTEMS

To answer the following questions, refer to the pilot's operating handbook for the airplane used for the practical test.

1. What is your airplane's total fuel capacity? Total usable fuel quantity?
2. What is the fuel grade and corresponding color of the fuel used in your airplane? If the recommended fuel grade is not available, what grade(s) of fuel can you use?
3. Explain fuel management for your airplane.
4. Where is the battery located in your airplane and what is its voltage?
5. Explain the information displayed by your airplane's ammeter or load meter.
6. What are the procedures for dealing with an electrical fire in flight?
7. What are the maximum and minimum allowable flap settings for takeoff?
8. Explain the cold and hot starting procedures for your airplane.
9. Explain the manual landing gear extension procedures for your airplane.
10. List the best rate-of-climb (V_Y) and best angle of climb (V_X) speeds for your airplane when loaded to its maximum allowable weight at sea level.
11. What is your airplane's stalling speed at maximum weight in level flight? In a 45° bank?
12. List the following speeds for your airplane: V_{FE}, V_{LO}, and V_{LE}.
13. What is the maximum demonstrated crosswind component for your airplane? Is this an airplane limitation?
14. What is the minimum required ground roll for takeoff at maximum takeoff weight if the field elevation is 5,000 feet and the temperature is 26°C?
15. Assuming the same conditions given in the previous question, what is your rate of climb with gear and flaps retracted at the best rate-of-climb airspeed?
16. What does the term "service ceiling" mean?
17. What are the service and absolute ceilings for your airplane?
18. Assume you are flying at a pressure altitude of 4,000 feet under ISA+10°C conditions. What are the predicted true airspeed and fuel flow values for 65% power?
19. What are the maximum allowable baggage compartment weights?
20. If you do not know an adult passenger's weight, what should you use for weight and balance computations? When should you not use standard weights?
21. Calculate the weight and balance for your airplane as it will be loaded for the practical flight test and assume the examiner weighs 180 pounds.
22. Explain how a constant-speed propeller operates on a multi-engine airplane.
23. What is the maximum continuous operating power setting for your airplane? Why is it important to comply with these limitations?
24. Explain the procedures to apply and reduce power.
25. Explain the propeller synchronizing system.

Multi-Engine Rating Course Briefings

These questions help prepare the student for flying a multi-engine airplane. Because a wide variety of multi-engine training airplanes exist, determine the questions appropriate to the specific training airplane. The student should demonstrate understanding of these questions and any additional questions that develop during the briefing before operating the multi-engine airplane.

MULTI-ENGINE OPERATIONS AND SYSTEMS BRIEFING

PILOT REQUIREMENTS AND SRM
1. Is a multi-engine rating a category or class rating?
2. What tests are required to obtain a multi-engine rating?
3. What is required if you are instrument rated and desire to operate a multi-engine airplane in instrument conditions?
4. Explain SRM considerations that apply to flying a multi-engine airplane.
5. Describe the risk factors that apply if you operate more than one type of multi-engine airplane on a regular basis.

PROCEDURES AND MANEUVERS
1. Explain the elements contributing to the left-turning tendency in a conventional twin (non-counterrotating propellers) with both engines operating.
2. Why does torque cause a rolling moment in conventional twin-engine airplanes? Why are the effects of torque eliminated in airplanes with counter-rotating propellers?
3. Explain the uses of differential power during taxi and takeoff.
4. Define the V-speeds for your airplane, and include the airspeed indicator color codes, where applicable.
5. Describe the preflight planning considerations necessary for a typical multi-engine cross-country flight.
6. Describe the correct procedures and sequence of events for a normal takeoff and a short-field takeoff with a maximum performance climb.
7. What guidelines determine the point of gear retraction following liftoff?
8. When is the first power reduction normally made during departure?
9. What determines the configuration of the cowl flaps during climb?
10. What are the advantages of performing a cruise climb to altitude?
11. Explain the procedure for maneuvering during slow flight.
12. Explain the procedure for setting up and performing stalls in the gear down and full flaps, as well as the gear up, flaps up configurations.
13. Explain the factors involved in planning the descent.
14. Explain the correct procedures and sequence of events for a normal landing and a short-field approach and landing over an obstacle.
15. Describe the correct procedures for performing a go-around.

Instrument/Commercial Syllabus

SYSTEMS AND EQUIPMENT
1. Explain how a constant-speed propeller operates on a multi-engine airplane.
2. What is the maximum continuous operating power setting for your airplane?
3. Why is it important to comply with these limitations?
4. Explain the procedures to apply and reduce power.
5. Explain the propeller synchronizing system.
6. Is an autofeather system installed on your airplane? If so, explain how the system works.
7. How does a reversible propeller system work? Can it be used in flight?
8. Diagram and explain the fuel system used in your airplane.
9. Explain the crossfeed system on the airplane. When is it used?
10. What is the normal fuel pressure and what are some of the things that cause low pressure?
11. Explain the fuel injection system.
12. Explain turbocharging operation.
13. Explain the electrical system including the primary sources of electrical power and how the electrical power is distributed.
14. What is the function of a voltage regulator?
15. Explain the purpose of an over-voltage relay.
16. Explain what adjustments have to be made with one alternator inoperative.
17. Explain the landing gear system. How do accomplish emergency landing gear extension?
18. Explain the following ice control systems, if installed on your airplane: propeller, wing and tail surfaces, and windshield.
19. Explain how the cabin heating system operates. How do you regulate the cabin temperature?

MULTI-ENGINE PERFORMANCE CONSIDERATIONS BRIEFING

These questions help ensure that the student understands the performance considerations that apply to a multi-engine airplane and can determine performance prior to flight operations in a light twin. The student should demonstrate understanding of these questions and any additional questions that develop during the briefing before performing maneuvers in the multi-engine airplane.

WEIGHT AND BALANCE
1. What are the maximum ramp, maximum takeoff, maximum landing, and basic empty weights for your airplane?
2. Which weights are required for weight computations?
3. Where is the basic empty weight found?
4. Which items are included in the payload?
5. What guidelines are used for making weight and balance computations if the weights of the passengers are unknown?
6. What is the purpose of a maximum zero fuel weight and does your airplane have this limitation?

7. If the airplane is loaded to maximum capacity, will the greatest movement in the center of gravity occur when weight is shifted from the fuel, baggage, or passenger loading station?
8. Assuming the listed conditions, determine whether your airplane is loaded within the center of gravity range.
   - Pilot and front passenger ....340 lbs
   - Rear passengers ....370 lbs
   - Fuel tanks...Full
   - Baggage...95 lbs
9. Assuming that your airplane is loaded with the CG at the extreme aft limit, explain the handling characteristics of the airplane during normal operations, such as takeoffs and landings.

PERFORMANCE CHARTS

1. Explain the relationship between power available vs. power required as it relates to engine-out performance.
2. Define accelerate-stop distance, and explain why it is an important performance consideration.
3. Given the following conditions, determine the accelerate-stop distance, the normal takeoff ground run, and the takeoff distance necessary to clear a 50-foot obstacle.
   - Field elevation ....2,000 ft
   - Temperature ....30°C
   - Altimeter setting..29.72
   - Runway......................................Hard surfaced
   - Weight......................................Maximum gross
   - Headwind component ....10 knots
4. Assuming the airplane is loaded to maximum gross weight, compute the average rate of climb at 5,000 feet and 20°C with both engines operating and with an inoperative engine.
5. Given the following conditions, determine the normal landing roll and the landing distance over a 50-foot obstacle.
   - Field elevation ....3,500 ft
   - Temperature ....30°C
   - Altimeter setting..30.32
   - Weight......................................Maximum gross
6. Explain why the climb performance of a twin-engine airplane is decreased more than 50 percent with one engine inoperative.
7. Explain the operational significance of the single-engine service ceiling an the single-engine absolute ceiling. How are V_{YSE} and V_{XSE} related to single-engine ceilings?

Instrument/Commercial Syllabus

MANEUVERS
1. When practicing stall recognition and recovery, at what point should you initiate the recovery maneuver?
2. What is an accelerated stall? Explain how to perform and recover from an accelerated stall.
3. Are the manufacturer's spin recovery techniques included in the POH proven for the airplane and, if not, why not?
4. What are the conditions required for a spin to occur, the indications of an incipient spin and a full spin, and the spin recovery techniques for your training airplane?
5. What are the most likely emergencies that might require an emergency descent in a multi-engine airplane? What are the steps to perform an emergency descent?

ENGINE-OUT OPERATIONS BRIEFING
These questions prepare the student to manage engine failures and perform engine-out operations. The student should demonstrate understanding of these questions and any additional questions that develop during the briefing before performing engine-out maneuvers and procedures in the multi-engine airplane.

AERODYNAMICS
1. What effect does induced flow have on the total lift generated by a multi-engine airplane, and what might result from a sudden power reduction during a slow final approach?
2. Define critical engine. Explain why airplanes with counterrotating propellers do not have a critical engine.
3. Define V_{MC}. Explain the factors that affect V_{MC}.
4. Why is the airplane directionally uncontrollable during flight below V_{MC}?
5. Is it possible for the airplane to enter a engine-out stall before V_{MC} is reached? Explain.
6. Why should you feather the propeller of the inoperative engine if you cannot restart the engine?
7. Identify and explain all the factors that contribute to the yawing and rolling tendency in the direction of the inoperative engine.
8. Explain why some airplanes might not be able to maintain altitude after an engine failure.
9. What guidelines should you follow when making turns with one engine inoperative?

Instrument/Commercial Syllabus

PROCEDURES AND MANEUVERS
1. Describe the steps you take immediately after an engine failure. How do you identify the inoperative engine? Why is the throttle of the suspected inoperative engine retarded prior to beginning the feathering process?
2. Explain why you should bank the airplane toward the operative engine during engine-out flight.
3. Explain why the takeoff and climb are considered to be the most critical phases of flight for an engine failure.
4. What indications do you have that the airplane is approaching V_{MC}?
5. What procedure do you use to regain airplane control if an engine failure occurs during flight below V_{MC}?
6. Is a successful engine-out go-around probable from a low altitude when the airspeed is below V_{YSE}? Explain your answer.
7. Describe the use of the landing gear and wing flaps during an engine-out approach and landing.
8. When considering an engine failure, which is more valuable, airspeed in excess of V_{YSE} or additional altitude? Why?
9. Does the shutdown of either engine affect the operation of the landing gear, flaps, hydraulic system, or electrical system?
10. If a positive engine-out rate of climb is not possible, how do you obtain the minimum rate of descent?
11. Explain the steps to secure the engine after complete shutdown.

MULTI-ENGINE INSTRUMENT FLIGHT BRIEFING

These questions help prepare the student for flying instrument procedures with both engines operating and with an inoperative engine. The student should demonstrate understanding of these questions and any additional questions that develop during the briefing before performing instrument operations in the multi-engine airplane.

NORMAL PROCEDURES
1. Why is important to know the proper power settings to maintain the desired attitudes and airspeeds?
2. Describe the recommended trim technique during airspeed and/or attitude changes.
3. What are the primary considerations for a departure under IFR?
4. What is the recommended holding pattern airspeed?
5. Why is preflight planning important for instrument approaches?
6. What are the main tasks you must perform during an instrument approach with all engines operating?

Instrument/Commercial Syllabus

INSTRUMENT PROCEDURES WITH ONE ENGINE INOPERATIVE

1. Describe the main tasks you must perform when one engine fails during instrument conditions.
2. What indications should the turn coordinator show during straight-and-level flight with one engine inoperative?
3. During engine-out flight, what approximate bank angle provides the best turning performance?
4. What type of approach should you request with one engine inoperative?
5. What deviations from normal procedures, if any, are recommended for an engine-out instrument approach?
6. What is recommended concerning an engine-out missed approach in instrument conditions?

MULTI-ENGINE RATING PRACTICAL TEST BRIEFING

These questions help prepare the student for the FAA Multi-Engine Rating Practical Test. The student should demonstrate understanding of these questions and any additional questions that develop during the briefing before taking the End-of Course Flight Check and the FAA Multi-Engine Rating Practical Test.

These sample questions are examples of the types of questions that the examiner might ask during the oral and flight portions of the practical test. The examiner may ask questions at any time to determine if the student's knowledge of a subject area is adequate.

AIRPLANE REQUIREMENTS

1. What documents are required to be onboard the airplane during flight? Explain the significance of each.
2. Explain FAR 91.213 with regard to how it applies to flight with inoperative instruments or equipment.
3. Review the V-speeds for your airplane, and include the airspeed indicator color codes, where applicable.
4. Calculate the weight and balance for your airplane as it will be loaded for the practical flight test and assume the examiner weighs 180 pounds.
5. Based upon the following data, determine the CG location.
   - Pilot and front passenger.....................350 lbs
   - Rear passengers......................................335 lbs
   - Fuel tanks...Full
   - Baggage..75 lbs
6. What does the term "zero fuel weight" mean? Does your airplane have a zero fuel weight limitation? If so, what is it?
7. Use the weight and balance data from the previous question and assume that when an intermediate stop is made, the airplane has consumed 28 gallons of fuel and a 150-pound center-seat passenger deplanes. How many inches will the center of gravity move, and in which direction?

APPENDIX ■ Multi-Engine Rating Course Briefings

189

Instrument/Commercial Syllabus

8. What grade and type of fuel and oil are specified for your airplane?
9. Determine the amount of oxygen required for a flight at 15,000 feet MSL for two hours with a total of three people onboard. How is the oxygen system checked and serviced?

PERFORMANCE

1. Define accelerate-stop distance and its significance.
2. Determine the accelerate-stop distance under the following conditions:
    - Field pressure altitude..........................2,500 ft
    - Temperature..52°F
    - Weight....................................Maximum takeoff
    - Headwind component..........................10 knots
3. Compute the takeoff distance over a 50-foot obstacle based on the following conditions:
    - Field elevation..3,000 ft
    - Temperature..68°F
    - Altimeter setting..30.20
    - Runway..Hard surfaced
    - Weight....................................Maximum takeoff
    - Headwind component..........................15 knots
4. Using the data from the previous question, determine the takeoff distance with no obstacles.
5. What power setting will produce 65 percent rated power at 7,000 feet if the temperature is 2°C.?
6. Determine the true airspeed and maximum range if the airplane is loaded to maximum gross weight.
7. Given the following conditions, determine the average single-engine rate of climb at 2,000 feet MSL.
    - Altimeter..29.92
    - Temperature at 2,000 ft. ....25°C
    - Weight....................................Maximum takeoff
8. What is the single-engine service ceiling for your airplane and what is its significance in relation to takeoffs and go-arounds?
9. Explain the relationship between density altitude and the single-engine service ceiling.
10. Given the following data, determine the landing distance required over a 50-foot obstacle.
    - Field pressure altitude..........................1,500 ft.
    - Temperature..27°C
    - Weight....................................Maximum landing
    - Headwind component.......................... 15 knots

Instrument/Commercial Syllabus

SYSTEMS AND EQUIPMENT

To answer the following questions, refer to the pilot's operating handbook for the airplane used for the practical test.

1. Explain the electrical system installed in your airplane.
2. During single-engine operations, are there any restrictions and/or recommendations placed on the electrical system?
3. Discuss the hot starting procedure for your airplane and explain how you determine when this procedure is necessary.
4. Describe the procedure for correcting an engine overheating problem.
5. Explain the correct and most accurate engine leaning procedure.
6. Explain and diagram your airplane's fuel system.
7. Discuss the proper procedure for fuel management for both twin-engine and engine-out operations.
8. Describe your airplane's landing gear system.
9. What is the purpose of the landing gear safety switch, and where is it located?
10. How many seconds are required for the landing gear to retract fully? In what situation could this become critical?
11. Explain the manual landing gear extension procedure.
12. Explain the landing procedure and configuration if the nosewheel will not extend and the two main wheels extend normally.
13. What action should you take in the event the propeller de-icing equipment fails on one propeller?
14. If the airplane is autopilot equipped, is there any limitation placed on autopilot operation during engine-out flight?
15. What type of system provides heated air to the cabin? Is there any limitation on restrictions on this equipment's operation?

ENGINE-OUT OPERATIONS

1. Does your airplane have a critical engine? Explain.
2. What procedure do you follow if an engine failure occurs below VMC on the takeoff ground run?
3. How do you determine the inoperative engine?
4. Explain the propeller feathering procedures.
5. Is there any engine RPM limitation on propeller feathering?
6. Explain the in-flight engine restart procedure if a propeller is feathered.
7. Explain why it is advisable to bank the airplane up to five degrees toward the operating engine during single-engine operations. What bank angle is appropriate for your airplane?
8. What airspeed should you maintain immediately after an engine failure? Why?
9. What gear/flap configurations and conditions were used to determine the published V_{MC}?
10. What is the proper recovery method if you inadvertently allow the speed to dissipate to V_{MC} after an engine failure?
11. Is the greatest amount of drag created by the extension of the landing gear, extension of full flaps, or a windmilling propeller?

APPENDIX ■ Multi-Engine Rating Course Briefings

This is to certify that

_____

is enrolled in the
Federal Aviation Administration

approved _____ course

conducted by _____.

_____
Chief Instructor

_____
Date of Enrollment

This is to certify that

_____

is enrolled in the
Federal Aviation Administration

approved _____ course

conducted by _____.

_____
Date of Enrollment

_____
Chief Instructor

This is to certify that

_____

is enrolled in the _____ approved _____ course

Federal Aviation Administration

conducted by _____.

_____
Date of Enrollment

_____
Chief Instructor

This is to certify that

_____

has successfully completed all stages, tests, and course requirements and has graduated from the **FEDERAL AVIATION ADMINISTRATION** approved _____ course conducted by _____ .

I certify the above statements are true.

_____
Chief Instructor

_____
School Certificate Number

_____
Date of Graduation

The graduate has completed the cross-country training specified in FAR Part 141.

o Instrument Rating Course — Appendix C, Paragraph 4(c)(1)(ii)
o Commercial Pilot Certification Course — Appendix D, Paragraphs 4 and 5
o Multi-Engine Course — Appendix I, Paragraph 4

This is to certify that

_____

has successfully completed all stages, tests, and course requirements and has graduated from the **FEDERAL AVIATION ADMINISTRATION** approved _____ course conducted by _____ .

The graduate has completed the cross-country training specified in FAR Part 141.

o Instrument Rating Course — Appendix C, Paragraph 4(c)(1)(ii)
o Commercial Pilot Certification Course — Appendix D, Paragraphs 4 and 5
o Multi-Engine Course — Appendix I, Paragraph 4

I certify the above statements are true.

_____
Chief Instructor

_____
School Certificate Number

_____
Date of Graduation

This is to certify that

_____

has successfully completed all stages, tests, and course requirements and has graduated from the FEDERAL AVIATION ADMINISTRATION approved _____ course conducted by _____.

The graduate has completed the cross-country training specified in FAR Part 141.

o Instrument Rating Course — Appendix C, Paragraph 4(c)(1)(ii)
o Commercial Pilot Certification Course — Appendix D, Paragraphs 4 and 5
o Multi-Engine Course — Appendix I, Paragraph 4

I certify the above statements are true.

_____
Chief Instructor

_____
School Certificate Number

_____
Date of Graduation